THE REMINISCENCES OF
Admiral Owen W. Siler
U.S. Coast Guard (Retired)

INTERVIEWED BY
Paul Stillwell

U.S. Naval Institute • Annapolis, Maryland

Copyright © 2004

Preface

A few years ago the Foundation for Coast Guard History was established "to promote the recognition and prestige of the United States Coast Guard by emphasizing its illustrious past." Captain Fred Herzberg is the foundation's executive director, and Vice Admiral Howard Thorsen is chairman of the board. In 2000 those two retired Coast Guard officers visited the Naval Institute and made a generous donation to sponsor Admiral Siler's oral history, the first project the new organization funded. It has been a special privilege for me to take part because I first met Admiral Siler in the early 1970s when both of us were working in St. Louis. Nearly 30 years later he and his wife were most hospitable as I visited their home in Georgia to record his memories of a career in the service of the Coast Guard.

That career began with an appointment to the Coast Guard Academy in 1940 and a term as cadet that was foreshortened by World War II. During the last two years of the war, Siler was an officer on board Navy attack transports that were manned by Coast Guard crews. His first ship was involved in the amphibious assault on the island of Bougainville in 1943, and his second carried occupation troops once the war was won.

By the late 1940s the young officer had embarked on a specialty as an aviator. In the ensuing years he served in a number of air stations that performed patrol duty, medical evacuations, and search and rescue. His travelogue from those years includes descriptions of service in Texas, Hawaii, Florida, and Alaska. A particularly interesting facet of his aviation duty was a tour from 1954 to 1959 as aide and personal pilot to Admiral Alfred Richmond, Commandant of the Coast Guard. The oral history provides Siler's insights into the personality and leadership style of Admiral Richmond.

As he became more senior, Siler used his administrative abilities in Coast Guard headquarters and as Commander of the Second Coast Guard District in St. Louis, where I initially encountered him. While he was there the Coast Guard demonstrated its inland role in providing aids to navigation, dealing with rising floodwaters, and defusing a potentially deadly situation when a barge went adrift near Louisville, Kentucky.

From that post Admiral Siler became Commandant in 1974. His discussion of his four-year tenure talks about both personalities and programs. Among the former are bestselling author Alex Haley and colorful Rear Admiral Mike Benkert. Among the latter are the introduction of women to the Coast Guard Academy and Coast Guard cutters; vastly increased territory for fisheries enforcement; patrols to interdict drug smuggling; the acquisition of modern ships and aircraft for the service; and dealing with oil pollution. During the interviews Admiral Siler demonstrated himself to be an innately modest individual who avoided the opportunity to brag about himself and his achievements.

Grateful appreciation goes to George Van, a Navy and Marine Corps veteran who did the initial transcription of the interviews. Admiral Siler provided his inputs to both the verbatim and edited transcripts. I have done some further light editing in the interests of accuracy, smoothness, and clarity. In addition, I have inserted footnotes to provide further information for readers who use the volume.

Rear Admiral Sid Wallace was a helpful source of encouragement. Dr. Robert Browning, Coast Guard historian, and his associates Scott Price and Chris Havern repeatedly supplied information that was useful in the preparation for the interviews and the completion of the finished product.

Finally, the Naval Institute expresses its gratitude to the Tawani Foundations and the Pritzker Military Library for their generous financial support of the oral history program that produced this memoir.

Paul Stillwell

Paul Stillwell
Director, History Division
U.S. Naval Institute
March 2004

ADMIRAL OWEN WESLEY SILER

UNITED STATES COAST GUARD (RETIRED)

Owen Wesley Siler was born on 10 January 1922, in Seattle, Washington. He was graduated from Santa Maria High School, Santa Maria, California, in 1938 and received an associate arts degree from Santa Maria Junior College in 1940. Appointed a cadet on 19 July 1940, he graduated from the U.S. Coast Guard Academy, New London, Connecticut, with a bachelor of science degree in engineering and with a commission as ensign on 9 June 1943, the usual four year-curriculum having been shortened because of World War II.

From the academy he was ordered to combat duty in the Pacific. On board the attack transport USS Hunter Liggett (APA-14) he took part in the invasion of Bougainville (November 1943) and other Pacific landings. During his two years of duty in that transport, he served in various billets including that of gunnery officer, assistant navigator, and deck watch officer. He was then transferred to the attack transport USS Bayfield (APA-33) in July 1945. While on board he participated in the occupation of Northern Honshu, Japan, following the surrender of the Japanese.

On returning to the United States in April 1946, he served briefly as personnel officer in the manning section of Alameda Training Station, California, and then served the remainder of the year as navigator of the cutter Taney (WPG-37) out of Alameda. By January 1947 he was stationed as communications officer at the 11th Coast Guard District office at Long Beach, California.

Assigned as a student aviator in June of 1947, he took his flight training at the Naval Air Training Bases at Corpus Christi Texas, and at Pensacola, Florida. After graduating from the latter with the designation of Coast Guard aviator on 28 July 1948, he performed his first aerial patrols and search and rescue missions out of the Coast Guard Air Station, Port Angeles, Washington. Following a course of advanced training at the Naval All Weather Flying School at Corpus Christi from February to May of 1952; he was next stationed for two years at the Coast Guard Air Detachment Barbers Point, Hawaii. He served his next tour of duty at Coast Guard Headquarters, Washington D.C., as aide to the Commandant, as well as administrative pilot from August 1954 to July 1959. During the following three years he commanded the Coast Guard Air Station at Corpus Christi.

From August 1962 to August 1964, he served as Chief, Search and Rescue Branch, at the 17th Coast Guard District Office in Juneau, Alaska. From there he transferred to the Coast Guard Air Station, Miami, Florida, where he first served as executive officer for a year and then as commanding Officer for a year. Under his command that station received a Coast Guard Unit Commendation for the Cuban Exodus operations during October and November of 1965. During this period the air station was involved in 85 assistance cases and, with other Coast Guard units, helped deliver 8,100 refugees to Key West.

After a year of student work at the National War College from August 1966 to June 1967, he began his second tour of duty at Coast Guard Headquarters in the post of Chief, Administrative Management Division. In February 1968 he was named Assistant Chief of Staff for Management, and on 1 July 1969, assumed the post of Deputy Chief of Staff. Meanwhile, he earned an M.S. degree in international affairs from George Washington University in 1968.

By nomination of the President in January 1971, and the approval of the Senate, the then Captain Siler was appointed to rank as permanent rear admiral from 1 July 1971. Subsequently, he began his first assignment as flag officer in the post of Commander Second Coast Guard District, St. Louis, Missouri. For his service during that tour of duty, he received the Meritorious Service Medal in 1972 for directing successful efforts to avert a potential major disaster near Louisville, Kentucky, where a barge loaded with deadly chlorine had smashed into a dam. In May 1974 he received the Legion of Merit for his overall performance as Second District Commander.

Following his nomination by President Nixon on 4 February 1974, Admiral Siler succeeded retiring Admiral Chester R. Bender, USCG, to the post of Commandant of the Coast Guard, with the rank of four-star admiral effective on 1 June 1974. On 30 May 1978 Admiral Owen W. Siler closed his 35-year Coast Guard career and retired.

The following is a resume of Admiral Siler's appointments in rank: Cadet, 19 July 1940; Ensign, 9 June 1943; Lieutenant (junior grade), 1 April 1944; Lieutenant, 1 November 945; Lieutenant Commander, 26 August 1952; Commander, 1 July 1959; Captain, 1 July 1965; Rear Admiral, 1 July 1971; Admiral, 1 June 1974.

Admiral Siler's medals and awards included the following: Coast Guard Distinguished Service Medal (1977); Secretary of Transportation's Award for Outstanding Achievement (1977); Legion of Merit (1974); Meritorious Service Medal (1972); Coast Guard Unit Commendation (1965); Norwegian Order of St. Olav, Commander's rank (1976); World War II campaign service medal and ribbons--American Defense Service; American Area; Asiatic-Pacific; World War II Victory; Navy Occupation Service (Asia); also the National Defense Service Medal (Korean and Vietnam).

Deed of Gift

The U.S. Naval Institute is hereby authorized to make available to individuals, libraries, and other repositories of its choosing the tapes and/or transcripts of five oral history interviews concerning the life and naval career of the undersigned. The Naval Institute may also, at its discretion, use the material in electronic/digital format, including posting on the Internet. The interviews were recorded on 10-14 December 2000, in collaboration with Paul Stillwell for the U.S. Naval Institute.

The undersigned does hereby release and assign to the U.S. Naval Institute the rights and title to these interviews, with the exception that the undersigned retains the right to use the material for his own purposes, as he sees fit. The copyright in both the oral and transcribed versions shall be the sole property of the U.S. Naval Institute. The tape recordings of the interviews are and will remain the property of the U.S. Naval Institute.

Signed and sealed this 6th day of January 2001.

Owen W. Siler
Admiral, U.S. Coast Guard (Retired)

Interview Number 1 with Admiral Owen W. Siler, U.S. Coast Guard (Retired)
Place: Admiral Siler's home in Savannah, Georgia
Date: Sunday, 10 December 2000
Interviewer: Paul Stillwell

Paul Stillwell: Admiral, it's a pleasure to get started on this oral history. We have a number of oral histories of your predecessors as Commandant in the Naval Institute collection, so this is a worthy addition as well. I wonder if you could start, please, by describing some of your family background, your parents, and how they had moved around somewhat before you were born.

Admiral Siler: My mother and father were married in Grove City, Pennsylvania. My father had been an instructor at Grove City College, and my mother was, I guess, his favorite student. They were married on the day after Christmas in 1918, and they moved shortly afterward to California, Atascadero, where my father was the accountant for the development of the Atascadero Colony. He wasn't happy with that arrangement, so he left—I don't know how soon afterward—and went to Seattle, Washington. There he taught in a business college, and that's where I was born. My parents moved shortly afterward to Los Angeles, California. On the way to Los Angeles my father stopped and was interviewed at the Santa Maria, California, High School and was offered a position there. So my father stayed for only a short time in Los Angeles, and then they went back to Santa Maria, where both my younger brother and my sister were born. That's the place that I remember as home when I was a child.

Paul Stillwell: And you had an older brother as well.

Admiral Siler: I had an older brother who was born in Atascadero; Walt was 20 months older than I. My younger brother was 26 months younger, and then three years later my sister was born in Santa Maria.

Paul Stillwell: Please describe your growing-up years and what you remember of Santa Maria.

Admiral Siler: Well, of course, my father being in the high school there, a large part of growing up was knowing the high school. My father frequently worked on weekends, and we kids ran all around the high school in the shrubbery and often visited the area where he taught.

With my father being on the school teaching staff, my mother at some time became a member of the school board of the elementary school that I went to, which was Orcutt School. Orcutt is six miles south of Santa Maria and was the school that all of us went to in our later years. The first few years I don't remember where my older brother went to school, but I went to Pleasant Valley School, which was a one-room school about two and a half miles out of Santa Maria. I don't know whether the school was closing or what. I went to Cook Street School in Santa Maria itself for part of my second grade education, and then I went to Orcutt School, which is where I went from the second grade through graduation. I can remember at the Orcutt School we had Frank Wycoff, who was an Olympic sprinter, as our graduation speaker.[*] Other than that, all I can remember is the school bus rides to and from school.

Paul Stillwell: How much interaction did you have with your siblings? Did you develop any relationships as far as recreational things?

Admiral Siler: My older brother and I played quite a lot with each other. We were both physically perfectly all right. My younger brother had a hernia and had poor eyesight, and so he didn't join into our games quite as much until we moved to a place where we had a row of eucalyptus trees on the back perimeter of our home site. Those trees grow over 100 feet tall, wonderful for climbing. My younger brother climbed those trees as much as I did, I guess, and about that time my older brother was getting interested in other things.

---

[*] In the 1936 Olympic Games in Berlin the American team consisting of Jesse Owens, Ralph Metcalfe, Floyd Draper, and Frank Wycoff set a new world record of 39.8 seconds in the 400-meter relay.

Paul Stillwell: What interests or hobbies did you have as you grew up?

Admiral Siler: I can't remember any particular hobbies. I can remember at one time I started a collection of birds' eggs and probably had a couple of dozen of the birds that were in the neighborhood and we could find the nests. I don't recall collecting much of other things of that sort. Both my older brother and I, and I guess my younger brother, were 4-H Club members at times. My older brother raised some chickens; I raised rabbits. I did a lot of bicycle riding down to the county park, about a mile and a half away, and around the park. Once I rode all the way to the beach—about 20 miles. I was happy to ride home after that!

Paul Stillwell: How much of a part did religion play in the family life as you grew up?

Admiral Siler: I can't say that we were deeply religious. We did go to church regularly. I was a member of a youth group in high school, and I was a member of the choir in the church. That's about it, I think. I was a regular attendee at the youth high school classes in the church when I was in high school and in junior college.

Paul Stillwell: What values would you say your parents imparted to you and your siblings?

Admiral Siler: Well, since we didn't have access to Boy Scouts or anything of that sort, the church and the 4-H Club and being good people is about it. I'd say that was the stress, that we were to do things the way they should be done.

Paul Stillwell: Did they put any emphasis on education?

Admiral Siler: I can't say there was a great deal of stress on it, although they expected us to do our best in school. My older brother graduated from high school two weeks after he was 16 and went to USC on a full-tuition scholarship.* I was never as good as he was in school, but I was a lot better than my younger brother. He struggled a whole lot more than the rest of us did. My sister had no problems at all. I don't know that she was offered scholarships, but she did quite well in school.

Paul Stillwell: You also graduated from high school when you were 16. Did your parents push you to shorten the normal time span?

Admiral Siler: I don't know that they pushed me; however, when I was in the fourth or fifth grade I was moved ahead one semester, so that I became an even-semester student instead of an odd-semester student.

Paul Stillwell: You were involved in sports when you were in high school. How early did your interest in sports begin?

Admiral Siler: Well, I tried to go out for sports when I was in elementary school, but we didn't have very much except the track meets and some speed ball and some basketball, which I never made the team for. When I was in high school, I participated in track and tried to go out for swimming. After a short period of time I developed best as a backstroke swimmer, but swimming on my back I got chlorine water in my nose all the time. I had problems there, so I dropped out of swimming. So track was really the only sport that I participated in regularly in high school.

Paul Stillwell: How much interest did you take in the current events of the time: Lindbergh's flight and the growth of the dictatorships in Europe and what have you?†

Admiral Siler: I can't say I took a great interest in those developments at all until I was in junior college. Then I was taking a course in Modern European History, so that it was

---

* USC—University of Southern California.
† Charles A. Lindbergh became a national hero when he made the first solo flight across the Atlantic Ocean in May 1927.

very interesting to follow along on those things that were occurring in Europe as we studied them in school.

Paul Stillwell: How much were your family or those around you affected by the Depression?*

Admiral Siler: That's interesting, because I think we were not affected as much. We lived in the country. My father felt that living out of town on a farm of some sort would teach good habits to children and young people. My father's teaching position paid only $2,000 a year in those days and nothing during the vacation months in the summer. We needed the income and food from living on eight acres in the country. So we had chickens all the time, we had pigs and we had a cow, and we had chores that had to be performed all the time. Those things provided us with a good assistance to subsistence. I raised rabbits and sold them most of the time for profit and 4-H Club. My father at one time wanted to develop enough laying hens that he had 1,000 hens at one time. I don't know whether he ever reached 1,000, but my duty every Saturday was to clean the chicken pens before I went to work at J. C. Penney, and it was a stinking duty. [Laughter]

Paul Stillwell: Literally.

Admiral Siler: Literally. [Laughter]

Paul Stillwell: So I would say that a work ethic was one of the things you inherited from your parents.

Admiral Siler: That's the reason my father said, "We need a place in the country." We had lived in town when we were small children. I went back recently, and a woman

---

* Following the crash of the New York Stock Exchange in late October 1929, the United States was plunged into the Great Depression, from which it did not recover until the nation geared up for World War II at the beginning of the 1940s. The Depression was marked by high unemployment and many business failures.

about my age said, "You used to live next door to us," and I had forgotten that completely. But we had lived on the main street of Santa Maria at one time, and we'd moved once in town. Then we moved from there out into the country, and that was the object of my father's moving us. We were to learn that work ethic. We always had something to do with the chickens, the pigs, milking the cow twice a day, etc.

Paul Stillwell: How much did you read as you were growing up?

Admiral Siler: Quite a lot, mostly things I wanted to read. I'll never forget Howard Pease wrote a whole series of books about someone who went to sea on merchant ships, and that always impressed me.* At one time I thought I wanted to go to the California Merchant Marine Academy to do the kinds of things that were in that book. As I got older, I sent off for information about California Merchant Marine Academy and Naval Academy and just accidentally learned about the Coast Guard Academy when I sent for some information about the Naval Academy.

Paul Stillwell: How did that happen?

Admiral Siler: I sent to one of the prep schools for the Naval Academy and asked for the admission requirements, and they sent along a booklet about the Coast Guard Academy and its requirements. I didn't know anything about the Coast Guard Academy at that time, so we got some books about the Coast Guard and not the academy necessarily but just the Coast Guard. As I read more about it, I decided that's what I wanted to try first.

Paul Stillwell: Well, before that was junior college. What was your objective in going there?

Admiral Siler: I didn't make it to the Coast Guard Academy. [Laughter]

---

* Howard Pease, The Ship Without a Crew: the Strange Adventures of Tod Moran, Third Mate of the Tramp Steamer "Araby" (Garden City, N. Y., Doubleday, Doran & Company, Inc., 1934).

Paul Stillwell: Oh, all right.

Admiral Siler: I was too young actually to make it to the Coast Guard Academy when I graduated from high school, so I enrolled to at least spend one year at the junior college. At the end of that year I took the Coast Guard Academy exam and didn't pass high enough to qualify to go. So I finished junior college before I left, and by that time I was well qualified to go to the University of California or UCLA, which was my next alternative.* I was thinking that if I didn't make it to the Coast Guard Academy again, I would go to either UCLA or the University of California and study foreign trade.

Paul Stillwell: So the family was evidently well enough off to be able to send you to the junior college.

Admiral Siler: Junior college didn't cost anything. Junior college in California was just like high school, except you bought your books.

Paul Stillwell: I see.

Admiral Siler: Other than that, there was no cost involved.

Paul Stillwell: Well, you evidently demonstrated some leadership qualities early, because you were president of your student body in high school and then president of your class in the junior college. How did those offices come about?

Admiral Siler: The presidency of the student body was, I think, largely as a result of some student body meetings that were held, and the then-student body president had the people who were attempting to take his office the following semester chair the meetings. I don't think there was much question about the other fellow, because he didn't have any training in that sort of work at all. So I made it to being student body president. As far as the junior college was concerned, there wasn't much involved with being president of my

---

* UCLA—University of California at Los Angeles.

freshman class, and in the student body itself I was business manager, which didn't really consist of anything except reviewing the reports of the professional bookkeeper. And so it was a pretty easy job.

Paul Stillwell: Did you get some experience in public speaking in those jobs?

Admiral Siler: Oh, yes. There were definitely some requirements there, and there was another thing that was involved with that. I had participated in a good many plays in high school and junior college, so I was at ease before audiences and many people were not.

Paul Stillwell: It teaches self-confidence as well.

Admiral Siler: Oh, yes, very definitely.

Paul Stillwell: Did you get into any more sports in high school than you'd been before that, junior high and elementary?

Admiral Siler: In high school I went out for track again, and there weren't many sports other than football and baseball that I could have participated in, and I really wasn't interested in baseball. We didn't have a tennis team at that time; we didn't till just about the time I graduated. My father didn't want me to play football, so I didn't go out for football until I was in junior college. [Laughter] Then I went out without telling him about it. But he always sold the tickets to the main entrance to the football field, so he was there the night that I first played football, and it was announced on the public address system that Siler was going in.

Paul Stillwell: Well, you look like you have the build for football, so that was probably a natural.

Admiral Siler: Well, I never felt that I was properly utilized. I always thought that I could make an end if they used me at that, but they used me as a center or a tackle. I remember in one game the center was hit on the head and really had a problem. He was a close neighbor of ours, and he couldn't even see his hands. So he was substituted for and the man they put in couldn't center the ball to anybody. [Laughter] So they put me in as center then, and I played the rest of that game at center. But as far as the end was concerned, I never played that until I was at the Coast Guard Academy.

Paul Stillwell: That was the era before linemen were gargantuan.

Admiral Siler: Well, it was also in the days when you played both ways, and so the center was also a linebacker, and I enjoyed that. I remember, though, tackling someone with my face, and that was not too good. [Laughter]

Paul Stillwell: There were no face masks in that time either.

Admiral Siler: No.

Paul Stillwell: Did you have any interest in following professional sports teams on the West Coast?

Admiral Siler: We didn't have many professional sports teams in those days.

Paul Stillwell: Well, the Pacific Coast League in baseball.

Admiral Siler: Never paid any attention to them at all, because we were too far from either Los Angeles or San Francisco. Now, in more recent years, why, there have been teams in Bakersfield and San Luis Obispo and places like that. Santa Maria may have teams. I don't know.

Paul Stillwell: Did you have any people as you were growing up that you would describe as role models?

Admiral Siler: No, I can't remember anyone I would have thought of as a role model.

Paul Stillwell: What was the appeal of the Coast Guard Academy? Was it partly the free education?

Admiral Siler: No, that didn't enter in too much, because my older brother went to the University of Southern California on a full-tuition scholarship, at least his first year. Of course, they pretty much made it a policy in those days to cut off that scholarship after the first year, so his second year my parents paid for. His third year he was on a half-tuition scholarship. But I went to junior college, because I could prepare myself for whatever I wanted to do later, and it didn't cost anything in those days.

Paul Stillwell: Was it this sense of adventure in going to sea that drew you to the Coast Guard?

Admiral Siler: Largely I think, yes.

Paul Stillwell: Anything about that period before going to New London that we haven't talked about but should?

Admiral Siler: Of course, Santa Maria is not right on the coast, but we were close enough that we could get to places like Port San Luis Obispo or places like that where there were at least boats that you could go to sea on and go deep-sea fishing. A lot of people would go to Avila Beach, which is the port of San Luis Obispo, and they would go either just plain deep-sea fishing or abalone fishing. Abalone is available only at low tide and extremely low tide, and very frequently people would go out and do that, but more frequently you'd find people going just deep-sea fishing, and we did that several times. I usually got seasick. [Laughter]

Paul Stillwell: And that didn't discourage you?

Admiral Siler: It did for a few minutes, but I never was truly discouraged. [Laughter]

Paul Stillwell: Please describe your experiences going to New London and becoming a cadet.

Admiral Siler: Well, of course, I went in 1940, and on the way there I took the train. Nobody flew airplanes in those days, and the bus would have taken just too long. So I went to San Francisco and spent the day at the Golden Gate International Exposition in San Francisco, Treasure Island today.* I saw, among other things, the Bear in its berth and gleaming in white paint.† I guess it was in pretty good shape in those days. And there was a demonstration of capsizing a lifesaving boat and righting it again and some other things that were impressive to me, like the first TV that was available. I don't think anything was available except for demonstration then.

Paul Stillwell: I interviewed a sailor who went to that fair, and he said the first time he ever saw a television he was on it, because they had a camera set up by the monitor.

Admiral Siler: Yes. I took the train all the way across country and got to New York and had to kill quite a bit of time before the New York, New Haven and Hartford went up toward New London. So that day I spent at the New York World's Fair, and I can't remember anything particular about it except that I went there. Then I went to New London and stayed at the Mohican Hotel, which in those days was the hotel in New London.

The next morning I went up to the academy and reported in. There were never any particular aspects of that that I remember except we were sworn in as cadets shortly after I arrived. Then we were sent to Fort Trumbull, which was in those days the operating base of New London. When we went down there, we drew our sailor suits and

---
* Treasure Island is a man-made island in San Francisco Bay, located between San Francisco and Oakland. It served as the site of a world's fair in 1939-40, then was converted for use as a Navy base during and after World War II.
† The Bear was a famous old cutter, built in 1873 in Scotland. In 1885 she began a long period of service as a Revenue Marine cutter; she often served in the Arctic.

all that sort of thing. Then went back to the academy, and my roommate was Ralph Peterson from Manchester, Connecticut.*

I opened our cadet regulations and studied them. There were certain aspects of it that we had to really study. There was one section that told about how you pack your clothes if you are going from one place to another. I don't know why that was in cadet regulations, but it was. Another section described how you made your bed, and the two of us studied that section and thought we'd made the bed exactly the way it said. Later in the morning, we had a visit from someone who had been at the academy the year before and had flunked out. Because of that he took the exam again to make himself a cadet and today is a retired captain. He came into the room and said, "Do you know how to make the bed with hospital corners? Well, I see you don't." [Laughter] So he invited us, along with several others, to a demonstration of how to make the bed, which was not exactly the way we had done it. [Laughter] We learned then how to make the bed properly.

Paul Stillwell: Was this the first substantial time you'd been away from home?

Admiral Siler: Well, I had been to YMCA camps for as much as two or three weeks several times when I was in junior college and in high school too.

Paul Stillwell: Was there any sense of homesickness being that far away?

Admiral Siler: Not that I can recall.

Paul Stillwell: They keep you too busy for that most of the time.

Admiral Siler: I would guess that's true. I was not homesick but sick that I was not home because of the girl that I'd left behind.

Paul Stillwell: Do tell. [Laughter]

---
* Cadet Ralph A. Peterson, USCG.

Admiral Siler: That came to a halt rather soon, and besides that we were introduced to the girls who were at Connecticut College for Women, and that made a good substitute. [Laughter] Conn. College didn't become open for males until after World War II, and I remember one of my classmates sent his son there. His wife graduated from Conn. College a year after we did, so it became a family affair.

Paul Stillwell: Was there any sense of motivation just from the deteriorating world situation of the time?

Admiral Siler: I don't think that we took any particular notice of that at that time. It was later in the year when we were drilling on the parade ground, I remember, and the tactics officer said, "We have now joined the Navy." Of course, that was an emergency that was declared by President Roosevelt.[*] But we were on the parade ground and drilling just the same then as we did an hour before. Didn't notice any particular change at that time. Most of us that time didn't get newspapers, and, of course, there were no radios or TV in fourth class cadets' possession, so we didn't pay much attention to the news at all then.

Paul Stillwell: How well did you adapt to the military-type regimen and the drilling and so forth.

Admiral Siler: I guess I adapted as well as any of them in the class did. I remember a man who took the entrance examination in Los Angeles with me. We had spoken at that time, because he was from Porterville and had played football for Porterville Junior College, and we had played Porterville Junior College. He had come across country and been sworn in as a cadet and decided he didn't want to be a cadet. He wanted to go home and get married. [Laughter] All you could say was, "Good luck," because off he went. I

---

[*] Franklin D. Roosevelt was President of the United States from 4 March 1933 to 12 April 1945. As authorized by Congress, Roosevelt ordered the Coast Guard to "operate as part of the Navy, subject to the orders of the Secretary of the Navy," on 1 November 1941. The Coast Guard returned to the Treasury Department on 1 January 1946.

have no idea what ever happened to him. I can't remember his name either. But there were several people who resigned in the first few weeks.

We had a period of about six weeks, which was called swab summer, and we were given a review in mathematics of a couple of kinds. We were given some military drill, and we were taken down to whaleboats on the water and taught how to row a boat. During that time, why, we lost several who resigned. We also lost some cadets when the regular program started. I don't recall how far we were into it, except that one of the cadets in our class was caught between a truck and a railroad car when the football team came down from Norwich University.* Norwich was a completely military school in those days, so this was the Army-Navy game of New England. This fellow was helping unload some equipment from the railroad car. The brakes on the truck failed or were not set properly, and he was caught between the two. He was hurt for a while, but before he came out of the hospital he was given a Naval Academy appointment, and so he went off to the Naval Academy. I do know he graduated from the Naval Academy, but that's all I know about that individual. Yet that happened after the regular program had started, and we were already into the football season, so I don't know how much he missed that made any difference.

Paul Stillwell: I wonder what would make a Naval Academy appointment more desirable at that point.

Admiral Siler: I think there were quite a few people who came to the Coast Guard Academy when they couldn't make it to the Naval Academy.

Paul Stillwell: I see.

Admiral Siler: In fact, we had one man who wanted to go to the Military Academy. Leo Kinnard couldn't make it to the Military Academy, so he took the Coast Guard Academy appointment and spent his entire first year at the Coast Guard Academy. At the end of the first semester he had failed two courses and had to take re-exams in order to stay in

---

* Norwich University is in Northfield, Vermont.

the program. At the end of his second semester he failed every subject he was enrolled in. He didn't care at all, because just before he left the Coast Guard Academy he received an appointment to West Point. He graduated from West Point with honors, and, of course, in some cases he was repeating the things that he'd taken at the Coast Guard Academy.* The other thing that was amazing, though, was he retired as a brigadier general, and after retirement he became, I think, the historian of the Military Academy.

Paul Stillwell: So would he have been in the class of '45 then at West Point? You were in '44, weren't you?

Admiral Siler: I was in '44 that graduated in '43. West Point changed the system and graduated the class of '44 in '44.

Paul Stillwell: Oh, so he would have been in the class of '44.

Admiral Siler: Yes.

Paul Stillwell: What sort of factors caused these men to drop out early in the program?

Admiral Siler: Some of them couldn't stand the heat, the military life, at all. Some of them realized they were in over their heads in certain subjects. There were quite a few probably left because of mathematics. I know there were times when I wondered about it when I was a third classman.† [Laughter]

Paul Stillwell: During swab summer did you encounter anything that would be called hazing?

Admiral Siler: Not in swab summer, because there was no one there to haze us.

---

* Leo D. Kinnard graduated from the Military Academy in the class of 1944 and eventually retired from active Army service in 1970 as a brigadier general.
† A third classman is a second-year student.

Paul Stillwell: I see.

Admiral Siler: The only people who taught us things were officers who were still there all the time, but swab summer is not the time for hazing.

Paul Stillwell: Did you encounter it later?

Admiral Siler: Some.

Paul Stillwell: What specifics do you recall?

Admiral Siler: Well, I was a pretty good guy, I think, so I didn't have very much trouble, but there was one time when I was in the barber shop and didn't realize that a second classman had come in and wanted a haircut. So when the chair became vacant, I bounced into the chair. That second classman didn't like it at all, and so I was out swinging a rifle and walking square corners for some time. Actually, that was the only time that I had very much problem that way, and it was as much my fault as anyone else's.

Paul Stillwell: Was there anything that would be comparable to the code of honor or the honor concept at the other academies?

Admiral Siler: Not then, but there is now.

Paul Stillwell: Was there any guiding philosophy in that area concerning cheating?

Admiral Siler: No, but there was a good example, because it was in the cadet regulations in those days. We had one of our class who was accused of cheating, and I don't think he did. In fact, I'm pretty well convinced he didn't because he was too brilliant. He was the kind of a person, though, who was so proud of what he was doing that he'd look around to say, "Anybody get it right, because I did?" [Laughter] With all that looking around in the exam, he was accused of cheating, and I don't think he could prove that he didn't cheat. But I doubt that they could prove that he did.

Paul Stillwell: What was the outcome in his case?

Admiral Siler: He was kicked out, very shortly.

Paul Stillwell: Of course, an example like that is taken up very readily by the others.

Admiral Siler: Well, one of the unfortunate things about it was that he was Jewish, and we didn't have very many Jewish cadets in those days at all. We did have one fellow there, Goldman.* He used to kid about being Jewish and put on a Jewish accent, and I recall his saying something like, "I go to the United States Coast Guard Academy." And he was very humorous. But he's retired now; I think he made captain. He is a doctor, a Ph.D. He's brilliant.

Paul Stillwell: I know that there had been some cases of discrimination against Jewish personnel at the Naval Academy. Was there any sense of that at the Coast Guard Academy.

Admiral Siler: I don't think there was sense of it at all, not that we could see. Most of us were not Jewish, and I don't think that except for the one who was kicked out and the one who graduated we were aware of others who were Jewish at all, so I don't know.

Paul Stillwell: And I take it there were no black cadets then at that point.

Admiral Siler: There was no such thing until after President Kennedy became President.†

Paul Stillwell: Didn't realize it was that late.

---

* Cadet Ernest H. Goldman, USCG.
† John F. Kennedy served as President of the United States from 20 January 1960 until he was assassinated on 22 November 1963.

Admiral Siler: Kennedy made the comment when he saw the review at the time he was becoming President, "You don't have any black skins among that cadet corps." That was the time they went out and recruited blacks for the academy. They had a great deal of trouble getting them in, because there had not been any interest in the Coast Guard built over the years. We had very few even enlisted personnel except for stewards.

Paul Stillwell: Or the rare person like Alex Haley who was able to break out of that.*

Admiral Siler: Yes, Alex Haley was one of the very few, and I worked with him back when we put the monument to the Coast Guard at Battery Park, New York. He had made chief by that time.

Paul Stillwell: I think he worked with Iceberg Smith at some point.†

Admiral Siler: I don't know when that was, but I don't think Smith was around at the time we did that.‡

Paul Stillwell: What do you recall about the academics at the Coast Guard Academy?

Admiral Siler: Pretty tough. [Laughter]

Paul Stillwell: But you undoubtedly were helped by having those two years of junior college under your belt.

---

* Alex Haley served in the Coast Guard as an enlisted journalist and retired as a chief petty officer. He subsequently had a civilian career as a writer and produced the Pulitzer Prize-winning book Roots that traced his lineage back to the days of slavery and to his ancestors in Africa. The initial telecast of the dramatization of the story was in early 1977 and drew 130 million viewers, making it the most-watched miniseries of all time. The cutter USCGC Alex Haley (WMEC-39) is named in the author's honor.
† See Charles A. Rawlings, "Admiral of the Ice: Rear Admiral Edward H. Smith of the Greenland Patrol," Saturday Evening Post, 8 July 1944, pages 26-27.
‡ Smith retired as a rear admiral in 1950.

Admiral Siler: I don't know how much that helped, because I took some math in junior college, but I shifted over to mathematical theory of finance. You don't have that at the Coast Guard Academy. I took analytic geometry and calculus as a freshman in junior college, and that may have helped a little bit, but I was never very good at it anyway. [Laughter] Most of the other subjects did not apply at all. Helped my study habits perhaps.

Paul Stillwell: Sure. What was the balance between academic subjects and professional subjects?

Admiral Siler: I thought professional subjects were far more interesting, for one thing. Some of the mechanical, the engineering-type subjects, were still rather difficult for me because I hadn't taken anything of that sort in college. Things like navigation and seamanship I loved, and I got just about my highest grades in navigation. Got good grades in Spanish, because I'd taken it an awful lot.

Paul Stillwell: Who were the instructors—mostly active duty officers?

Admiral Siler: Mostly. We had a few civilian instructors, and some of them were very good. We had one Spanish instructor that I recall who was a reserve officer, but as far as being an instructor in Spanish was concerned he was Spanish. His name was Santa Cruz, and he was a true Spaniard. He downgraded the Spanish grade of my classmate who had always gotten the highest grade in Spanish of anyone in the class. His reasoning for it was no one should get a 90 or higher unless he speaks and writes Spanish like a Spaniard. I got an 89. I thought it was great. [Laughter]

Paul Stillwell: What other faculty members do you remember?

Admiral Siler: Well, the other Spanish instructor, who had taught us freshman Spanish, fourth class Spanish, was a man named Colby, who was quite good. But there was a French instructor whom I never had to take anything from, I'm happy to say, because his favorite statement was, "You do better, but you still flunk." [Laughter] There was a man who made admiral who was a chemistry instructor, and his favorite expression was "What do you think about that, Mr. Steele?"[*] Joe Steele, who was a classmate of mine and graduated number two in the class, already had a degree in either chemistry or physics, so "What do you think about that? Obviously you have a degree in it. What do you think?" So he was an obvious one to call on.

Paul Stillwell: And the instructor probably didn't have a degree in it.

Admiral Siler: That's right. [Laughter] He had taken probably one semester of postgraduate instruction in it at the University of Connecticut, and I don't think he had any interest in being an instructor, but he was a pretty good soccer coach.

Paul Stillwell: Was this a period still when essentially everybody took the same classes?

Admiral Siler: Everything was exactly the same. We had a good seamanship instructor in Miles Imlay, who was just about two inches taller than I and must have outweighed me by 50 pounds anyway.[†] He made a movie that was shown as a military instructional thing. Years later, when we were in Corpus Christi, Texas, there was polio all over the place, and so we borrowed movies and somehow got a projector and used to show that movie of him rowing a boat for hours. Then we'd show it backward just for fun.

Paul Stillwell: What was the point of all the movies, to keep kids off the streets?

Admiral Siler: Well, we got the movies because we had absolutely nothing else to do at night. We were not taking any ground school at all. We were just flying.

Paul Stillwell: Did the instructors or the active duty officers throw in a lot of sea stories to get you sort of pointed toward that profession?

---

[*] Cadet Joseph R. Steele, USCG.
[†] Captain Miles H. Imlay, USCG, later served as commander of LCI Flotilla Ten and as deputy commander of Assault Group O-1 for Omaha Beach when the Allies invaded Normandy on 6 June 1944.

Admiral Siler: Not necessarily to appeal to us, but just because they would find that they'd fit in with what they were teaching. The man who taught us seamanship was the man who wrote a book about bringing the Eagle to the United States, Gordon P. MacGowan, and he had had some interesting experiences on a small ship right in this vicinity, I think Savannah and Charleston.* He used to throw in the actual experiences a lot, because it many times would demonstrate exactly what he wanted to talk about in seamanship, knowing other ships and things of that sort.

Paul Stillwell: How much emphasis in the training courses was there on the military roles of the Coast Guard?

Admiral Siler: Not a great deal. Of course, in gunnery, there would be some talk about firing the 5-inch gun for one reason or another. But the 5-inch guns hadn't been fired very often in those days. They'd been fired in drills and very frequently nothing else. On our cadet cruise in 1942, I guess it was, we were on the Atlantic, which was a beautiful schooner, and it was given by Lambert of Lambert Pharmaceutical to the Coast Guard.† We were sailing in Long Island Sound, and there was a tug that started crossing the bow of the Atlantic. Of course, the sailing vessel always has the right of way, but the towboat figured that towboats have right of way over everything else [laughter], so he was going to cut across our bow. On board was this man who had been our seamanship instructor, but at that time I don't think he was associated with the academy except for reserve training. He sent down below for a Tommy gun, loaded that thing with a magazine, and started to fire it across the bow of the tugboat. It slowed down. [Laughter]

Paul Stillwell: I'll bet he did. [Laughter] Did you enjoy going to sea?

Admiral Siler: Very much.

---

* Gordon McGowan, The Skipper and the Eagle (Princeton, New Jersey: Van Nostrand, 1960).
† In 1941 Gerard Lambert donated the Atlantic to the Coast Guard Academy. He was a noted corporate executive who was quite successful in selling Listerine to the public.

Paul Stillwell: What appealed to you about it?

Admiral Siler: Oh, just the open space and getting where you wanted to go. The navigation aspect of it was always appealing to me. I have to say I got seasick the first time we were out from New London going down the coast to St. Thomas, but I wasn't as seasick as some of them. One of my classmates was so green after two days of being at sea that he wasn't sure he wanted to stay being a cadet. Of course, as soon as he got ashore he decided he did want to stay in. But his fitness reports on the cruise were written up in such a way that he was let go. He went into the submarine service, hoping that they'd get below that.

Paul Stillwell: Did it work?

Admiral Siler: No. He did go to sea as a submarine officer, but he was not too helpful. Someone had seen him after he had tried that for a while. He had lost an awful lot of weight. He looked green, even though he was ashore. So I don't know what he did after that.

Paul Stillwell: Did the seagoing part of it tie in with this desire you'd had back in California to go the Maritime Academy? Was it that same sort of sense?

Admiral Siler: Yes, I think so. In fact, I don't think that I would have thought about the maritime academies at all if it hadn't been for the fact that they went to sea.

Paul Stillwell: What are the benefits of training under sail?

Admiral Siler: Well, I think that the great advantage there is you see some of the advantages of using the wind to do what you want to do. The other advantage is that you realize that in many cases in going to sea you'd better do what you have to do immediately, not think about it for a whole day and then say, "Well, maybe that's a good idea." [Laughter]

Paul Stillwell: Which had great applications later when you got into aviation.

Admiral Siler: You bet.

Paul Stillwell: Well, you also made a cruise in the Danmark.* Please tell me that.

Admiral Siler: Well, one of the things that I remember best about the Danmark was that we didn't have bunks to sleep in; we had hammocks.† By the time you rig a hammock so that you can get into it, you have to get some bend to it. I can't sleep on my back all the time, and I can't bend that much anyway except on my back, so I didn't sleep too well. I think one night I tried the hammock. The next night I slept on the table someplace [laughter] and slept a whole lot better.

The sailing station I had on the Danmark was the second highest on the ship, the fore royal, which was way up there, and I did enjoy that. The other thing was that we saw how much ability in seamanship the captain of that ship had.‡ He sailed it under full sail into the harbor of one of the islands out there, Long Island, and then some other ones out. He sailed it right into the harbor under full sail and dropped the sails just as if he did this every day. I don't know how strong a wind he could have done that with, because he had a bunch of dumb cadets with him.

Paul Stillwell: What do you remember about a developing sense of camaraderie with your fellow cadets, not only on board ship but in New London?

Admiral Siler: Well, of course, the first year we were on ships for quite some time. We took a pretty good cruise. The first year we went down to St. Thomas, San Juan, Havana,

---

* The Danmark was built in 1933 as a training ship for Danish merchant mariners. When Germany overran Denmark early in World War II the crew kept the ship in the United States. Once the United States declared war in December 1941, Captain Knud L. Hansen and his crew turned themselves and their ship over to the United States. She then became a training ship for Coast Guard cadets.
† The Danmark could accommodate about 120 cadets.
‡ Captain Knud L. Hansen was master of the Danmark from 1937 until 1964.

then up the coast to what later became Camp Lejeune.* In those days it was just a Marine base and nothing more. Then we went out to Bermuda. We spent two days with liberty other than the two days we went out in the middle of the harbor and made water because Bermuda was having a water shortage. I don't know that we developed anything except a dislike for being out in the middle of the harbor and not being able to get ashore.

Paul Stillwell: What do you recall of liberty in some of those spots you've named?

Admiral Siler: Well, St. Thomas and San Juan and Havana were all great fun. And we didn't have much time for liberty in what was later Camp Lejeune, because we were on the rifle range most of the time, and we were supposed to be clear-eyed the next day to shoot at the target. So we didn't have an awful lot of time for anything except shooting those rifles. We had very little time to do anything with pistols.

We were not scheduled for Bermuda at all, but the ship was ordered out there because it had the largest water evaporators available to the U.S. Navy at that time except the Saratoga and Lexington.† The Saratoga and Lexington were both in the Pacific, and we were told to go out and make water for the people in Bermuda. Of course, it rained every night we were out there. [Laughter] It was so hot we had to sleep on deck when we could, but when it rained we'd have to go back down below, and it was hot.

Paul Stillwell: They have white painted roofs there so they can catch the water in cisterns.

Admiral Siler: Yes, but it just plain didn't rain for I don't know how long. Anyway, we went out for that reason. Then, when we finally were relieved of that duty, we just went back to New London. It cancelled out a port call at Larchmont, New York, and I don't know where else, but we thought we were going to meet lots of girls in Larchmont. We didn't meet any of them. We went right into New London.

---

* Marine Corps Base Camp Lejeune, Jacksonville, North Carolina.
† USS Lexington (CV-2) and USS Saratoga (CV-3) were large Navy aircraft carriers, both commissioned in 1927.

Paul Stillwell: Did you get ashore in Bermuda at all?

Admiral Siler: The first two days, if you didn't have the duty, you could get ashore, so I got ashore once. The rest of the time our recreation was swim calls when the ship was at anchor. Unfortunately, there were a lot of Portuguese men-of-war jellyfish in that water, so that if you happened to swim through them you were in deep trouble. There was one enlisted man who had been on the ship I don't know how long before we got on the ship, and he decided he was going to take a sponge bath. The only way to do that was take a bucket, fill it with fresh water, and take your bath in that. He did it with a bucket that had had a Portuguese man-of-war in it and had the gook all over the place. He sponged that all over his body, and he was in agony. Had to get the doctor out of bed in the middle of the night to do something about that.

We had good liberty in St. Thomas, although there weren't enough girls for us to have a great time. In San Juan, again, there were not enough girls. A few people met girls, and I had a classmate who knew a Navy junior whose father happened to be stationed in San Juan. In Havana I had more luck than most of the guys, because we met a family that had about six girls and one young man who was a graduate of the Cuban Naval Academy. One of the subjects he'd had to take was English, and the father spoke excellent English. The father had written a book called Lo Que yo Vie en Europa, What I Saw in Europe on a Cruise. I had that book for years, and I kept telling myself, "I'm going to read that someday." I finally decided I was wasting time and packing space, so I threw it away.

Paul Stillwell: But your Spanish must have helped you out there.

Admiral Siler: Some, yes. Not a great deal.

Paul Stillwell: Did you get to the Royal Navy Dockyard in Bermuda?

Admiral Siler: That's where we went initially. We first went in and transferred all of the water that we'd come out with into the royal dockyard, and then when we went out into the middle of the harbor I think all that water went into someplace else.

Paul Stillwell: It's a fascinating place. It was from Bermuda that the expedition was launched in the War of 1812 that burned down Washington, because that was the big Royal Navy base in the Western Hemisphere.

Admiral Siler: I've been on a cruise of the Caribbean where there are royal dockyards all over the place, and it is fascinating to see how many places had to have royal dockyards in those days because they couldn't go very far.

Paul Stillwell: Anything else about that cruise that sticks in your mind?

Admiral Siler: No, I don't think so.

Paul Stillwell: And the <u>Danmark</u> cruise was probably shorter because the war had started by then I would think.

Admiral Siler: Well, the <u>Danmark</u> cruise was the next year, and we only had, I guess it was, two weeks on the <u>Danmark</u> and two weeks on the <u>Atlantic</u>, and that was it. So particularly that was it for us who played football.

Paul Stillwell: Please tell me about your football experiences at the academy.

Admiral Siler: Well, that first year I was just a substitute, but I didn't play until the last couple of games. I know I was told as an end at the end of the season to get in there and catch a pass because we needed to score badly. I know it was the year when Muddy

Waters, who wrote a couple of books about Coast Guard operations, ended the season on the floor of locker room crying.*

Paul Stillwell: Did you catch any passes?

Admiral Siler: No. [Laughter] The man who was playing opposite me, I think, was using an illegal system of banging me on the head to make sure that I didn't have my balance to get out there where I should have been to catch a pass. It was fortunate that I was still on my feet. And, of course, then too we played both ways, so that we had to play defense as well as offense. I think that was the year we lost every game.

Paul Stillwell: Who were some of the opponents that you played?

Admiral Siler: Trinity, Wesleyan. I'm not sure whether we played Colby then or the next year. We used to play Middlebury, Rensselaer, and Worcester Tech. That was about the schedule for a good many years. The next year I was brought back from those cruises on Long Island Sound early for the practice of football, and the third day of practice the coach said, "Okay, full suits and hit hard." I was blocked from the side, and that was the end of my football career.

Paul Stillwell: Hurt your knee.

Admiral Siler: Yes.

Paul Stillwell: Was it a torn cartilage?

Admiral Siler: I don't know. It probably was, but it was never X-rayed.

Paul Stillwell: Sports medicine was not nearly so sophisticated then.

---

* Cadet John M. Waters, Jr., USCG. His books: Bloody Winter (Princeton, New Jersey: Van Nostrand, 1967) and Rescue at Sea (Princeton: Nostrand, 1966). Waters graduated from the academy in 1942 and eventually retired from the Coast Guard in 1968 as a captain.

Admiral Siler: No. The man who was the number-one trainer was a warrant pharmacist, Mickey McClernon. I don't know that he had ever had any training other than he was a boxer and the head boxing coach. He was promoted to lieutenant commander in World War II, and we served together on Bayfield.*

Paul Stillwell: So after that you worked with the football team as a manager.

Admiral Siler: Yes.

Paul Stillwell: What did that entail?

Admiral Siler: Mainly keep checking on all the equipment, making sure that we had enough towels and enough—everybody brought their own equipment so it was not very demanding.

Paul Stillwell: What do you recall about your own boxing experiences?

Admiral Siler: Well, that first year I was told very little about style, because the coach was this warrant officer who had been boxing for a good many years. The assistant boxing coach was a chief petty officer who was also a boxer and a pretty good one. But neither one of them could coach too well. They just watched you. Maybe when the match was over they'd say, "Next time try such-and-such," but not much until then. I was heavy enough that I was classed as a heavyweight, and we had two men who were both six feet four, which was the maximum, and both of them probably weighed 20 pounds more than I did. I was afraid I'd go in against them sometime.

Fortunately, I boxed more against a light heavyweight who was a little closer to my weight except since he was an excellent football player and he would put on a little more weight during the football season and then take it off so that he could be a light heavyweight. He was a hard hitter and a rugged individual. And the 165-pounder that

---
* Lieutenant Commander Harry K. McClernon, USCG.

we had never won or lost a bout other than a TKO or a knockout.* When he boxed me, I had a black eye that lasted two weeks. The rest of that season I had a black eye on one eye or the other and usually alternate eyes every week.

Paul Stillwell: These were all intramural matches?

Admiral Siler: Well, these were in the training before we'd go off someplace and box another place.

Paul Stillwell: I see.

Admiral Siler: They used to box against Catholic University and Western Maryland University and West Point, and we beat West Point during my senior year. But I'm happy to say I didn't box that match. I had broken my nose already. [Laughter]

Paul Stillwell: How well did you do overall?

Admiral Siler: The best that I ever did was when I was listed in the newspaper as being the heavyweight boxer for the academy. I didn't make it because I broke my nose that week.

Paul Stillwell: Did you wear headgear?

Admiral Siler: Well, we did in training. I guess we didn't during the actual match, you see. But knockouts were not uncommon, particularly people like that light heavyweight and the 165-pounder. The 165-pounder, as I say, never won or lost but with a knockout.

Paul Stillwell: Did you win or lose any by knockouts?

---

* TKO—technical knockout.

Admiral Siler: Yes. [Laughter] At the end of my fourth class year we had inter-company matches so that we could say who was the best inter-company. And I boxed against a man that I played football against a lot. He was shorter than I but probably a little heavier and had shoulders like this. And I outpointed him and won that one. The next year I had decided there was no future for me in heavyweight because of these two big guys, so I tried to go down to light heavyweight, where again a rugged guy was there, but I figured I was closer to his weight and so I'd try that. I lost some strength, I'm sure, when I lost that weight. So when it came to the final match, I was matched against a fellow who again was as tall as they come, and six feet four was the maximum then. He was a lousy boxer. There were movements like that.

Paul Stillwell: A roundhouse punch.

Admiral Siler: Yes, and so I figured all I needed to do was look out for that, and I would be in good shape. Well, I missed one that was coming, and so the bout had hardly started and I was on the floor. [Laughter] But I remembered, "If you're knocked down, take the eight count and then get up. You'll be okay." So I took the eight count, and the referee was the fellow who had won the intercollegiate championship. He saw that I had taken the eight count, and so he figured I was all right. He wiped off my gloves and said, "Okay, go at it." And I didn't see the next one coming either. It was exactly the same thing. So with two of those in too short a time, I was not too great. So he stopped the match, and I was ready for that. I could not remember the day afterward what had happened that night except that I could remember coming back from the gym to the barracks, and I couldn't remember doing anything like going to dinner or anything like that. I was still too groggy.

Paul Stillwell: So that probably qualified as a TKO.

Admiral Siler: At least, and I was ready to quit then, though I didn't. I boxed. Well, I didn't box very much in my first class year, because I told myself at the beginning of the season, "If I don't have some success right away, I quit." The first match I had, I knocked out the guy who was bigger than I was again, and so I was encouraged enough to stay around until I boxed the other man who was pretty good-sized. He was heavier than I, and he connected with something on my nose and broke my nose. So that was the end of my boxing career, and I've been away from boxing every since.

Paul Stillwell: What do you recall about your social life as a cadet?

Admiral Siler: It was fortunate that Connecticut College was close enough, although I didn't concentrate on Connecticut College. I dated some town girls quite a bit. I had a good time and particularly my first class year. My second class year I enjoyed. My third class year I dated a Conn College girl all the time, and she was a nice girl from Andover, Massachusetts. She and her best friend from Andover dated my roommate and me. We met at the first dance that was for the Conn College girls and the fourth classmen. And we went together all year, both of us. That didn't last into the second year. [Laughter]

Paul Stillwell: I'll bet there've been a lot of marriages between the alumni of those two schools.

Admiral Siler: I think so. I don't know what it's like now with Conn College being coed and the Coast Guard Academy being coed. It's interesting that quite a few of the young women who've graduated from the Coast Guard Academy are married within two years. I don't know who they marry. [Laughter]

Paul Stillwell: Well, we were talking about Quentin Walsh at lunch, and he found his bride at Connecticut College.*

Admiral Siler: Well, there's quite an age difference between the two of them too.

Paul Stillwell: Yes.

---

* Commander Quentin R. Walsh, USCG, was a hero in the American capture of a German-held fort at Cherbourg, France, in June 1944. See "The Capture of Cherbourg" in Paul Stillwell, Assault on Normandy: First-Person Accounts from the Sea Services (Annapolis: Naval Institute Press, 1994).

Admiral Siler: I think he was back as an instructor after his whaling time.

Paul Stillwell: Right. He was, yes. But there was also a merchant marine training facility there at Fort Trumbull. Was there any connection between that and the Coast Guard Academy?

Admiral Siler: No. There may have been instructors from the Coast Guard that went down there but not from the academy that I am aware of.

Paul Stillwell: Your yearbook entry described you as "An oil on troubled waters type." What brought that about?

Admiral Siler: I don't know. I have no idea where that came from unless I said sometime, "Well, let's consider it," or something like that.

Paul Stillwell: Would you say that was an accurate description?

Admiral Siler: Not that I'm aware of. [Laughter] Not that my wife would say. [Laughter]

Paul Stillwell: What do you recall about getting the news that Pearl Harbor had been attacked?*

Admiral Siler: I was a third classman then, and I was working on a term paper on photography.† I had gone to a classmate's room to use his typewriter to type this thing. He had one of these little RCA Victor portable radios that was about that long, about that

---

* In late November 1941, the Imperial Japanese Navy dispatched from the Kurile Islands in the North Pacific a task force built around six aircraft carriers. A force of some 350 fighters, dive-bombers, and torpedo planes attacked U.S. military installations on the island of Oahu, Hawaii, on Sunday, 7 December 1941. The principal focus of attack was the collection of American warships at the naval base at Pearl Harbor. The U.S. Congress declared war on Japan the following day.
† A third classman is the equivalent of a college sophomore.

thick, and about that wide. It would fit in the middle drawer of a desk in a cadet's room. He had his radio on while I was typing across from him, and we heard the news.

So we knew the news before we should have known, because you couldn't have a radio in your room in those days. You couldn't have the door to your room closed officially. Nobody enforced that door situation very much with anyone except the fourth classmen. They couldn't have their doors closed, period. We were third classmen, and so we were working in there, heard the news, and were perking up to listen to the news. The man who was the senior cadet in the wing had wanted to get married just as soon as he could. He came down the hall, and when he saw the door closed he swung the door open and said, "Have you heard the news? Oh, I see you have." [Laughter] That's all that he said about that radio.

There were just two of us in the room, and we both started wondering how much effect this would have on us. We had no idea what it would mean. And I don't think very many in Coast Guard at all did. But that was the way we discovered it, and I don't think that we realized how much it was going to affect us. Now, the fellow who swung the door obviously knew. "And I'm getting married in the morning," almost. I don't think it was in the morning, but it was within a week.

Paul Stillwell: You said you didn't know then what the effects would be of the beginning of the war. What effects did you see after that?

Admiral Siler: At the academy not a great deal except we had guards posted at more sites on the academy reservation than we ever had before. We blacked out the place at night. Of course, before too long we had women in one wing of the barracks, which made for an interesting situation with female cadets in one wing and male cadets all over the place other than that.

Paul Stillwell: Where were the women from?

Admiral Siler: They were OCS.[*]

---

[*] OCS—Officer Candidate School.

Paul Stillwell: Oh, I see.

Admiral Siler: And the male OCS candidates were put in the wooden barracks that were built just for them. And for some reason they couldn't trust the women in there, but really they were in one wing of the academy barracks. And the only time that that made any difference was when we had an air raid, we blacked out the entire building and everybody went into the basement. And the women would be there and the men would be there, and supposedly there was a barricade in between, and we never knew for sure whether it was booby-trapped or not. [Laughter] But there were good rumors that it was.

Paul Stillwell: So there was a strict prohibition against fraternization, I take it.

Admiral Siler: Oh, absolutely. In fact, I don't know that anyone in my class anyway ever dated a woman OCS cadet.

Paul Stillwell: What effect did it have on the curriculum? I take it it was shortened down to three years.

Admiral Siler: Oh, yes. It was shortened to three years, but the academy class of '42 graduated two weeks after the war began, so they had no chance to shorten their program. The next class didn't shorten all the courses. They shortened some courses, but the majority of them were just dropped. Our course was the same except it was shortened. We had some things that were rather so short that you really couldn't consider very much. For example, we had a lecture by an eminent professor from Yale who used to come up and lecture on maritime economics. I think he gave us two short lectures, and that was the entire course, so obviously you don't learn much about maritime economics. Our civil engineering course consisted of a very short time in the summertime, and we had to read some material on civil engineering. It wasn't much of a course.

Paul Stillwell: The object was to get you out and serving.

Admiral Siler: And having exposure to most of these things so that if you at later times were brought back for some postgraduate training you would have had at least some exposure to what they were about but not necessarily much more than that. But I don't think we got as much on ordnance as we would normally have done, although they tried to give us as much as they could in that short period of time that they were allowed with us graduating a year early.

Paul Stillwell: Is there anything else to mention about your time as a cadet?

Admiral Siler: Our summer leave didn't amount to much. The first year I had enough time that I came home. My brother at that time was working for the airline, so he got me a pass where Western Air Express or Northwest had routes. I started out in Chicago with a free pass on Northwest to someplace in Montana. At that point I took the train—because there was nothing available at that particular time—to West Yellowstone where the park is and got off the train there. I knew that Western Airlines would be available later that day, and I took the airline flight from there to Las Vegas. Spent the night in the hotel as an associate of Western Airlines and then flew into Los Angeles. Pretty nice way to go.

Didn't work that well going back the other way, but anyway I ended up eventually after taking the Karstt Stage, as they called it. This was a panel truck with two extra seats in it into Bozeman, Montana, and caught the train there. Took the train to Fargo, North Dakota, and I thought I'd catch Northwest there. Eventually a vice president of Northwest came in in a Lockheed private airplane, and he took all of the people who were on passes from there into Minneapolis. From Minneapolis into Chicago was cinch, and then I took the train the rest of the way.

The next year one of the cadets had done some research about what the best way to get to California was from Chicago, because we figured the best way to get from New London to Chicago was by train. He didn't know what train we should take from Chicago on. He found out that the fastest train, even faster than the Super Chief, was a thing called the fast mail train. The only trouble was it had no passenger facilities, and I do mean no. It had half of one railroad car that had seats that went this way or they went that way, and that was it. As far as coolness was concerned, you opened the window. What else? In the middle of winter they had a coal-burning pot-bellied stove in one corner.

A bunch of us decided we could do that, because it was as fast as the Super Chief. We took a good car from Chicago to St. Louis, and then we all went, other than what the trainmaster figured that we were going to take, and went to the fast mail train. They searched us down, passed the word for the Coast Guard cadets and so on. They eventually found us and said, "We're going to tell your commanding officer." And we said, "Go ahead." [Laughter] Of course, they never did. We got on the fast mail train, and the only way you could get food was to tell the conductor and he'd drop a rock or something with a note tied to it and say, "At the next station give me X number of lunches." [Laughter]

He'd slow down going through the next little station and take a bunch of box lunches, and that was all we had to eat for a day or so. It was hot, and we'd get perspiration circles like this under the arms. We all wore sailor suits that nobody'd know what they were anyway. We took the fast mail train into Los Angeles, and I remember as we went through Pasadena one of my classmates got off there. We all envied him, because he got off ten minutes before we did. [Laughter] The rest of us were trying our best to clean up, and, of course, we had a little washroom that big and the basin that big, and that was where we washed. The only thing we had. So we cleaned up a little bit, put on our blue uniforms with white shirts and paper collars probably, because that's what we were wearing in those days. I'm not sure about that paper collar because I threw away both the shirt and the collar it was so black by the time I'd worn it that night.

Then we got into Los Angeles, and I had a date that I'd arranged by mail with a girl I'd never had a date with before but whom I'd seen with my older brother who had life-guarded at the Los Angeles Country Park, a big park up above Los Angeles. It was way out in the extremities of the county. But this girl was a real glamour girl. She had glamour photographs that I used to keep in the room just to give me inspiration.

Paul Stillwell: Build your morale.

Admiral Siler: Yeah. I had a very pleasant evening with her. When I got back to her house that night, where I guess I shared a bedroom with one of her two or three brothers, I took off my shirt and the cuffs were absolutely black and, as I say, I threw it way. I don't know what I wore to get home, but anyway that was a tough way to get home, and I don't think that I came back that way. I probably took one of the Chiefs that was a whole lot better than that. One fellow arrived in Phoenix, Arizona, and his parents looked at him and said, "You look terrible. You're not going back that way. Before we leave this station, let's buy your ticket back another way."

Paul Stillwell: And, of course, you weren't as eager to make the trip back east as you had been to make the one west.

Admiral Siler: No, that's true too. But we didn't have much time for leave at that time because the war was on.

Paul Stillwell: What do you remember about a sense of patriotism in the country then? I've heard of servicemen being treated extremely well by civilians.

Admiral Siler: I think we were treated well, but I can't say anything strikes me as being outstanding.

Paul Stillwell: Your discussion of the northern route reminds me once I heard a talk by a woman who was in South Dakota working with the USO.[*] They would feed pheasant sandwiches to the servicemen as they came through on trains.

Admiral Siler: I didn't see anything of that. In fact, I didn't see anyplace where the train stopped and you'd get out and have sandwiches. I have had only the possibility of getting a small cup of Coke or something like that.

---

[*] USO—United Services Organization is a group of U.S. civilians who put on entertainment programs for service personnel and provide hospitality for them in many parts of the world.

Paul Stillwell: As your time passed as a cadet did you have an eagerness to get out into the fleet?

Admiral Siler: I think any time you've spent three or four years at the academy you have an eagerness to get out of there. [Laughter]

Paul Stillwell: What do you recall about your graduation?

Admiral Siler: Well the speaker was Forrestal, and I don't remember what he said.[*] I remember a good many years after I retired when Tom Moorer spoke to the Coast Guard Academy graduates.[†] One of his statements was, "I don't expect anybody here to remember what I said tomorrow." [Laughter] And I thought, "How accurate that is." [Laughter] And I have no idea what Forrestal said at graduation.

One of the very funny things to me—I'm not sure that my wife feels it's as funny—but, of course, I didn't have any family coming to graduation across the country. There wasn't any way to get there in those days. So I had asked the girl I'd been dating if she would come to graduation. And she wasn't too anxious to go, I guess. She was pretty much engaged to a man who was in, I'd guess, the submarine service because the sub base was right across the river.[‡] Finally she agreed to come to graduation. After graduation a Coast Guard photographer asked if my girl and I would pose for a picture with her kissing me in congratulation for graduation. We posed for the picture. He took the picture and distributed it all over New England at least. And it appeared in her hometown paper, which was Stamford, Connecticut. Her mother was furious because she was a society girl, and here I was just one more cadet, although she'd been very nice to me the times that I had been in Stamford. Later I visited in the town as well. The parents

---

[*] James V. Forrestal served as Under Secretary of the Navy from 22 August 1940 to 16 May 1944.
[†] Admiral Thomas H. Moorer, USN, served as Chief of Naval Operations from 1 August 1967 to 1 July 1970. He was later Chairman of the Joint Chiefs of Staff from 3 July 1970 to 30 June 1974. His oral history is in the Naval Institute collection.
[‡] Naval Submarine Base New London is the site of the Navy's Submarine School. Despite its name, it is on the Groton side of the Thames River.

bought us tickets to go see Oklahoma.* So I just have always remembered how furious that mother was that I posed for that picture.

Paul Stillwell: Did she think that a cadet was beneath her daughter in social station?

Admiral Siler: Oh, absolutely. I have no idea where that girl is today. [Laughter] I think she's in Florida because other girls have said something, not because I've kept track of her.

Paul Stillwell: And your wife has prevented any thorough investigations probably.

Admiral Siler: I have never mentioned any investigation, and I'm not about to. [Laughter]

Paul Stillwell: That's right. Well, after that how soon did you have orders to go to your first ship?

Admiral Siler: I had orders already. Before we graduated we had orders, but we were kept at the academy for a period of about three weeks to give us some indoctrination into antisubmarine warfare so we'd at least understand what went on there. Then we'd go out on the Coast Guard 83-footers in those days, wooden 83-footers, and we'd cruise up and down Long Island Sound pinging on the submarines that would come out from the sub base. Then after the three weeks, we were just told, "Good-bye. Get on your way and get to your ship."

Paul Stillwell: Who provided the training in ASW?

Admiral Siler: The Coast Guard. We had the 83-footers, and we would have recordings that we'd listen to for the pinging and have some instruction on how you did that. We

---

* Oklahoma was a popular Broadway musical of the period.

had actual stacks that we could listen to in basement of buildings.* Of course, a lot different now, but anyway it was an exposure to how submarine warfare works, and it wasn't expected to be much more than that. Of course, if you were going to something that had some real equipment, you'd have to do a lot more training.

Paul Stillwell: Like the Secretary class.†

Admiral Siler: Yes. We had time to kill very frequently when we were headed to our first assignment. In San Francisco you'd report in to the Navy for transportation. You'd go to the Coast Guard and report in there, and they'd say, "Okay, go to the Navy and report in there." When you'd get to the Navy, they'd say, "These courses and classes are available. Which would you like?" You could choose among them, depending on what kind of a ship you were going to. I don't think I went to any ASW at that time, but in San Diego later I got more ASW training.

In San Francisco—not then but a later time—I took a 5-inch/38 course.‡ We didn't have a 5-inch/38 on the first ship I was on. The later ship that I went to did have 5-inch/38, and I went to the class there. But that first time I can't remember what courses I took, but I think probably I went to one or two courses of some kind. Then eventually they put four of us Coast Guard officers on a ship that was headed to the South Pacific. We spent I think it was 19 days getting to Noumea, New Caledonia.

Paul Stillwell: Was this a Navy ship?

Admiral Siler: This was on a Dutch ship which had been converted to transport-type duty. The first place we went was to Port Hueneme down the coast, and we picked up a whole battalion of Seabees.§ While we were in there, we were told, "Go where you want

---

* The assembled components of sonar gear are referred to as the sonar stack.
† The Coast Guard's Secretary-class cutters were built and commissioned in the mid-1930s and served for many years. Each ship was 327 feet long, 41 feet in the beam, a maximum draft of 15 feet, and a maximum speed of 19.5 knots.
‡ This refers to a gun with an inside barrel diameter of 5 inches. Those in World War II were dual purpose, for use against either air or surface targets.
§ Seabees is the nickname applied to members of the Navy's mobile construction battalions (CBs).

to, but be back here such-and-such a time on Monday morning, and we'll be sailing." So we went into Los Angeles.

There were two people in the group who were reserve officers and a fellow named MacFarland and myself. We all went to Los Angeles. One of the fellows went home, the other one went to his girlfriend's, and I don't know where I stayed now at all. But, anyway, we spent a day or so in Los Angeles. Then got back to San Barbara. I remember some of my classmates from junior college were at Santa Barbara State. That was Santa Barbara State College then instead of the University of California, Santa Barbara. Soon we went back to the ship at Port Hueneme, and they'd loaded the Seabee battalion. We sailed from there and never saw land at all until we finally got to Noumea, New Caledonia. My ship was in, so the four of us went over there and introduced ourselves on the ship, because we didn't know a soul on that ship.

Paul Stillwell: Did you have any watch-standing duties during that long transit?

Admiral Siler: No. Sunbathing was the main thing.

Paul Stillwell: And you reported on board the Hunter Liggett?

Admiral Siler: Yes, that was on the Hunter Liggett. We went out on a Dutch ship; Weltevraden was its name. We got on the Hunter Liggett and went north to what is today a different country than one of those that became independent.* We did some amphibious training there, with the landing craft from the ships, and we had New Zealand and Anzac training.†

Paul Stillwell: Fiji?

---

* USS Hunter Liggett (APA-14) was a Navy attack transport that was manned by a Coast Guard crew in World War II. She was commissioned 9 June 1941. She displaced 21,900 tons, was 535 feet long, 72 feet in the beam, had a maximum draft of 31 feet, and a top speed of 15 knots. She was armed with four 3-inch guns and carried a variety of landing craft for amphibious warfare operations.
† During World War II the Anzac area comprised the land and water areas of eastern Australia, New Zealand, British New Guinea, the Solomons, Loyalties, and Fijis.

Admiral Siler: No, no, we weren't that far up. We were on a line between Noumea and Guadalcanal. That was one of the New Hebrides in those days.*

Paul Stillwell: Was she a converted passenger ship?

Admiral Siler: The Hunter Liggett was, yes.† It was 535 feet long, twin-turbine power. It would make about 18 knots. Rather comfortable ship and had still not been completely converted to troop use. In fact, we went into Wellington, New Zealand, in November of '43 for some more conversion, and they tore out about a ton more of plywood. Some of the places that they tore the plywood out they still had the paintings that had been on there when she was decorated as a passenger ship. We went into Guadalcanal on that first trip and took all the troops off and headed south. On the way south we had a Navy escort for a while, and the destroyer would zigzag out in front of us. A Japanese plane dove out of the clouds and dropped bombs on us on the way south. I was at the conn and had just turned to port, and the bombs dropped out here to starboard, where we would have been if we hadn't turned.‡

Paul Stillwell: Interesting that that's an antisubmarine maneuver, but it helped in this case against aircraft.

Admiral Siler: That's right. It was the normal cruising maneuver for zigzagging.

Paul Stillwell: What was your job when you reported to the ship?

Admiral Siler: I was assistant first division officer, which meant that I was supposed to oversee the cargo handling and the boat handling up there on the forward part of the ship, forward of the bridge. My station at general quarters was the number-one 3-inch gun up there. There were two guns up forward and then the break and the holds number one,

---

* In October 1943 the ship went to Efate in the New Hebrides.
† The ship was built in 1922 as the SS Pan America. After years of merchant service she was transferred to the Army in 1939 and became Hunter Liggett. She kept the name when transferred to the Navy in 1941.
‡ The individual with the conn—normally an officer—directs the ship's movements in course and speed.

two, and three. Number three was usually covered with the two big LCMs.* I don't recall whether we had boats on the number one and two at all, but number three was always covered with the big LCMs. The LCVPs were off on the sides of the ship.†

Paul Stillwell: Welin davits?‡

Admiral Siler: Yes. But the number three had to be handled by the big boom on the ship. And we always sort of wondered about whether it was going to make it because it was so big.

Paul Stillwell: Probably hadn't been designed for that job.

Admiral Siler: That's right. Hadn't been at all. In fact, I don't know when they put it on. Probably back about '40, I guess. But we went back to Wellington, and as I say that Japanese plane tried to get us. When I was in Wellington, either the first or second night I went ashore and found an officers' club, which was a civilian officers' club. One of the women there was a WREN from New Zealand, and she looked at the shield on my sleeve and said, "Oh, you're from the Hunter Liggett. You were attacked by a Japanese plane."§ I thought, "Who else knew about this?" But she knew all the dope. I think we spent about two weeks there, and we went into dry dock. The entire underwater body of the ship was painted. It was hard to get that ship into position because it was so big, and by the time it took out as much ballast as it could, the wind would flop it this way or flop that way. Finally they just had to say, "Okay, drop it. Let's see what happens." And it worked. We got it in on the dry dock, and then we were pumped out of the water.

---

* LCM—landing craft mechanized, a type of craft equipped with a bow ramp that can be lowered on a beach during an amphibious landing. It was large enough to hold large trucks and small tanks.
† LCVP—landing craft, vehicle and personnel.
‡ Welin davits are lifting devices for putting the boats into the water and recovering them later.
§ WRNS—Women's Royal Naval Service. When pronounced, the acronym sounded like "wrens." The shield device on his sleeve indicated he was in the Coast Guard. Navy line officers wear a star in a comparable position as part of the rank insignia.

Paul Stillwell: Why had so much ballast been taken out?

Admiral Siler: Well, the ship was heavy when it was operating, and it certainly didn't need to be that heavy when it was going into dry dock.

Paul Stillwell: I see.

Admiral Siler: We had the same trouble later when we went into dry dock in San Francisco. It was really bad when we went to San Francisco. We were in winds that were probably 40 miles an hour or more. We'd go one direction, and the wind would flop us this way and turn around, and it would flop us that way.

Paul Stillwell: A lot of sail area.*

Admiral Siler: A very big ship.

Paul Stillwell: Well, I wonder also if adding the boats topside added to that effect also.

Admiral Siler: Probably. Instability.

We had I think it was two weeks there in Wellington, and then we went back to Guadalcanal and picked up the troops there that we took to the New Hebrides. It's now a private country, Vanuatu.† We did training with some more troops before we went to Bougainville. When we went up to Bougainville, the first day we didn't have much escort at all, and then we accumulated a whole bunch of destroyers. I think we were escorted by about 10 destroyers, and there were 12 ships in our transports group. We

---

* "Sail area" is a term for a ship's vertical surfaces on which the wind exerts force.
† Before achieving independence and being renamed, the New Hebrides were under joint British and French administration.

went into Bougainville. We were the second ship to go in.* The first one was the American Legion, which was an exact sister ship. She was to fire on the beach as she went in. Then we were to go in, and we were to fire on the beach. I was told several times by my friends and cohorts, "Now, remember, as you'll get closer you're going to have to spot down." We spotted down, and it filled the water with shells. [Laughter] The trouble was the first shot was not on the beach, and so none of the other ones were.

Paul Stillwell: Were you concerned about an air threat going in there?

Admiral Siler: Not concerned when we went in, but once we got in we sure were. In fact, the day after we had gotten there, we talked to people who had been in the radio room or in the code room immediately across from the radio room. They were scared to death, because they could hear the communications and knew that the aircraft were there all the time. There were quite a few times when they were told things that sounded as if we were in deep trouble. We didn't have any trouble with the ships, but I was in one of the landing craft. I was the wave commander on one of the later waves. One of the earlier waves had gone in, not from our ship, and the landing craft dropped the ramp directly across from a Japanese machinegun. It just mowed down most everyone in that boat.

Paul Stillwell: That would be an LCVP?

Admiral Siler: Yes. The problem with our wave was the surf was much bigger than our people were used to, and a good many boats broached on the beach. Then the boat group commander operated a boat that had no ramp at all. It was pretty maneuverable, and so it was going to help get those boats, pull so that they could get off the beach. While it was there, why, the Japanese planes came over and strafed the beach. The coxswain of that boat, which was our boat group commander's, was hit with a shell that had gone into the water, ricocheted off and went through the side of the boat and went into his chest. He

---

* On 1 November 1943 U.S. forces made an amphibious assault on Bougainville, the largest island in the Solomons chain.

breathed through that for months before he finally died. He had had malaria, and it probably recurred when he was very ill. The boat group commander himself was later my roommate, and he hated it when someone asked him how he got his Purple Heart. I think he did wear it, but he didn't want anyone to ask, because he was hit in his backside when he was face down in the boat. [Laughter]

Paul Stillwell: How close did your boat go in?

Admiral Siler: Well, we went in and let our troops off.

Paul Stillwell: You beached.

Admiral Siler: Yes, and all of the boats in my wave got off again. But we went out into the middle of the bay, and our ship was gone because they'd gotten the warning that Japanese planes were coming, and so there they went.

Paul Stillwell: Gives you kind of a helpless feeling.

Admiral Siler: Oh, it sure does. "What do we do now?" We didn't even have enough equipment to spend the night someplace on the beach. A good many of the boat crews had been told to expect something like that, and so they should take equipment along. One of our people unfortunately was court-martialed, because he took more than he should have, and he was accused of preparing to spend months on the beach at Bougainville. He was returned the next time the ship came in and then court-martialed for going over the hill on Bougainville. [Laughter] I never heard of such a thing as being over the hill in a combat area. We went back to Tulagi and loaded up again and took those people back to Bougainville a second time.

Paul Stillwell: So the ship did come back.

Admiral Siler: Yes. [Laughter] And at that point we took this guy back aboard, court-martialed him, and finally he was acquitted. One of the court members, I think the president of the court, said, "I don't think this guy should be court-martialed. I think he ought to be decorated." Anyway he got off. And most of the people were not prepared to spend any time I know. I'm pretty sure that most of the officers who were in the boats supposedly just for that wave and coming on back were not equipped to spend time on the beach. So when the ships pulled over the horizon, it gave us quite a start. While we were there, milling around in the middle of the bay, the Japanese planes came over and strafed the beach. That gave us a second concern. However, most of them just made one pass, and that was it.

Paul Stillwell: How soon did the ship come back for you?

Admiral Siler: Probably two hours at most.

Paul Stillwell: So you weren't stranded overnight.

Admiral Siler: No. We got back on the ship and went to work unloading. The ships were all unloaded completely. I think they took a day and a half to get everything off. They went back from there to Tulagi.

Paul Stillwell: Did you have any more air raids other than that one?

Admiral Siler: Not that we could see, but we didn't have air-search radar, so we didn't know.

Paul Stillwell: That's what the destroyers were for.

Admiral Siler: Yes.

Paul Stillwell: What do you recall about interaction between the ship's crew and the Marines?

Admiral Siler: I wasn't in a position to know that at all, so I really don't know.

Paul Stillwell: Just had them as passengers briefly then going ashore.

Admiral Siler: Yes, and we had a transport commander who was a Marine colonel, full colonel, so we didn't expect any problems and didn't have any. I'm not sure about other ships.

Paul Stillwell: What was the mechanism whereby a Navy ship was operated by a Coast Guard crew?

Admiral Siler: Here's the ship and get a crew. I don't know that there was anything to it except here it is.

Paul Stillwell: Were there any differences in procedures between the way a Navy ship would be run and a Coast Guard ship?

Admiral Siler: I doubt it. I was on two Navy ships, and in both cases they were just Navy ships. If anything was to be different, we were to learn what it was like in the Navy and use their procedure. Someone else asked me a very similar question recently, and my feeling was that it's a Navy ship. Regardless where the people come from, it's a Navy ship.

Paul Stillwell: Well, and the Coast Guard didn't have any independent amphibious capability, so you would use their procedures.

Admiral Siler: Sure. Although one of the reasons why the Coast Guard went into amphibious warfare was because we handled the boats better in surf than most Navy people did.

Paul Stillwell: Which is understandable.

Admiral Siler: Well, it may not be true today when you have amphibious training the way the Navy does, but over the years the Coast Guard has probably had more time operating in a surf situation than the Navy.

Paul Stillwell: Well, during some of the Navy's amphibious warfare development in the late '30s, they had boats that were not suited to it at all, like motor whaleboats, for example.

Admiral Siler: And we tried them. [Laughter] When I was on cadet cruise, I guess in the second cruise, we went to an offshore island near New London and spent the whole day operating not motor lifeboats but rowed lifeboats. One of the things we did particularly was get in the surf so that the thing would capsize, and we experienced that. The coxswain would stand back there with a big steering oar trying to keep it as straight as he could.

Paul Stillwell: What other adventures do you recall from the Hunter Liggett?

Admiral Siler: Well, after the invasion of Bougainville and another trip to Bougainville we were ordered to go to Espiritu Santo, Samoa, and back to the States. We went into Oakland and went through a semi-overhaul. Then we were ordered to San Diego to join the amphibious training group in San Diego as a training ship there. First we started with the Army's troops from Fort Rosecrans, and we trained them, and then in between we'd take crews from the Navy's amphibious training base and operate with them so they'd operate the boats. Then we started taking troops from—in those days they didn't call it Camp Pendleton. It was the Marine installation at the mouth of the Santa Margarita

River. The last landing that we would make would be at the mouth of the Santa Margarita River. I was always impressed by the navigating ability of the man who was the navigator. I was the assistant navigator on the Hunter Liggett, and this guy would check that radarscope and say, "Change course five degrees." We'd always be right in the spot he wanted to be.

Paul Stillwell: You said that navigation was something that had interested you at the academy.

Admiral Siler: Yes, but here he was navigating with a new method completely, and we were not introduced to radar at all at the academy.

Paul Stillwell: Well, it was highly classified thus far.

Admiral Siler: Yes, and, of course, I think we had loran by this time, but it was highly classified.* In fact, you had to keep a cover on the thing because it was so highly classified. Any time you wanted to use it, you had to unlock the tables, because there was nothing known as a loran chart. You would chart the position using two points that were given to you from these tables and draw a line in between.

Paul Stillwell: So you got lines of position out from the stations? Was that it?

Admiral Siler: Yes.

Paul Stillwell: Do you have any memories about formation steaming when you were with other ships? Was radar a help there?

Admiral Siler: We didn't have radar when I first got on the ship.

---

* Loran (long-range aid to navigation) is a system of electronic navigation that involves the reception of pulse signals transmitted simultaneously by paired stations ashore.

Paul Stillwell: I see.

Admiral Siler: We got radar when we were in New Zealand, and at that time we tried not to use it for station keeping because we felt it was important to know who else was out there. We had operated for years without radar for station keeping, so we still didn't use it most of the time. As I remember, there was one time when we were off the coast of California, and I was the senior OOD.* One of my junior OODs was actually senior to me, and it was time that he got to the point where he could navigate and be in position. So I said, "Okay, you have the conn." I walked out on the port wing of the bridge, and all of a sudden here was this ship that was supposed to be astern of us passing us. [Laughter] So I notified the old man in a hurry and told him what had happened. And we ended up in San Diego in last position. [Laughter]

Paul Stillwell: Did you use mostly stadimeter for station keeping?†

Admiral Siler: In the daytime, but you couldn't at night. At night you had to use binoculars and see how much of the field of your vision you'd get the distance you were supposed to be.

Paul Stillwell: Well, and after a while also you develop what's called the seaman's eye and are pretty good at judging distances.

Admiral Siler: Well, the best way to measure distance at night is with the field of vision of the binoculars.

Paul Stillwell: What do you recall about the officers and the training that you got going to sea?

---

* OOD—officer of the deck.
† The stadimeter is a mechanical device for measuring the range to another ship when the height of her mast is known.

Admiral Siler: Well, a lot of the training that we got was just talking about the experience and on vessels that were entirely different from the transports. A transport is a lot bigger and a lot slower to maneuver than a Coast Guard cutter, and the instructors at the academy usually were talking about what the Coast Guard cutter does. A transport is an entirely different animal.

Paul Stillwell: Probably had a very big turning circle.

Admiral Siler: Yes, a big turning circle, and yet if you tried to anticipate on a turn, if you turned inside, you were in deep trouble. So there were a good many things that you just had to learn by being junior OOD on the ship.

Paul Stillwell: Do any of the senior officers particularly stand out in your mind?

Admiral Siler: I think two of them particularly. Captain Patch was very interesting, because he had spent a good part of his career in the Army.[*] He'd graduated from the Coast Guard Academy I think in 1913 or '13 to '17, somewhere in there, and he served first in the Army because he became dissatisfied with being in the Coast Guard away from World War I.[†] He was about that tall.

Paul Stillwell: You're indicating about three or four feet.

Admiral Siler: Well, that's just about right. [Laughter] At least that's the way it seemed to me. And the exec was another one who was about that high. It was very funny to see the two of them on the bridge, because someone had realized that they were so short that they could not see over the windbreakers out on the wing of the bridge. But there was a place just about that wide—

Paul Stillwell: About two feet wide.

---

[*] Captain Roderick S. Patch, USCG.
[†] Patch's date of rank as an ensign was 1 September 1915.

Admiral Siler: Well, maybe a little more than that but no more than three.

Paul Stillwell: Like a shelf maybe?

Admiral Siler: Well, like there was a window there.

Paul Stillwell: Oh, I see.

Admiral Siler: And you could drop the windscreen from that area and lean out and see what was going on right down below you. The two of them used to fight over those positions all the time. [Laughter] It was so funny that you had to get on the other wing of the bridge to control your laughter at their wiggling into the little viewing space. Commander Hahn's son was on the ship for a while, and the son was a signalman.[*]

The exec was a commander most of the time. He'd been made captain and had to be transferred off because he was too senior to be the exec. People just loved him. He knew what went on on that ship. The first thing in the morning, of course, we'd be at general quarters an hour before sunrise. About the time the sun would come over the horizon, he'd say, "Goddamn it. I wonder what horrible thing will happen today." [Laughter] A New England accent—really funny to hear.

I searched all over the ship one day for him—I thought all over the ship. And probably the messenger was searching right behind him everyplace he'd go. So I finally used the PA system, knowing that he didn't like it. And he said, "Mr. Siler, don't ever use that public address system to get me. I'll either be in my stateroom or in the office." BANG! I'd gotten him, though. [Laughter] He had answered the phone by this time, because we only had one phone from off the ship, and it went to the gangway. And Captain Patch was, as I say, the same height and a real funny guy. He retired in San Diego. When I was Commandant he came to hear me speak one time.

Paul Stillwell: I'll bet you enjoyed that reunion.

---
[*] Commander Edward E. Hahn, Jr., USCG.

Admiral Siler: Yes, it was interesting to see him again. I don't know how old he would have been at that point. I'm sure he's dead now. Both of them are probably dead now.

Paul Stillwell: Well, if he was in World War I he was probably in his 80s by then.

Admiral Siler: Probably. Hahn was not quite that old. He had served in the merchant marine before he became a Coast Guard officer, and we did have his son aboard for a while.

Paul Stillwell: Did you have division officer responsibilities also?

Admiral Siler: I was assistant first division officer, but my responsibilities after that became assistant navigator. I really enjoyed that more, and I always liked the navigation responsibilities.

Paul Stillwell: What do you remember about the quality of the enlisted personnel?

Admiral Siler: Some of the people in the first division were amazingly capable. There was one man who was older than a good many of them, and I know he was a college graduate. Turned down a commission because I guess he just plain didn't want it. And they ranged every place in between. The most interesting thing was the way some of the blacks were integrated into the crew sooner or later, particularly later. There was one young man who was in not my division but either the division that had the after part of the ship or the boat division, I'm not sure which it was. I used to see him playing around with the other crew members just the same as anybody else, as if his skin were painted white.

Paul Stillwell: Was he a steward?

Admiral Siler: Oh, no. Never had been a steward. I don't know how he managed to go straight into deck work, but he was a deck man.

One of the interesting stewards was a man who had been John D. Rockefeller's personal valet.* He was initially a third class petty officer and obviously far more capable than most of our first class petty officers. And, of course, some of the most serious fights you'd have among the crew were in the black stewards' quarters. When this man was a third class petty officer he started taking some responsibility to maintain discipline, and very shortly afterward he was coming up to second and first class. I don't know if he ever made chief while I was aboard, but he was the man in charge very soon after he got on the ship and showed his capabilities.

Paul Stillwell: Did that cut down on the fighting?

Admiral Siler: I don't know for sure about the fighting, but he certainly got a lot more done in the division.

Paul Stillwell: Now, were these black versus white incidents or black versus black?

Admiral Siler: Black versus black.

Paul Stillwell: Did you have any racial disharmony?

Admiral Siler: Not that I can recall. I think if we had any it was between blacks and Filipinos, because they'd be competing for the same thing in the steward division. But we had almost all blacks, not Filipinos.

Paul Stillwell: What happened as far as the operations after you got back to the States and were involved in that amphibious training?

---

* John D. Rockefeller (1839-1937) was one of the richest men in the United States as a result of founding and operating the Standard Oil Company. His son, John D. Rockefeller, Jr. (1874-1960) was involved with his father's business interests.

Admiral Siler: Well, then the problems didn't become anything racial at all, but it was geographical problems, because so many of our enlisted people were from Los Angeles and they'd go to Los Angeles. Every time they had two days off, they'd go to Los Angeles, and if they couldn't get a ride back, huh, so what. They'd all be AWOL, and they didn't care.* About that time I was put on the court for the ship, and we had a permanent summary court. And there was one time when I was requested as the counsel.

Paul Stillwell: Defense counsel?

Admiral Siler: Yes. Obviously I was not on that court, but I was asked to be this guy's counsel. It turned out that he was picked up by the shore patrol when he was ashore because he was trying to break into a house. The reason he was trying to break into it was because that was his girlfriend's house. [Laughter] The only trouble was she was gone for the weekend and he didn't know it. So he was trying to break into the window where the housekeeper for the weekend was sleeping, and she immediately called the shore patrol and they came out and picked him up. We had to testify to the fact that he had been trying to get into the girlfriend's house. The girlfriend came to testify that that was where she normally slept.

Of course, the whole thing was thrown out as fast as we could possibly do it, but the captain in the meantime had said, "We'll have a summary court." For some reason we didn't get the word to the captain that, "This thing's all been solved, and it's a big mistake." So the man who was the permanent prosecutor on the ship, who was a well-qualified attorney, kept saying, "Don't worry about it. We'll just get it thrown out." But we got it all the way up before the court and the court sworn in and the first testimony, "I do this all the time." [Laughter] So that one was kind of funny.

Paul Stillwell: Made you look good as a defense attorney.

Admiral Siler: Oh, absolutely. [Laughter]

---

* AWOL—absent without leave. The Navy equivalent for this term is UA—unauthorized absence.

Paul Stillwell: What other operations was the ship involved in after that?

Admiral Siler: Well, it wasn't until after I left that it went back on the Magic Carpet run.* It was going to Japan and the Philippines and loading up troops and taking them back to the West Coast, because if it got out on the ocean and was just cruising along, it could make 18 to 20 knots, and there were very few ships that were that size in particular that could do that. That was a big ship, 535 feet, and it probably could carry I'd guess 3,000 troops anyway, maybe more.

Paul Stillwell: That's a lot of men to take care of.

Admiral Siler: It sure is. And whoever cooks the food for them has a real job. One interesting thing was that the troops ate all their meals standing up. Got them out of the mess hall in a hurry. The troop officers ate in what used to be the passengers' dining room, and we used that space when the ship was under repair at times. It was a pretty good spot to have a dining room and not too far away from where the enlisted personnel were. One other interesting thing about that ship, we had quite a few enlisted men who wore the old uniform of the surfman before the surfmen were integrated in the total Coast Guard.†

Paul Stillwell: How did that uniform differ?

Admiral Siler: Their shirts were this style instead of sailor's jumper. And it seems to me that the trousers were creased instead of inside-out creases.

Paul Stillwell: They were creased front and back.

Admiral Siler: Yes.

---

* Magic Carpet was the nickname for the use of Navy ships, including combatants, to bring servicemen home to the United States from overseas once World War II ended.
† In 1915 the Lifesaving Service, including its surfmen, was amalgamated into a new organization known as the U.S. Coast Guard.

Paul Stillwell: Well, did they have some kind of a grandfather clause exception on those?

Admiral Siler: Yes. When they were moved over from surfmen to seamen, they were told they had a certain number of years that they could wear the surfman uniform.

Paul Stillwell: Well, now the merger was in 1915. Did they go back that far?

Admiral Siler: Oh, no. They didn't assign those people to regular ships for a good many years after that merger.

Paul Stillwell: So they were just in a specialized branch of the Coast Guard.

Admiral Siler: Yes. They were still kept on lifesaving stations, and I don't know when that changed. But we had quite a few surfmen at that time.

Paul Stillwell: I have never heard that.

Admiral Siler: We had a good many of them, believe me. Well, of course, a good reason for that was that they were taking these people and putting them into seagoing operations when they never had before. They were all always on a shore station before.

Paul Stillwell: Well, and the other part of it was that if they were manning those landing craft they were going into the surf.

Admiral Siler: Yes. So it changed but not too fast.

Paul Stillwell: Did you spend any time down in the troop compartments?

Admiral Siler: Oh, yes, because in the first division we had responsibility for all of the troops and troop spaces forward. Now, that would be number-one and -two holds.

Number three didn't have any troops. It would have cargo only. But when we'd check those compartments, we'd go down and look at the bunks and the heads. The bunks were either four or five high, and I don't know how anybody got in those top bunks unless they were—you'd have to get the ship rolling the right way. Just hang on if you're rolling the wrong way.

The heads were very interesting, because they were all the way forward in the ship. When the wind was blowing 70 miles an hour, as it did when we were headed into San Francisco, the ship would go up, up, up and back down. And there you were, still there. [Laughter] If you were sitting on one of those things you might end up on one three away. [Laughter]

Paul Stillwell: Well, I've heard from some of those troops that that was a miserable experience.

Admiral Siler: I'm sure it was. I think the troops today might have it a little better but I'm not sure how much.

Paul Stillwell: Well, they hardly had room to turn around or roll over in their bunks, and there would be an aroma of seasickness throughout the compartment.

Admiral Siler: Oh, now that was pretty bad. When we were coming back from Samoa to San Francisco it was miserable. And the wind was blowing 75 a good deal of that time.

Paul Stillwell: Well, they said it was almost a relief to be able to get out of the ship and go ashore on an invasion. [Laughter]

Admiral Siler: Well, I don't think that was quite so true in the South Pacific, because most of the time the sea in the South Pacific was not bad. You'd find some bad surf when you'd get into some of the practice landings that would be on islands down around New Zealand or someplace like that, but even when you'd land on the New Hebrides, the surf was like that.

Paul Stillwell: Maybe a foot or foot and a half.

Admiral Siler: At most. And when we went to Bougainville the sea was two to three feet high, and that's when a good many of our boats were broached on the beach. So it didn't take much to upset those boats if they didn't know how to operate them.

Paul Stillwell: Was it up to the troop officers to maintain discipline in those compartments?

Admiral Siler: Yes. We didn't have to do that.

Paul Stillwell: That was their territory, and you had a different one.

Admiral Siler: Right.

Paul Stillwell: How much did you learn in terms of being a mariner from that shipboard experience?

Admiral Siler: I can't say I learned an awful lot. Most of the seamanship aspects of it I had learned at the academy from lectures, and so exposure to it in the actual case was pretty much what I expected.

Paul Stillwell: And probably you wouldn't have any experience taking her in or out of port.

Admiral Siler: No, because most of the time that size ship under Navy command was told to take a pilot. We were told to take a pilot in and out of San Diego Bay, and both the captain and the exec had operated in and out of there for years. There were times when the pilots were on strike when the exec would take it right up to the dock and say, "Okay, put the lines over." [Laughter] And he'd say, "Well, if they don't like it they can do something about pilots." But he had no hesitation about that. He was an excellent seaman.

Paul Stillwell: This was Captain Patch?

Admiral Siler: This was Hahn. I'm not sure that Captain Patch would have done it.

Paul Stillwell: Anything else that you remember from that ship before we move on to the Bayfield?

Admiral Siler: I think that's most of the Liggett.

Paul Stillwell: How did the transfer come about? What led you to go from one to the other?

Admiral Siler: Well, Captain Hahn didn't like the idea of an academy officer spending as much time on one ship as I did. He figured that an academy officer ought to be experienced on something other than a ship that spent a lot of time in San Diego Bay. So he suggested that I write a letter asking for a transfer. The other thing was that he had just been on leave, and he had gone to San Francisco and Alameda. And he talked to one of the officers at Alameda, either my old friend Captain Evans, who later became Admiral Evans, or somebody else who was up in the assignment area.* So I wrote the letter asking for a transfer to the Alameda manning section, hopefully for assignment to one of the new gunboats the Coast Guard was building, which was a 255, which weren't supposed to be 255 but ended up that way.†

The letter ended up in officer personnel in Coast Guard headquarters as a routine thing, and they wrote back and said I was transferred to the Bayfield, which was, of

---

* Rear Admiral Stephen H. Evans, USCG.
† These were 255-foot-long cutters of the "Indian Tribes" class. The first was USCGC Owasco (WPG-39), which was commissioned 18 May 1945.

course, the same type as I was already in.* So I went on to Alameda and reported in there. I talked to Captain Evans, who had been the tactics officer at the academy years ago, and told him what we had had in mind when I put in the letter. He said, "Well, I agree. I think that you could do better here. But I'll have to send a message to headquarters to see what we can do." And in the meantime I stayed in the process to go out to the Bayfield. That's when I went to training courses on the 5-inch/38 to learn more about it and modern warfare in those days. A few days later the Navy said, "Be at such-and-such a location, and we'll get you to the Bayfield."

So I called Captain Evans and told him what was happening and he said, "Well, let me send one more message, and maybe we can do something about it." In those days personnel matters were all sent deferred messages for precedence, and he sent this priority, which was unheard of for a personnel matter. He got back an answer saying, "All right. Cancel his orders and assign him to the manning section, provided you can assign someone else equally qualified to the Bayfield."

He said, "No possibility I can do that, so you'll have to go to the Bayfield." So I went on to the Bayfield, and how did I get out there? Went on a Filipino merchant ship. My roommate on the trip out was a man who had been the commanding officer of a PCE.† We had a Navy chaplain as a passenger and two Catholic priests who were designated to go to the cathedral on Guam. The Navy chaplain who was with us was also a Catholic, because that would make the three of them compatible. So, anyway, I went to Guam on this transport and spent 16 days, I think it was, on Guam waiting for the ship to come or to tell us where they were or whatever. Eventually they came in. Apparently nobody told the personnel section when they were there, because they told me that the ship was in and I was to be on board by a certain time because it was sailing at 4:00 o'clock that day for San Francisco. [Laughter]

Paul Stillwell: Now, what time period was this?

---

* USS Bayfield (APA-33), an attack transport, was the name ship of her class. She was commissioned 30 November 1943. She displaced 8,100 tons, was 492 feet long, 70 feet in the beam, had a maximum draft of 26 feet, and a top speed of 18 knots. She was armed with two 5-inch guns and carried a variety of landing craft for amphibious warfare operations.
† PCE—patrol craft escort.

Admiral Siler: It was July of '45. Anyway, I got on the ship after spending those 16 days, censoring mail. And when I wasn't censoring mail, why, I'd go to the beach, because you could stand out on the road and go like that and get a ride with the first car.

Paul Stillwell: You're just showing me holding your thumb up. [Laughter]

Admiral Siler: Yes. And it's a favorite beach today. Of course, nobody had cleaned up the sea slugs on the bottom in those days, but other than that, it was a pretty nice beach. So I got on the ship after 16 days and headed for San Francisco again.

I had been told that I would be the gunnery officer when I first came aboard, so I was fully qualified to relieve him just before we got in so he could say "Good-bye" as soon as he left. One of the first nights in San Francisco we had a ship's party. I don't know where the girls came from. But the next morning the exec called me and said, "We need somebody to go up to shore patrol headquarters to get the chaplain." [Laughter] This was a Catholic chaplain, so he was not in the least hesitant to imbibe, but he had imbibed far too much. [Laughter] He'd had a brawl with the shore patrol officer and everything else. But we got him out of there, got him back to the ship. I'm not sure what happened to him after that, whether he was ordered someplace else or not, but, anyway, I lost track of him.

Paul Stillwell: Where did the ship go in San Francisco? Was it Hunters Point or one of the docks?

Admiral Siler: We eventually went into one of the docks for a short time. I spent an awful lot of time at Moore's Drydock area over in Alameda, and I'm not sure whether that time was one of the times or not.

Paul Stillwell: She was different from the Hunter Liggett . . .

Admiral Siler: Oh, quite a difference.

Paul Stillwell: . . . because she was not a passenger ship before. That was a straight cargo hull that was converted.

Admiral Siler: It was a C-3. There were quite a few C-3s that were made attack transports. The Bayfield, the Calvert, the Cavalier—they were all Coast Guard manned. There were only a total of eight attack transports manned by the Coast Guard like the Leonard Wood, the Liggett, the—thought I knew more than that.

Paul Stillwell: Well, Bayfield had quite a history even before you got there, because she had been the command ship for Utah Beach at Normandy.*

Admiral Siler: That's right. And, of course, she was also in the Pacific at Okinawa and Iwo Jima. But I missed all that. We made the initial landing of Northern Honshu at Aomori. We sailed into Aomori Harbor not knowing whether they had truly mineswept that area or not, so we rigged the paravanes as we went in. Didn't hit a thing. I still have someplace a sake bowl that I picked up in Aomori.

Paul Stillwell: Where were you when you got the news that the war had ended?

Admiral Siler: San Francisco.

Paul Stillwell: What do you recall of that experience?

Admiral Siler: Madhouse. A lot of service people had gotten into hotels, and dropping a wastebasket full of water from the sixth floor was not unusual. So the best place to be was in the middle of the street. [Laughter] It was crazy. As far as streetcars were concerned—and, of course, streetcars were a common way to get around then—the streetcars were so full that if you were able to get onto the rear step of a streetcar that was pretty good transportation. But hold on tight, because if you fell off, they were not

---

* When U.S. forces invaded Normandy France on D-Day, 6 June 1944, the U.S. landing beaches were code-named Utah and Omaha.

stopping. [Laughter] God. Betty was at a meeting in the Palace Hotel, and I told her I would meet her there. By the time I got there, there was nothing we were going to do except try to get to her apartment and say goodnight and head back. By the time we got out and tried to get to a streetcar—I think we watched about three go by—and finally we got onto the rear platform and managed to stand on the rear platform while it went up. People would fall off, and it made no difference. It was really a terrible night.

Paul Stillwell: You've just introduced your future wife's name into the conversation for the first time. How had you become acquainted?

Admiral Siler: I made it a practice to visit at the junior officers' club on Taylor Street in San Francisco, and a classmate of mine and I had made dates through a girl I had met there. We went there for dinner, because it was a home-cooked meal and tasted home-cooked, not the kind that we'd find at service places or in restaurants. After we had finished dinner and while we were waiting for it to be time for us to go and pick up our dates, two women arrived, one of whom was my wife. We knew that they came on the same nights each week, and so we decided right then we'd come back the next week on that day.

Paul Stillwell: Without dates.

Admiral Siler: Without dates. That's right. [Laughter] We came back, and I found Betty, but he didn't find the other girl. [Laughter]

Paul Stillwell: Must have been fate.

Admiral Siler: Yes. So we dated rather busily for a short period of time, and the next time the ship was in, I believe it was the next time, why, we decided that we would be married. We had a little trouble getting everything lined up in the short period of time we had, but we were married in Palo Alto and honeymooned at Carmel.

Paul Stillwell: When had you met her and when did you get married?

Admiral Siler: We got married October 27 of '45.

Paul Stillwell: Navy Day by the way.

Admiral Siler: Not any more.

Paul Stillwell: It was then. [Laughter]

Admiral Siler: I know, but the Navy became ashamed of themselves [laughter] and decided that they couldn't celebrate the same day we did [laughter], so they changed it. I'm not sure exactly when we met, but it wasn't very long before.

Paul Stillwell: But it obviously was before the war ended.

Admiral Siler: Oh, yes. In fact we were on a date when we first heard that the war had ended. Well, that was what, August I guess it was.*

Paul Stillwell: Right, mid-August.

Admiral Siler: And we were married in October.

Paul Stillwell: What was the mood in the ship when that news came in?

Admiral Siler: I wasn't on the ship. I was in San Francisco.

Paul Stillwell: So where was the ship?

---

* V-J Day—Victory over Japan Day, marked the end of the war in the Pacific on 15 August 1945. Because of the time difference it was 14 August in the United States when combat ended.

Admiral Siler: The ship was in Oakland, and the day that the news became definite we had all sorts of ammunition that had just arrived and we were loading on the ship. We needed the crane from the dry-dock company there in Oakland, and the man said, "I quit. I'm going ashore." We managed to get him to lift that stuff up on the deck of the ship instead of on the dock, but that was as much as we could hold him. We'd put a guard on the ammunition and said, "We hope that it will be there in the morning."

One of the interesting things that happened about that time my—I'm not sure what position he had on the ship at that time, but I had one other academy officer who worked rather closely with me. He was a year junior to me from the academy, and he had the duty while I was going to go ashore. Just about the time I was getting ready to leave, whoever had the OOD duty came and said, "We've lost the captain's gig. We heard the engine going on it, and it went off, and we've lost track of it."

It turned out that this other fellow had taken the captain's gig to go across to the Alameda Air Station and pick up his date [laughter] and bring her back to the ship for dinner because he had the duty. Of course, over there at the air station he didn't have the duty, but anyway he went over and got the girl. In the meantime, the OOD had noted the fact that the boat was gone, told the shore patrol, told the captain and the exec and everyone in San Francisco Bay knew that Bayfield's captain's gig was stolen. [Laughter] At this point it came back with the duty officer and the date. I'm not sure he went ashore again for some time [laughter] but he did have the girl aboard a good many times; I know that. [Laughter]

Paul Stillwell: Was there a feeling of relief in the crew that your trip to Japan would be a peaceful one?

Admiral Siler: I think so.

Paul Stillwell: I mean, a lot of people had foreboding about the planned invasion during the war itself.

Admiral Siler: I'm sure there was a feeling of relief, but I don't know how much that was. To a lot of young people, why, it was, "Shucks, we won't have that thrill."

Paul Stillwell: Interesting.

Admiral Siler: I'm sure that there were a good many people who looked on it as an opportunity for a thrilling operation.

Paul Stillwell: Probably wouldn't have found as many Marines that felt that same way.

Admiral Siler: I don't imagine so.

Paul Stillwell: You were probably a fairly rare exception being a regular officer on board at that point. What do you remember about the reservists you served with?

Admiral Siler: They varied a tremendous amount in quality and their dedication. The majority of them, though, I think were very fine officers. They were very dedicated to doing a good job, because they knew they would not be called upon regularly or often for this kind of work, and there were a good many who were dedicated to making certain that what they did do they did well.

Paul Stillwell: For the most part where had they been trained? At the OCS in New London?

Admiral Siler: I think probably so, although we had some who were direct commission because they owned yachts of their own or something of that nature.

Paul Stillwell: Now, you've talked about the captains in Hunter Liggett. What do you remember about the captain in the Bayfield?

Admiral Siler: The first captain, the one I had most to do with, had been at the academy and was my instructor in ordnance at the academy. He was a real brain, or he is a brain. Maybe he's still alive. He loved to talk about the technical aspects of things like a Fathometer. And he was a very good officer. He was a little fussy, but I guess you'd have a right to be fussy when you're a captain. The exec was about as much the opposite as he could possibly be. He was a big guy, had been a real football player at the academy, big grin on his face most of the time. Even when he was being bawled out by the captain, why, he'd still have that grin on his face.

Paul Stillwell: Probably made the captain madder. [Laughter]

Admiral Siler: Probably. He was an aviator. He had been a football player at the academy, and I knew the man who played next to him in the line at the academy because he'd been my commanding officer in Port Angeles when I was there.

Paul Stillwell: What were the names of these gentlemen?

Admiral Siler: The captain was W. R. Richards, and the exec was J. P. White.*

Paul Stillwell: That's not the normal stereotype for an executive officer.

Admiral Siler: No, but he had been the commanding officer of an AKA, and he'd enjoyed that.† He was a little bit lost, I think, because he was only the exec in this case.

Paul Stillwell: It's understandable.

Admiral Siler: But a real difference in the two personalities.

---

* Captain Walter R. Richards, USCG; Commander Justus P. White, USCG.
† AKA—attack cargo ship.

Paul Stillwell: What do you remember about the voyage to Japan and what you did once you got there?

Admiral Siler: I don't remember much about the voyage to Japan at all. It was a fairly simple trip, as I recall. You're speaking now of that first trip?

Paul Stillwell: Yes.

Admiral Siler: Well, we didn't go directly to Japan. We went to the Philippines first with a bunch of replacement troops, and there was a bunch of unhappiness on that ship because many of them had enough points to get out.* But they weren't in a position to say, "I have enough points," because the ship was headed for the Philippines. Of course, when they got to the Philippines they'd march up to someone and say, "I want to go back," so they did I guess. We let off the troops in the Philippines, and then I think we went to Saipan and then to Tinian.

At Tinian we were hit by a hurricane while we were at anchor. It came up very suddenly, and we had no warning of it. But around 4:00 o'clock in the morning, why, all of a sudden you could tell something was happening, and it turned out to be that the anchor was flopping over and over. Didn't have enough holding. It was just flip-flopping over and over with the hurricane pushing us farther out of the harbor. We'd had quite a few boats in the water tied up at the boat boom, and they were most of them blown away and off over the horizon. We got up and got the ship under way and got the rest of the boats back on the ship, but there were something like six of them that were missing. We sailed out downwind and eventually found two of the boats and got them back under the booms and got them hoisted aboard. But the rest were just lost.

Paul Stillwell: So you had the captain's gig that had gone AWOL with somebody in charge, and these went AWOL on their own.

---

* For the demobilization of the U.S. armed forces after World War II, the services had a point system to determine individual priorities for leaving the service. Points were awarded for length of service, overseas service, battle stars, decorations, and dependent children. Those with the highest number of points were the earliest discharged.

Admiral Siler: Yes, that's right. [Laughter] We had all kinds of boats in the Bayfield. Then once we loaded up in Tinian, I think we had enough troops to head back to San Francisco. And there we didn't stay very long. We turned around and went back, this time to Korea, to pick up troops and bring them back from there. We started out for Yokohama, Japan. We spent about two days studying all of the notices to mariners about Yokohama and got a change of our orders to Sasebo. So we started studying that area. Two days more, and they changed again—to Jinsen, Korea. So we studied that, but we didn't have much of that, so we read what we had and went into the Yellow Sea and headed up to Inchon, which is another name for Jinsen. One is the Korean name, and the other is Japanese. Fortunately, when we arrived there, they met us with an LCI, and they said, "Just follow me."* We went into the outer entrance to the harbor there. You can't get into the actual harbor because the tide range is 30 feet.

Paul Stillwell: Well, Inchon has that lock in a tidal basin, but I don't know if it was there then or not.

Admiral Siler: No. This ship may have been too big for it too.

Paul Stillwell: Oh, that's right. It would have been.

Admiral Siler: So we went to anchor outside and took boats in, but we'd have to leave people in the boat, because you'd have to back it out as the tide went out or take it in as the tide came up. So I got the sailing orders, and we picked up a load of troops and headed back to Long Beach and unloaded them. We were going to be in long enough, so that was when Betty and I were married.

We got back into Long Beach and picked up sailing orders back to Inchon again and went back that time. Now we had the sailing orders. We'd gone right through the mine lines to get there. As we left Inchon we had seen a mine on the surface and loaded up the 20-millimeters. It was exactly at the spot where we were told to head. [Laughter]

---

* LCI—landing craft infantry.

So we went back to Inchon this time and picked up another load of troops and took them back to San Francisco this time. That time we were to prepare to turn the ship over to the Navy. So we inventoried everything that we could think of and had all those inventories ready and turned the ship over to them. That was the end of our use of the Bayfield, and now it became a Navy-crewed ship again.

Paul Stillwell: Well, your biography says you made a trip to Northern Honshu. Where was that in this whole itinerary?

Admiral Siler: The Northern Honshu was to Aomori. We went into the harbor at Aomori and that's the time when we had the minesweeping, the paravanes out in place. And I do have a sake bowl still from that.

Paul Stillwell: So what did you make, about three or four trips altogether?

Admiral Siler: On the Bayfield we made the trip, but that one to Aomori and then we went from there to—can't remember how the Philippine trip worked in there.

Paul Stillwell: And you had the one to the Tinian and Saipan in the Marianas. Was that the same one as the Philippines?

Admiral Siler: That was the same as to the Philippines. I can't remember how the Honshu trip worked in with that.

Paul Stillwell: So you had one to the Philippines and Marianas and one to Japan and two to Korea. Is that essentially it?

Admiral Siler: Two to Korea for sure.

Paul Stillwell: You had learned the route pretty well by then.

Admiral Siler: Yes. Navigating in the Eastern Hemisphere was very interesting, I must say.

Paul Stillwell: What do you mean by that?

Admiral Siler: Well, you use entirely different tables, and you're on eastern longitude instead of western. And it's different.

Paul Stillwell: Had loran become less of a secret by then?

Admiral Siler: Oh, yes. I don't know when it was completely declassified. But it was still not in great use, although we had a good many loran stations around. It was interesting when I was in flight training that a lot of people still didn't know how to use loran at all. All of my classmates had received an AlCoast when I was in the Philippines.* It said, "We're ready for your class for flight training." One of my classmates who was a football player when I was the manager came over to my ship from the ship he was on, which was an attack cargo ship, and said, "I'm going to go get a physical. What do you think?"

I said, "Well, I've been trying for this for some time, but maybe I better go now." So he and I went to the Philippine base that had American airplanes and took our physical while we were there. I don't think he had any trouble at all. He was a little guy but a backfield man obviously.

I had no trouble until they took my chest X-ray. I think the film was old so that it was all misty, and they said, "We wouldn't even bother to send that in."

I said, "Send it in anyway and let the Coast Guard determine what they want to do. Maybe I'll get out of the Coast Guard." I didn't know. Anyway, they did send it in, and it was a good many months after that. I didn't get orders to flight training, obviously, and I stayed on that ship. We got back to Alameda and turned the ship over to the Navy. I went ashore in Alameda, and they made me a personnel officer, which really amounted to signing my name on personnel data sheets. In those days every time that you moved a

---

* AlCoast—a message to the entire Coast Guard.

person you made a new sheet, and you had to have a signature on it. I quickly learned how to sign my name without lifting up the pen.

Paul Stillwell: [Laughter]

Admiral Siler: Anyway, I ended up in Alameda and was personnel officer there for some time. Finally Coast Guard headquarters came and said, "We have examined your application for flight training and notice that you say that the Army says that you have a lightening or whitening of the chest area, so take another chest X-ray."

So I went over to the medical section and said, "I'm supposed to take a chest X-ray."

They said, "Gee, we took our chest X-ray machine and put it in a storage space."

I said, "Well, what do I do then?"

They said, "Well, let me see if we can still take a chest X-ray." It was right next to the wall. So I could get down to the proper level if I stood like this you know, with my feet far apart.

Paul Stillwell: Spread-eagled.

Admiral Siler: The only trouble was it's like this. So here was the machine over here and I was supposed to go like this. Anyway, it was very difficult to get down there without twisting and turning. When I got down there finally they did take the X-ray and sent it to Coast Guard headquarters and they said, "We see no problem with your chest. However you do have curvature of the spine." [Laughter] Obviously.

Paul Stillwell: Since you were all twisted out of shape. Well, I wonder if this is a convenient breaking place for today.

Admiral Siler: Well, it was at that point that I moved over to the Alameda Training Station as personnel officer. I was there until the Alameda Training Station was decommissioned. At that point, we could pretty much have our choice of what was available, and I asked for the Taney, because it had just come in from the East Coast and had just had a recent conversion. So I asked for a Coast Guard cutter for a change and went to the Taney in 1946, I guess.

Paul Stillwell: Well, you want to cover that tomorrow?

Admiral Siler: Okay.

Paul Stillwell: Thank you for a fine first interview.

Interview Number 2 with Admiral Owen W. Siler, U.S. Coast Guard (Retired)
Place: Admiral Siler's home in Savannah, Georgia
Date: Monday, 11 December 2000
Interviewer: Paul Stillwell

Paul Stillwell: Admiral, after we finished up yesterday you said that you might think of some things during the night that you wanted to add to the record from yesterday. Do you have any such items?

Admiral Siler: The only thing that I wondered about whether we should have put into the record or did we put into the record that thing about the chest X-ray?

Paul Stillwell: Yes.

Admiral Siler: All right, because that occurred in my visit to the Philippines in early '45 when all my classmates with the exception of I think myself and about two or three others went to flight training, and I didn't get to go. The endorsement that was put on my request was that I should not be allowed to leave the <u>Bayfield</u> until it was turned over to the Navy, so I didn't leave the <u>Bayfield</u> until March of the following year.

Paul Stillwell: Did you have some desire or disposition to get into aviation, or was that just a thing for your class?

Admiral Siler: I had a desire to get into aviation, yes. My older brother was in the Army Air Corps and had flown B-26s in Europe during the war, and so I had a desire to do that kind of thing.[*] I didn't until I went to flight training in June of '47.

Paul Stillwell: What percentage of your class went into aviation, would you say?

---
[*] On 20 June 1941 the U.S. Army Air Corps was officially redesignated the U.S. Army Air Forces.

Admiral Siler: About a half of them who stayed in at all. There were quite a few who got out after the war was over.

Paul Stillwell: Did you have anything to add on that period when you were at Alameda signing your name with one push of the pen on the paper?

Admiral Siler: It was an interesting and a very difficult time, because it was just after the war was over, and not too many people wanted to come into the service. But they still had the requirement for some compulsory service, so we were getting some people at times who were really the dregs of the people who were eligible. Quite a few of them we discharged because they couldn't even read. I was on one of the boards that considered these people for adaptability and capability, and if they couldn't even read the simple words in a newspaper, we frequently recommended that they be discharged at that point.

Paul Stillwell: Had the bulk of the demobilization taken place before you got into that job?

Admiral Siler: It was still going on. There were still people coming from places in far Asiatic ports, the Philippines and Japan and Korea, who would come through. A good many of them would be either discharged or given transfers to farther locations on the East Coast. This was, of course, the West Coast receiving center.

Paul Stillwell: Did you have to process that paperwork as well?

Admiral Siler: I had to sign my name in order to get rid of them. [Laughter] Fortunately, I didn't have that particular job very long. That was the kind of thing that they would ease you into the first day that you reported. Then because I'd guess that there were probably stacks of those things that were a foot high, we'd give someone a letter that authorized them to sign "by direction" in matters of having to do with personnel. Someone who had never been in personnel before or didn't know what they were doing would get the assignment of signing his name.

Paul Stillwell: What sort of staff of personnel enlisted people did you have to handle these records and prepare them for your signature?

Admiral Siler: I'd guess that we had probably a dozen yeomen and that kind of person. We didn't have people who had a personnelman rating as the Navy did, so these people were just yeomen, and they were eligible to do anything that had to do with written work. Fortunately, there was a chief petty officer who was in that department, and he knew his business quite well. Good thing he did because I didn't. [Laughter]

Paul Stillwell: You depended on him.

Admiral Siler: Very much so.

Paul Stillwell: Well, on the other hand, it was probably the sort of job that was not that challenging, so you could relax when you got away from the office.

Admiral Siler: Oh, yes. I had no concerns about it at all. In fact, there was another officer, a warrant officer as I recall, at that time. I saw something about him just within the past week about his—I guess he had passed on or was honored by the warrant officers, I can't recall which. But he retired as a commander at this point, and he's been retired a long time. Of course, he was older than I, and he handled all the disciplinary cases, so I didn't get involved with that at all.

Paul Stillwell: Well, and Gregory was born in 1946 so that was a change in your family life.

Admiral Siler: Very much so.

Paul Stillwell: What do you remember about that part of it?

Admiral Siler: Well, that was after I had left the training station.

Paul Stillwell: I see.

Admiral Siler: I was told that the training station was being decommissioned, and it wasn't started again for several years. They let us have our choice of the assignments that were available. The Taney had come into port one Sunday when my wife and I were at that time living in San Francisco, and I was commuting across the Bay every day, which was hellacious.*

Paul Stillwell: Was housing hard to find in that period?

Admiral Siler: Very difficult. Most of us who were eventually going to be at the training station or on the ships that were working out of Alameda lived at a housing unit called Tassafaronga Village, Tassafaronga being the place in Guadalcanal, and these were pretty cheap plywood construction.

Paul Stillwell: Was that a Navy housing development?

Admiral Siler: It wasn't Navy. It was public housing, though, and I forget how we went about getting into it. But I ended up living next door to an academy classmate of mine. They gave me a choice of going on the Taney or going into the district office and being a duty officer in the operations center. I definitely didn't want to go ashore at that point. I wanted to be on a Coast Guard cutter, and I asked for and was assigned to the Taney.

Another shipmate, a warrant officer, was on the other side, and upstairs were a brand-new ensign and his wife. He had just graduated from the academy. She was about four feet tall, as I recall [laughter], very small woman, but she insisted on wearing high heels. And with those floors constructed the way they were, every time she walked

---

* USCGC Taney (WPG-37), a Secretary-class cutter, was commissioned on 24 October 1936. She was 327 feet long, 41 feet in the beam, and had a maximum draft of 15 feet. She had a maximum speed of 19.5 knots. She remained in active service until decommissioned on 7 December 1986 and transferred to the city of Baltimore as a memorial.

across the room upstairs, you could here her go "Click, clack, click, click, click, click." [Laughter] They went away one weekend, and we didn't have refrigerators; we had iceboxes. She forgot to empty the water bucket in the refrigerator, and we had waterfall wall. The classmate of mine next door saw Greg when he was quite young, and his comment was, "He looks just like a monkey, doesn't he?" [Laughter]

Paul Stillwell: Not very complimentary.

Admiral Siler: I don't think my wife forgave him for that for years, but we still exchange Christmas cards with them every year. The man on the other side who was the warrant officer—we were all demoted on the first of July of '46 when we went back into the Treasury Department.

Paul Stillwell: What do you mean by demoted?

Admiral Siler: All our promotions during World War II were temporary, and if you happened to be in the right slot you might keep your rank, but the great majority of us went back. The people who had been warrant officers had been chiefs and had worked up to warrant officer or to jaygee, and a good many of them went back, and that warrant officer went back to chief.[*] He was well educated, and so was his wife. I'm sure they resented it a great deal, but he stayed around for a long time.

Paul Stillwell: What was the demotion in your own case?

Admiral Siler: The entire class went from lieutenant back to jaygee. We had dates of rank that were so early that we were always the most senior jaygee around. [Laughter]

Paul Stillwell: But probably jaygee is about what you would have been anyway.

---

[*] Jaygee—lieutenant (junior grade).

Admiral Siler: Probably. Our dates of rank were sometime in '44, and we had made full lieutenant in November of '45, but we were back to jaygee then.

Paul Stillwell: Who was the classmate who lived there with you?

Admiral Siler: Ward Emigh was his name, and he went into naval engineering; he's now retired. I think he may have been a private professional engineer in St. Louis, Missouri, for a long time. He still lives in St. Louis.

Paul Stillwell: Well, the Taney had quite a history. She had been at Honolulu when the Japanese attacked in '41.

Admiral Siler: That's right. I understand they're having celebrations on that right now.

Paul Stillwell: And she is now in Baltimore as a tourist attraction.

Admiral Siler: I took my family to see it one time when we were all there, and my grandson was there also. We went aboard the ship, and unfortunately they have closed off certain areas so I couldn't get back into the room that I had had. We could see the door to it, but that's all, because you went into the wardroom, and as you looked aft, the next room was my room as the navigator. The exec had a stateroom that you could see into just forward of mine, and that was about all that you could see of the living quarters of the officers. But that was a pleasant time to be on the Taney, although we were on ocean station at that time. We were providing weather reports every couple of hours, and we'd release weather balloons every so often. The weather balloon would have a little transmitter on it, and we'd follow it with radar and get the winds aloft that way. And then we'd get the pressure reports from the balloon as it went up.

Paul Stillwell: Was the idea of the ocean stations to support commercial airlines and provide a safety net?

Admiral Siler: Just exactly that. Initially we had about three of them in the Pacific, two well off the West Coast, one that was off of and slightly north of Puget Sound. When the ship was on station we would take those weather readings. I think it was every three hours, and then every other one they would attach the transmitter on. Sometimes when those things would get strong winds they'd come ashore, which was a long distance for them to go, but if they'd go to very high altitude and not burst, they could go a long distance. Sometimes they'd pick them up on the shore, and they'd think that the Japanese had been doing something again. Of course, the Japanese reported nothing, and the weather report after a certain time had no useful application.

Paul Stillwell: The Japanese had killed one family during the war with those balloons that traveled on the jet stream.

Admiral Siler: That's right.

Paul Stillwell: Had explosives on them.

Admiral Siler: And they probably weren't any farther offshore when they released them than we were at this time, if as far.

Paul Stillwell: Where was your ocean station in the Taney?

Admiral Siler: We were almost exactly halfway between San Francisco and Honolulu, and that was called Ocean Station Papa, as I recall. But being halfway out there, loran was very little help to us. The intersection of the loran lines from the West Coast and Hawaii was so close that you could be 20 miles off station and not know it. So if you had access to the sun or to the stars, it was far better. In the evening and the first thing in the morning we'd take our position by sights usually.

    I was the navigator, so I was up to take the morning star sights, and after dinner I'd go up and take the evening star sights. And during the day we'd usually get some sun lines. Occasionally Venus was so bright that we could take a star sight on Venus in the daytime. The intersections sometimes were useful; sometimes they weren't. But we used to do it just because daytime Venus sights were so unusual. [Laughter] Moon sights, of course, were available, too, but they weren't as much fun because you've got the actual size of the moon. You have to reduce that to where the center of the moon should be, and you have to figure out whether it was the lower branch of the moon or the upper branch or what. So navigating was fun. I thought that was the ideal assignment on the ship.

Paul Stillwell: At least you didn't have dawn-and-dusk GQs the way you had during the war.

Admiral Siler: That's right. Never had to do that.

Paul Stillwell: I remember a movie that came out in the '50s with John Wayne called The High and the Mighty, and it had to do with a plane between Hawaii and the West Coast.

Admiral Siler: I saw that movie and enjoyed it.

Paul Stillwell: Probably brought back some memories for you.

Admiral Siler: Yes, indeed.

Paul Stillwell: How did the ship ride out on those lonely patrols?

Admiral Siler: Well, the 327 class had a rather interesting roll and pitch.* It was like a corkscrew when you got in certain conditions. I can remember one time we were called out of Alameda to do some search and rescue, and we just had gotten outside of San Francisco. We had taken the channel that was fairly shallow but went north faster than it went out all the way to the Farallons, so we were staying fairly close to the shore. We

---

* The ships of the Secretary class were also known as 327s because of their length in feet.

got into a pitch and, well, a sea condition that was very uncomfortable. I lost my cookies. [Laughter] Usually I was not bothered when we went to sea, but that particular time I was.

Paul Stillwell: It was kind of a broad-beamed ship wasn't it?

Admiral Siler: Well, it was 41 feet, as I recall, and it wasn't really steady, but when it would get up to speed it would have an interesting corkscrew roll.

Paul Stillwell: I served in an LST, so I got some of that unpleasant experience too. [Laughter]

Admiral Siler: LSTs were about as uncomfortable as anything, I think.

Paul Stillwell: What do you recall about the skipper and some of the other officers on board?

Admiral Siler: Well, the skipper had been an aviator who was sent back to sea during World War II because he asked for it. He got a little bored with being a CO of an air station doing not much except saying, "Go out and patrol here." And most of the time the patrols didn't do anything, although one of the patrols that I think would have been when he was CO in Biloxi, Mississippi, went out, and it was a little J4F that was carrying a depth charge.* The depth charge was so heavy that you could hardly get that airplane in the air with it. You had to take off from the water there in Biloxi. There was no runway. Later they built Keesler Air Force Base just a stone's throw down the road, but there was no land airport at all except they used the water there, and that little J4F with a depth charge under the wing had a lot of trouble getting airborne. He did get airborne, and he went down into the Gulf of Mexico and spotted a German submarine. And I think he got

---

* The Grumman-built J4F Widgeon was a two-engine amphibian flying boat that first entered Coast Guard service in 1941. The J4F had a wingspan of 40 feet, length of 31 feet, gross weight of 4,500 pounds, and top speed of 165 miles per hour.

credit for sinking the submarine. That particular J4F now is in the Naval Aviation Museum, but it's been modified since he flew it. Has a different engine completely.

Paul Stillwell: What was the skipper's name?

Admiral Siler: Carl Bowman, and he went from there to I think headquarters for a while.* Then he went to the academy, and he was the skipper of the Eagle at one time. And now he, I think, still maintains the position of skipper of the sailing vessel that's on display in San Diego.

Paul Stillwell: Oh, the Star of India?

Admiral Siler: Yes. They take it out once a year and turn it around, and he'll be the skipper, I think, on that. He was an interesting person. He didn't get along with the exec at all. The exec had been ashore for quite some time, and he'd been to some postgraduate training on finance, and he loved paperwork. The first thing that he decided we'd better do was to change the entire watch, quarter, and station bill. So he worked on that for weeks. Finally had a product, and he took it up to the captain, and the captain said, "I don't think this is worth the paper it's written on." [Laughter] I used to have to go in with position reports for the captain, and so I saw a lot of this going on, and I have to say I thought the skipper was right. [Laughter] I couldn't sympathize with the exec too much.

On Thanksgiving we were going to have dinner in the wardroom for any officers and their families who wanted to come down and eat in the wardroom. I think I originally said I'd like to, but that particular day, the day before Thanksgiving, was when they said a second time that my class could be considered for aviation, and I had gone over to Alameda Naval Air Station to take my flight physical. So the word was passed for me to contact the captain, because he wanted to invite me and my wife and small child to Thanksgiving dinner.

---

* Commander Carl G. Bowman, USCG.

I'd planned beforehand to be in the wardroom when I came back from Alameda and I got this message, "Contact the captain before you go ashore," so I phoned the captain and got no answer. I didn't want to stay on that ship all night, so I called the exec and said, "What do I do?"

He said, "The message was contact him before you go ashore, so don't go ashore."

I thought, "Ye gods, how long is this going to be?" So I finally contacted the captain and got the invitation. The next day, Thanksgiving, the officers and their families gathered in the wardroom, and the exec looked around and said, "Well, where are the Silers?"

Somebody said, "He's having dinner with the captain." [Laughter] That settled that rather quickly. [Laughter] But the captain and I always had gotten along very well except he had two little hellion kids. One was nine years old, and the other was six. The six-year-old was a sweet little kid. The nine-year-old was a little brat. I know that the nine-year-old came into the Coast Guard when he was old enough. First he went to the academy, and I think he flunked out. Then he went to OCS sometime later and became a Coast Guard officer for a while at least. I think he asked for integration as a regular officer and was turned down. But, anyway, he was a real brat at that time, although he was smart as could be. We gave him the exam that we were giving to regular enlisted recruits.

At that time there was no boot camp for Coast Guard kids at all, and so they'd be put aboard the Taney, one of the biggest cutters that was operating. After a certain period of time, why, they'd give them a test to see if they qualified to be a seaman second class instead of apprentice seaman. He got the highest grade of any of the kids. Of course, he wasn't qualified. In fact, he was still nine years old when he got the highest grade.

Paul Stillwell: Why was there no boot camp?

Admiral Siler: Monetary limitations of the Coast Guard at that time.

Paul Stillwell: Just on-the-job training.

Admiral Siler: That's right. They'd come aboard, and you knew that they had no training, but they were supposedly going to be qualified seamen after a cruise or two, and I don't recall when we said that they were ready.

Paul Stillwell: Did the ship have a stepped-up training program to account for the fact there was no boot camp?

Admiral Siler: Yes. Had to.

Paul Stillwell: Well, the exec would probably excel at that making out training plans and what have you.

Admiral Siler: Probably. [Laughter] I'm not sure he did that, because he was so busy with that watch, quarter, and station bill. [Laughter]

Paul Stillwell: How was the captain operationally?

Admiral Siler: Great. He really knew his stuff. I think he went from there to Coast Guard headquarters as chief of the floating units of the Coast Guard.

Paul Stillwell: Was that kind of boring duty, just sitting out there day after day doing weather reports?

Admiral Siler: Oh, yes. You'd take reading material along, and we'd take correspondence courses or anything of that nature because it was boresome. And, of course, we had movies every night. It was very tempting to have three or four every night [laughter], but usually we'd have just one because we had about enough movies to spend the entire time at sea with a movie a night.

Paul Stillwell: I've heard of some ships that had to watch the same movie so many times the sailors would do the dialog right along with the actors. [Laughter]

Admiral Siler: Probably.

Paul Stillwell: What other forms of entertainment? Play cribbage, acey-deucy?*

Admiral Siler: There used to be a poker game in the wardroom every night. They didn't have poker chips, so they had nuts and bolts and things of that sort that were given values. I don't know what they were, because I didn't play poker. But I watched it occasionally, and when the cruise was just about done they would look at the nuts and bolts and figure out how much money each person had won or lost, and there was a limitation on how much you could lose. So during the entire cruise no one would lose any more than I think $25.00. If they had actually lost $250.00, they'd just divide the whole thing by ten so that the man who thought he had made a fortune won one-tenth of that, and the loser lost one-tenth of what he had. So no one lost very much money, in spite of the fact that the captain was a good poker player. [Laughter] And the chief engineer was a good one too. The chief engineer was academy class of '38; his brother was '39.

Paul Stillwell: What was the engineer's name?

Admiral Siler: That was Art Pfeiffer.† And at one time the exec was ordered to other duty. He was Bub Boyce, and he always had a pipe in his mouth, but he was ordered off the ship, and so the engineering officer should have been the exec.‡ He said, "I've got so much to do down here in engineering," because the ship had just come out of the yard. After being ordered out of the Pacific, the ship was sent to the yard in Charleston, South Carolina, to be modified back to a Coast Guard cutter, then sent through the Panama Canal to San Francisco. There was a lot that needed to be done in the engineering area,

---

* Acey-deucy is a variation of the board game backgammon.
† Lieutenant Commander Arthur Pfeiffer, USCG.
‡ Lieutenant Commander George R. Boyce, Jr., USCG.

and he said, "I really think it would be better if I stayed in engineering." So I became the exec for about a week until this other man came; I think he was at a training station for a while. His name was Benjamin B. Shereshevski, but he'd changed it to just Sherry.* And he loved the paperwork.

Paul Stillwell: You said converted back to a cutter. What had she been converted to?

Admiral Siler: The Taney was modified more than most of the Coast Guard cutters, because she was at Pearl Harbor during the attack on December 7.† Shortly after that she was taken to a yard someplace and put four 5-inch guns on her, two forward and two aft. Her profile from a long distance was just like a battleship. Of course, the 5-inch guns were not like the battleship at all, but you couldn't tell that from a distance, and the whole ship looked like a battleship.

Paul Stillwell: Was this for convoy escort work?

Admiral Siler: I guess so. I really don't know for sure, because she was the only one that was modified that way, and they must have decided after running it someplace that it was top-heavy, so they didn't use her very much for that. Then the next thing was they modified all of the 327s to be communications ships in the invasions, and so they had antennas all over the place. Most spaces that they could convert were converted to bunk space, because they had so many people on them for communications. And every space topside was used for a communications workroom.

Paul Stillwell: Did she have a depth-charge capability as a matter of course, or was that added on as well?

Admiral Siler: That probably was added on after the seventh of December, but I don't recall exactly where or what the depth charge capability was. But that was taken off

---
* Lieutenant Commander Benjamin B. Sherry, USCG.
† At the time of the attack the ship was moored in Honolulu Harbor rather than at Pearl Harbor, which is some distance away.

when they converted them back to Coast Guard ships, of course. Then it was pretty much the configuration she has today, with one exception. All of the Coast Guard 327s were converted back to a certain configuration for the ocean stations, but the Taney was the last one that was kept for weather reporting. She got a balloon-type of construction that went forward, because it had more capability for radar than any other of the ships. The other ships were being decommissioned at that time, but the Taney was kept on weather patrol on the East Coast because there was an area pretty much offshore from Baltimore that was not covered adequately from shore radars, so it was the last weather ship that we had.*

Paul Stillwell: There was a famous picture taken during the war, and I think it was from the Spencer looking aft over the fantail and you see a huge geyser of a depth charge rising up.

Admiral Siler: Right.

Paul Stillwell: The photographer on that was a man named Jack January, and 30 years later, when we were in St. Louis, he was a photographer for the St. Louis Post-Dispatch.† I met him there. Small world.

Admiral Siler: Yes.

Paul Stillwell: Any other operations you remember with the Taney other than that one search and rescue you mentioned as a break from the routine?

Admiral Siler: We were more involved with the ocean station duty that anything else. I don't recall any search and rescue that we were on during the time I was out there, except

---

* The program was terminated in June 1974, except for Ocean Station Hotel, in which the Taney monitored Gulf Stream currents north of Cape Hatteras. See Michael R. Adams, "Ocean Weather Hotel: A Stormy Address," U.S. Naval Institute Proceedings, April 1975, pages 100-102.
† In the early 1970s, when Admiral Siler was Commander Second Coast Guard District, the interviewer was working in St. Louis at the same time.

that one incident when we went offshore. There was one other time when we were told to go down near Santa Barbara. We were going out of San Francisco Bay and headed down in that direction, but it was cancelled very shortly afterward, and we just turned around and went back.

One of the more interesting things for me was we were coming back from ocean station, and the engineering officer said, "One of these times soon we're going to have to make a full-speed run because of the requirement of the engineering regulations." Normally, it was done for only an hour or two.

But the captain said, "Well, let's do it on the way home so we get home faster." So we cranked up everything we could and came all the way back from ocean station at full speed.

Paul Stillwell: What kind of a plant did she have?

Admiral Siler: It was a twin steam turbine. The 255s had a single steam turbine, and so they could make about 15 knots, and that was it. But the Taney class was supposedly able to make 21 knots, and we did for a little over 48 hours. Got us in in a hurry. When we got to San Francisco, the news said that all the shipping in San Francisco Bay was on strike, so there was nothing moving in San Francisco. So when we got to the Farallon Islands I relieved the normal officer of the deck and had the conn up the channel from the Farallons into San Francisco and under the Golden Gate Bridge. As we went under the Golden Gate Bridge, the captain relieved me, because he was going to take it into the channel over to Oakland. So we rang up one-third speed as we went under the Golden Gate Bridge. When we went under the Bay Bridge we were still going at about 15 knots because it had so much way on her.

Paul Stillwell: Momentum.

Admiral Siler: Yes, we went into the Oakland Estuary with a wake that was about four feet tall. [Laughter] We were still coasting all the way up the channel. It was a real thrill going across San Francisco Bay at about 15 knots.

Paul Stillwell: So you're suggesting that wouldn't have been done if the normal shipping had been there.

Admiral Siler: You'd better not. [Laughter]

Paul Stillwell: Well, I guess on an ocean station deal you hope nothing happens so no planes go down.

Admiral Siler: Well, we had planes going over all the time. Being there on that station between San Francisco and Honolulu, all the airliners would use us as a position fix as they went over. So we were trying to maintain our position as closely as we could, because we would use radar and locate those planes in the air and give them a position fix as they went over. It was always kind of fun to see if the stewardesses would respond. [Laughter]

When I was flying the plane in the '50s, the Commandant would get on the radio and call down, just because we thought they would be interested to hear the Commandant speak to them.[*] It had been so long since he had done that sort of thing that he was not too anxious to use the radio.

Paul Stillwell: He wasn't up on the latest procedures?

Admiral Siler: That's right.

Paul Stillwell: Well, you probably enjoyed hearing a friendly voice passing over when you were on that detached duty sort of.

Admiral Siler: Oh, yes.

---

[*] This was during Siler's tour of duty as aide and pilot to the Commandant, Vice Admiral Alfred C. Richmond, USCG.

Paul Stillwell: What ways did you grow professionally during that tour of duty?

Admiral Siler: Well, we learned more Coast Guard procedures than we had used in a good many years. Everything that was Coast Guard had been stopped during the war except for the buoy tenders that would still do the buoy tending. This class of ship did nothing that was Coast Guard oriented during the war except occasionally the search and rescue that they'd be called upon for. Well, I think we had something like two incidents in the six months I was on the Taney. My duty on the Taney lasted only from the first part of June until the end of December, and I was transferred off and went to shore duty in Long Beach.

Paul Stillwell: Was there any difference in the internal procedures of running a Coast Guard cutter as opposed to the Navy ships you'd been in?

Admiral Siler: Yes, the organization's quite different.

Paul Stillwell: How would you describe that difference?

Admiral Siler: Well, much of what the Coast Guard is doing today has been modified to be more technically oriented.

Paul Stillwell: Anything else to mention about the Taney before you move on to Long Beach?

Admiral Siler: One of the collateral duties I was assigned to on the Taney was I was the exchange officer, so I would go over to the Navy supply depot about once a week when we were in port and see what new goodies they had gotten in. We had things in the exchange there like electric irons that were not available on the market yet after the war, and we were still able to get the wristwatches that had been the issue type, quite accurate watches, and we were selling them for $20.00. It was fun to see what the latest goodies were, get them in the exchange. And, of course, we made huge profits on cigarettes in those days, because there was not the pressure on stopping smoking. The cost of sea stores in particular was amazingly cheap. I never smoked, so it didn't bother me, but a lot of people were stocking up on sea stores when we were at sea and using them all of the time we were in port. That was an interesting aspect of being at sea, when once you got beyond the continental limits, the price of cigarettes was amazingly low.

Paul Stillwell: Maybe ten cents a pack or something like that?

Admiral Siler: I don't recall what it was. We sold them all by the cartons rather than by packs, but I think that it was never any higher than $2.00 for a carton.

Paul Stillwell: What were the differences in the internal running of the Coast Guard and Navy ships?

Admiral Siler: There were differences, because for one thing we didn't have some of the responsibilities that the Navy had. For example, we had ASW but on some of the ships—and the Taney class had ASW, but there were some things that we didn't have responsibilities for. The gunnery was a whole lot simpler than it would be in the Navy.

Paul Stillwell: In what way?

Admiral Siler: Well, our guns didn't have the fire control systems as complicated by any means.

Paul Stillwell: How did you aim them then?

Admiral Siler: Well, we had some of the simpler types of gun control, but the computers that were used by the Coast Guard were far simpler than the Navy's fire control systems.

Paul Stillwell: So was it mostly just by optical gunsights and directors?

Admiral Siler: Frequently the directors were Navy-developed for things like the 20-millimeter or the 40-millimeter, but the 5-inch gun was very frequently pretty much line of sight.

Paul Stillwell: So you wouldn't have, say, a plotting room?

Admiral Siler: No. The CIC was simpler by far.*

Paul Stillwell: What was the communication capability? Was it still as good as it had been when she had been involved in those invasion communication roles?

Admiral Siler: No, nowhere near as much. It was far simpler. The communications was mostly just to the nearest Coast Guard radio station. We would send the messages there, and they would relay it to the Weather Bureau.

Paul Stillwell: Did you still have Morse code communications, or had you gotten into the Teletype?

Admiral Siler: I'm not sure of that from the time, because although my next assignment was communications I wasn't that concerned at all at that time.

Paul Stillwell: Well, please tell me about serving in Long Beach. Was that just another waiting station?

Admiral Siler: It really turned out to be that, but it wasn't supposed to be. I was ordered to assistant communications officer for the district, and that district was fairly simple, because we had only a couple of rescue stations. I had one air station, and we had no ships except for a 165-footer, and that was about it.

Paul Stillwell: Where was it based? Was it near Terminal Island?

---

* CIC—combat information center.

Admiral Siler: The 165-footer was on Terminal Island, and it's been decommissioned for many, many years now.

Paul Stillwell: Where was your office?

Admiral Siler: In downtown Long Beach. It was I think the Times Building when I was there. It's been moved an awful lot of times since then.

Paul Stillwell: About how many people were in the district office?

Admiral Siler: Probably a couple a hundred. But the duties of the district office, except for a small amount of operations, were mostly personnel, pay, and things of that nature as far as the operations were concerned. And, of course, my responsibility at that time was encryption and things of that nature, making certain that everyone had the up-to-date codes they were supposed to have, and there were not very many stations that had a lot of codes that they had to keep up on.

Paul Stillwell: Did you use Navy crypto systems?

Admiral Siler: Yes, completely.

Paul Stillwell: There was an Adonis machine that had the rotors back then. Might that have been it?

Admiral Siler: Probably. I remember the rotors at that time.

Paul Stillwell: It was a laborious process.

Admiral Siler: Yes, it was, but I don't think we had but one or two stations that had anything except just straight communications. The air station had encryption and we did.

I can't recall where else the radio stations. We did have one radio station. It was a good place to start in communications because it was simple.

Paul Stillwell: Well, it was probably good professional background for you to learn about communications.

Admiral Siler: Yes, undoubtedly.

Paul Stillwell: Do you remember any specific events that stand out during that tour?

Admiral Siler: No, not at all. I was only there from the first of January until June, and then I went to flight training.

Paul Stillwell: It was probably time for family life there in Southern California.

Admiral Siler: Not at all. There was no housing. We spent two months living in what they called a beach cottage, and I do mean beach cottage. It was the kind of a thing that in the middle of summer would be tolerable, but through the winter when we moved in in January it was terrible. The rats were not taken care of. It was cold and drafty. Then we found a place that was being built over a garage, a personal type garage, so that there were two bedrooms and a living room and kitchen, and that was about it. We didn't have much furniture, but this was rented unfurnished, so we went out and one night bought furniture for the living room and found a place to buy a mattress. And the senior chief radioman said, "Well, I have a box spring you can borrow." So we started out with the one night's purchase of living room, and we bought a refrigerator from Montgomery Ward after standing in line day after day after day to see if they even would have any, because they were coming in so slowly. We finally got a very simple refrigerator.

That was about the extent of our purchases, but we lived with that furniture for exactly two months, and I was ordered to flight training. The furniture could not be moved, because it was temporary duty in Corpus Christi, and the permanent duty would be in Pensacola. But I was afraid if I was not a successful aviator I might be ordered someplace else before I ever got to Pensacola. So I put all the things that we could in storage to be shipped on later when we got orders to Pensacola. Of course, when we got orders to Pensacola there was a railroad strike and nothing went by van in those days, so we waited and waited and waited to get things in Pensacola.

Paul Stillwell: Did you have similar problems getting a car after the war?

Admiral Siler: We had gotten a used car. It was a '41 model that we bought in San Francisco before we had left there, and it got us to Pensacola. Then we disposed of it. We got rid of it and replaced it with a '46 model Dodge which gave us plenty of room

Paul Stillwell: New cars were hard to come by also during that era.

Admiral Siler: Yes, they sure were.

Paul Stillwell: What do you remember about Corpus Christi and your introduction to aviation?

Admiral Siler: Well, again housing was a real problem. In Corpus Christi we lived in a motel for a little while and went on a radio program that had to do with "Any rooms today?" or something like that. Eventually we heard about a Navy lieutenant who was taking a child of his to a hospital for a month's stay because it was a blue baby, and they had to operate and treat the baby. So we took care of his house for one month and still hadn't been able to find anything. Then we moved onto the naval air station, and we lived in three BOQ rooms. There was three heads on each floor in a two-story BOQ, and so over a men's head would be the women's head and the next one around would be the other way around so that if you wanted to walk halfway around the barracks, you could always find a head. We lived in the BOQ for a couple of months.

As far as the flight training was concerned, we started with ground school, and it was not too difficult. The navigation was rather easy for me. I don't think we had any loran at that time. We were introduced to loran later when we were flying multi-engine.

The first training we had was what you would have to do if you were flying a fighter airplane and just had no way to navigate except on your kneepad. So we worked on that in the first phase. I was the first one in the class to solo the plane.

Paul Stillwell: What plane was it, SNJ?

Admiral Siler: SNJ—in my class.* I don't know how that happened, but anyway I had no problems with my learning to fly the airplane.

Paul Stillwell: Were your cohorts Navy men and Coast Guardsmen both?

Admiral Siler: Both. We had about ten Coast Guard people in that class.

Paul Stillwell: Out of how many would you say?

Admiral Siler: Out of 25. And, as I say, I was the first one to solo. I remember when I took the plane off and was flying it that I was amazed by the feel of the rudder pedals, because the tail wheel was steerable in the SNJ in those days and completely swivelable too. Quite a few of the class had had problems with that tail wheel that would swivel at the wrong time, because if you really booted the rudder, you'd go into full swivel. With complete swivels, ground loops were not too uncommon. I remember as I was taking my safe-for-solo check we flew over one of my classmates who had just ground looped.

Paul Stillwell: What do you remember about the instructors and instruction?

Admiral Siler: The instructing was terrible, I thought. They did a lot of yelling at you. In the SNJ we had intercom, not the gosport, but the gosport was what they had in the

---

* The SNJ Texan was a training aircraft manufactured by North American Aviation. The Navy first ordered a version of the airplane in late 1936; the Army designation was AT-6. Versions of the Texan continued in use for Navy training well into the 1950s.

N2S, which was just before that.*

Paul Stillwell: That gosport was a one-way communication.

Admiral Siler: Yes, a tube was what it amounted to, and we were required to use the microphone at times to respond to orders or something of that nature. The instructor did yell a lot. I know he thought he needed to yell at me. [Laughter] I ran into him years later when he was stationed at Whidbey Island and the Korean War was on.† He had been ordered out of flight training to actual operational training at Whidbey while I was at Port Angeles. He came into Port Angeles and told me that there were times when he doubted that I would ever make it. [Laughter]

Paul Stillwell: Do you remember his name?

Admiral Siler: No, I don't now.

Paul Stillwell: Was he a naval officer?

Admiral Siler: Oh, yes. In those days I think we had just one instructor assigned to Pensacola, and I was at Corpus Christi for all of the basic training. I went to Pensacola for some of the formation flying and PBY training, which we didn't complete.‡

Paul Stillwell: Why not?

Admiral Siler: They did away with the complete PBY syllabus and felt that there was no reason to train Navy officers in PBYs. There were two Coast Guard people in my group

---

* The Stearman N2S Kaydet was the Navy version of a biplane trainer first ordered by the Army as the PT-13. It was 25 feet long, had a wingspan of 32 feet, gross weight of 2,717 pounds, and a top speed of 124 miles per hour. Deliveries of the plane to the Navy began in 1935.
† Whidbey Island Naval Air Station is in the state of Washington.
‡ The PBY Catalina was a twin-engine flying boat that performed extensive service before and during World War II. Built by Consolidated, it first entered fleet squadrons in 1936. The PBY-2 model had a wingspan of 104 feet, length of 65 feet, gross weight of 28,400 pounds, and top speed of 178 miles per hour. Cruising speed was 103 mph.

who had gotten through the PBY syllabus. My partner and I had completed the entire PBY syllabus except the last flight, and then it was cut out. We operated the PBY with no wheels, so it was always a matter of beaching the PBY. Then we were sent to Whiting Field to supposedly learn how to fly the Beechcraft.* We spent half a day learning how you get into the operating pattern at Whiting Field and all that sort of thing and the station regulations and so on.

Then they decided the Coast Guard didn't need that either. So we were all told to go back to Mainside Pensacola and get our orders to Jacksonville, where we would fly PBMs.† The only thing was when we got to Jacksonville they'd been told that they were moving to Corpus Christi. [Laughter] So we didn't fly for all the time we were there except we would get our flight time in order to get flight pay, and all we'd do was sit in the belly of the PBM. Couldn't even look out because there were no windows. [Laughter] After about a month there, a month and a half maybe, we were told to go to Corpus Christi, and we'd be picked up there sometime. We spent an awful lot of time playing hearts in Corpus Christi until the first of July. They had graduated as many Navy officers as they possibly could to make a quota, and on the second of July the Coast Guard could fly. And they flew us every day of the month of July.

Paul Stillwell: What were you flying then?

Admiral Siler: PBMs. I got my wings on the 28th of July, and there were I think six or eight of us who all got our wings that day, all of us Coast Guard.

Paul Stillwell: Did you find that you enjoyed flying?

Admiral Siler: Yes. I could see things happening a lot faster in that, and, of course, we still had administrative duties at a Coast Guard air station. That kept us quite busy when

---

* Naval Air Station Whiting Field, Milton, Florida. The SNB Kansan was a training aircraft manufactured by Beech Aircraft Company. The Navy first ordered a version of the airplane in 1941; the Army equivalent plane was AT-11.
† The Martin PBM Mariner was a two-engine flying boat that first entered fleet patrol squadrons in 1941. The PBM-5 was 80 feet long, had a wingspan of 118 feet, a gross weight of 58,000 pounds, and a top speed of 182 miles per hour. Each PBM-5 was equipped with two Pratt & Whitney R-2800-22 engines.

we were not flying. When we were flying, there was a lot that had to be done administratively to report exactly what went on and how our flight plans worked out and that sort of thing. I was moved from there to Port Angeles, and that was a very interesting location to be assigned to as a junior birdman.[*] At that time it was a single runway, oriented east and west down the Strait of Juan de Fuca.

Paul Stillwell: One more thing. At Corpus you got your instrument training there, didn't you?

Admiral Siler: Sort of. [Laughter]

Paul Stillwell: Please tell me about that.

Admiral Siler: Well, we got our basic instrument training there, and then we went from there to formation flying at Pensacola. We were exposed to instrument flying again in the PBM, but it was quite different when it was flying multi-engine planes. The instrument-training introduction that we had in Corpus Christi was really only an introduction to it, and that was in the SNJ. But I was ordered to advanced instrument training before I left Port Angeles.

Paul Stillwell: What sort of duties did you have at Port Angeles?

Admiral Siler: Well, I was started to be aviation material officer, so I was the supply officer for engineering parts. We had aviation parts around that were left over from World War II. This would have been late '48 when I got there. And there were parts of helicopters, and we didn't have any helicopters. They had brought the Northwind with helicopters through there and transferred off the helicopter, but it was not flown after that at all.[†]

---

[*] Port Angeles, Washington, which is about 65 miles west northwest of Seattle, is on the Strait of Juan de Fuca, opposite Victoria, Canada.
[†] The Northwind (WAGB-282) was a Coast Guard icebreaker.

We had an amazing assortment of airplanes there in Port Angeles. At various times we had a PB-1G, which was a B-17.* We had PBYs all the time. We had R4Ds some of the time.† We had JRFs and J4Fs all the time.‡ I never flew a J4F off the water, and I'm just as happy. [Laughter] But I loved to fly the JRF off the water, and I volunteered a good many times to take medical evacuation flights from a fishing port up the coast someplace on either Vancouver Island or out at Neah Bay or Friday Harbor, which was north of us. We'd land on the water with the JRF and then go into Boeing Field with a man who needed to see a doctor. Always, of course, he'd wear his Sunday-go-to-meeting clothes, because when he finished seeing the doctor he was going to enjoy the weekend. It might be more than a weekend, but anyway it was obvious that they were counting on seeing Seattle while they were there.

Paul Stillwell: What was the main mission of that station?

Admiral Siler: Search and rescue primarily until the Korean War started, and at that time we also had to patrol the coast to see if anyone was coming in from Korea.§ We would fly out just as far as we could on the route toward Korea to see what was coming in, and if it were something that could not be identified. Usually we had the list of ships that were coming in to the pilot station in Port Angeles. The pilots always had their station right there next to the Coast Guard air station, and so we knew what ships were supposed to be coming in. And if they were standard to be coming into Port Angeles, we didn't pay too much attention to them except to fully identify them and go on and see who else was out there. But we had that and a lot of search and rescue.

It was an interesting search and rescue station, because for many years we did mountain rescue work as well the water rescue work. The mountains get pretty high

---
* Boeing's B-17 Flying Fortress was one of the principal bombers employed by the U.S. Army Air Forces throughout World War II. PB-1G was the Navy-Coast Guard designation.
† The DC-2 and DC-3 were superb cargo or passenger planes; the design was quite innovative for its time. In World War II the DC-3 carried the Navy designation of R4D and the Army Air Forces designation C-47.
‡ The Grumman-built JRF Goose was a two-engine flying boat that first entered Navy and Coast Guard service in 1939. The JRF-5 model had a wingspan of 49 feet, length of 38 feet, gross weight of 8,000 pounds, and top speed of 201 miles per hour. Cruising speed was 191 mph.
§ The Korean War began on 25 June 1950, when six North Korean infantry division and three border constabulary brigades invaded the South Korea. In New York that same day the United Nations Security Council adopted a resolution condemning the invasion.

pretty quickly there. Mount Olympus was just behind to the south of the air station, and there are some snowfields up there that we could not have landed the aircraft on unless we really had to. But we'd fly up over them and do some searches for the people there. And we had an agreement with a couple who did a lot of movie work up in the Olympic National Park that we'd fly up and drop them supplies to give us some more familiarity with flying around the mountains. Other times we'd be flying around the lakes that were up in the Olympic National Park. It was beautiful flying.

Paul Stillwell: Was that mainly in PBMs?

Admiral Siler: No, that was more in the JRF. The PBM was too big to fly there. We only had one PBM.

Paul Stillwell: Well, if you would not be able to land in the mountains was your role to find the people so you could locate them and they'd be rescued from land?

Admiral Siler: Well, part of the time we had a helicopter in Port Angeles. We had an HO3S for a while till we wrecked it.*

Paul Stillwell: A big dragonfly.

Admiral Siler: Yes. We had the third commanding officer reported on a Friday, and on Sunday we wrecked the helicopter. [Laughter] I was the duty officer. We had dispatched the helicopter to a place that was inland a little bit and a man who was at an observation station in the National Forest Reserves. He had fallen off of one of the lookout towers and thought he needed to be evacuated to the hospital. He said, "It's 5,500 feet high," and we said, "Well, we can make that in the HO3S but not much higher." So we went over, and fortunately I didn't go. I was the one who sat at the desk and dispatched it.

---

* The Sikorsky HO3S was a two-rotor helicopter that first entered Navy service in 1946. The main rotor diameter was 49 feet, length of the aircraft 45 feet, gross weight, 5,500 pounds; maximum speed, 103 miles per hour.

The pilot went there and made one approach over the area and said, "I think I can land the next time around." We had sent a JRF with him for better communications. The JRF was higher and was reporting a blow-by-blow description. When the helicopter pilot came over to slow up the helicopter, it stalled and he went in and cartwheeled over the landing area and ended up leaning against a tree on the edge of a cliff. He would have gone down at least 1,500 feet if he'd made one more roll. The station's doctor had just come back from going to church, and so he was wearing his go-to-meeting shoes and had put a flight suit on over his suit, trousers and no coat.

The pilot got back on the radio after the plane had wrecked and was upside down and said, "We're okay, but obviously the helicopter's in trouble." Then there was a pause and the doctor came on the radio and said, "Don't believe it. He's nutty as a fruitcake" [Laughter] The doctor had broken a hand, and the doctor's worst injuries were blisters on his feet because he had to walk out. [Laughter] Since he was just wearing church-type shoes somebody loaned him a pair of boots that were two sizes too big. Every time he'd step in them going down the hill he'd go this way with his feet, and he had terrible blisters. As far as the hand was concerned, it was broken, but he ignored it and took the bandages off it and got all right after a while.

Paul Stillwell: What happened to the people that they were originally trying to rescue?

Admiral Siler: He walked out too. [Laughter]

Paul Stillwell: And the JRF just flew home.

Admiral Siler: Yes. I think that as far as the other man was concerned, he may have been carried out. I just don't know, but we couldn't do anything for him anymore. The helicopter was definitely out of commission.

Paul Stillwell: How far out did those reconnaissance patrols go looking for unidentified ships?

Admiral Siler: I'd say something like 600 miles. The PBY had pretty good range, and they were usually PBY flights. Sometimes we would use the B-17 or a PBM. The PBM was taken away for overhaul that one time I recall, and so we didn't have a PBM for months on end. The B-17 was only assigned from time to time. We always had the same one, but I don't know why they moved it elsewhere. It was too small a runway actually for the B-17.

Paul Stillwell: Where had the B-17 come from? Was it an Army cast-off?

Admiral Siler: Well, if it were it had been cast-off to the Coast Guard a long time before. There were quite a few of the B-17s that were converted to a rescue-type configuration. They'd have a rescue boat that they had under them, and we had the boat, but I never saw it actually dropped. In fact, most of the time we didn't use it at all. We would figure that if we covered the surface of the ocean with life rafts that was as good as having a boat there.

Paul Stillwell: What do you recall about going on search-and-rescue missions yourself?

Admiral Siler: Well, we didn't have quite as many urgent ones where you thought you had to get up in the air immediately because a plane was in trouble someplace, but ours were more frequently boats that were in trouble. Medevacs were not too uncommon.[*] I volunteered for the JRF flights where we would land on the water at Nootka Sound, which is up on the Vancouver Island coast, over on Neah Bay, which is out next to Cape Flattery and Friday Harbor, which is northeast of Port Angeles. Those cases would all have to be flown into Boeing Field in Seattle because that was near the Marine Hospital.

Paul Stillwell: So you'd land on the water and pick the people up?

Admiral Siler: Yes. They'd usually come over with a small boat from the fishing boat that they were normally assigned to, and we'd take them on into Boeing Field. There was

---

[*] Medevac—medical evacuation.

one time that I was flying the JRF, and the JRF had notoriously bad brakes, particularly when they were wet. When I was taxiing out of Boeing Field down to the end of runway, I turned on the taxiway toward a B-36 and realized that the brakes were wet, and I might not be able to turn. [Laughter] When I finally did turn, I didn't do a thing to the B-36, I'm happy to say.

Paul Stillwell: What is the excitement or satisfaction or experience that goes from rescuing people that are in trouble?

Admiral Siler: Just a feeling of satisfaction that you've helped someone. There was one time when there was a serious forest fire that burned almost the entire city of Forks, Washington, and it may have been the entire city because I never got there afterward. The forest fire we saw was leaping the tops of the trees up there in the Olympic Forest, and it really looked grim. Most of those people came to Port Angeles to find someplace in the barracks to sleep for a little while, because it was really a rugged thing. It was one of those incidents where you know you've helped people a lot. We didn't do a great deal that time except make our barracks space available so that they could find a place to get some rest.

Paul Stillwell: What do you remember about open-water landings and takeoffs in the JRF or PBY?

Admiral Siler: Well, the JRF you couldn't land on the open ocean. You had to have a place that was pretty well sheltered. Nootka Sound and Neah Bay and Friday Harbor all had that capability, so it was not at all difficult to land there. We used to practice the rough-water landings, but I'm happy to say I never participated in one that was truly a rough-water landing.

Paul Stillwell: Well, if somebody were stranded out beyond, is that the case where you'd use the B-17 and drop the boats?

Admiral Siler: Yes. Once in a long while, the PBM or the PBY could be landed in fairly rough waters, but most of the time you tried to avoid it if you possibly could. The PBM could be slowed down well enough that it could land in fairly rough water.

Paul Stillwell: Well, operating a flying boat is pretty much a lost art these days. What were the techniques involved?

Admiral Siler: Well, you'd sort of hang the airplane on the propellers. And when you found a place that you thought was smooth enough that you could stay on the water for a short period of time while the plane slowed down, you'd chop the power and stall the airplane into the water at about as slow a speed as you could get while still having some control. Then once you were on the water, later we had the PBM that had reversible pitch props. It wasn't built that way to begin with, but the Coast Guard modified it for that.

Paul Stillwell: So that essentially acted as a brake?

Admiral Siler: Yes. The PBY never had reversible props, but the PBM would operate with reverse props. You could turn rather shortly with one engine back and one engine forward.

Paul Stillwell: I've heard that for takeoffs the water couldn't be too smooth, that you had to have at least a little chop on it.

Admiral Siler: A little chop is a good thing, but too much chop is not too good. [Laughter] It's been a long time since I did it. I can't think of the term for it, but when the nose comes up and falls back so that you can't get airborne because you can't get enough speed.

Paul Stillwell: Well, the idea was to get up on the step, wasn't it?

Admiral Siler: Yes, and most of the time, and particularly with the PBM if you applied just a little backpressure, it would get up on the step rather easily. If you tried to force it up so that it got on the step sooner than it should, then it would fall through. You'd get a bouncing effect, and that was not good. You'd lose control rather quickly then.

Paul Stillwell: So you really had to get a feel from experience on just when to apply the power.

Admiral Siler: Well, you'd put the power on and then apply some back pressure and just hold that until the airplane would come up, and it would generally fall through so that you'd be on the step in the right attitude to gain the additional speed. Then you could lift off without too much trouble. It was when you were in rough water that was the problem.

Paul Stillwell: I've also heard that you needed a fair amount of physical strength to manhandle one of those PBYs.

Admiral Siler: I don't know about that. The PBY was not that difficult. The PBM was much harder.

Paul Stillwell: Not that much help from hydraulics?

Admiral Siler: The PBM didn't have hydraulics at all. Now, on the P5M, it had hydraulics, but it had the hydraulics more for flaps that were underwater, so it was steerable with those underwater flaps and they were hydraulic.* I only flew that a couple of times. I was someplace with the Commandant, and usually he'd get in the airplane, and they'd let me sit there and pretend I was flying. [Laughter]

Paul Stillwell: What was family life like in the Pacific Northwest, your native region?

---

* The Martin P5M Marlin was the U.S. Navy's last operational flying boat. It entered fleet service in 1948 and was last used in 1966. In 1962 it was redesignated P-5.

Admiral Siler: It was a very pretty area. In the summertime it was lovely. But one problem with Port Angeles was that we had a wind down the Strait of Juan de Fuca all the time, and the Coast Guard air station was out there with a strong wind. And believe me, in the wintertime that wind was strong and cold. It would shift around then and come over Canada, and it was really freezing out on the spit. We had one storm when they wiped out the road to the air station, and we'd go down the railroad track then. [Laughter] There were rather frequently times when you didn't want to go out on the small boat dock and investigate the condition of the small boats because it was just too damned cold.

Paul Stillwell: What was your housing situation there? Had that improved?

Admiral Siler: Yes, we were told about a place the day we got into town. I had three classmates who were stationed there who'd been in the earlier group that went to flight training, and so one of them told me that the place across the street from them was available. So we moved in rather quickly there. It was not that wonderful a house, but it was two bedrooms, one in that corner of the house and the other in the other corner of the house. The only heat was a floor furnace that was oil-fueled, and it was in the floor in a third corner. [Laughter] So it was very frequently cold in the house or too hot in that part of the house and cold elsewhere. But we lived there for the three years we were there.

Paul Stillwell: Summers are very nice there.

Admiral Siler: Well, they're not too nice at the air station where the Coast Guard is because it's out in the strait, but in town it can be lovely.

Paul Stillwell: Did those prevailing winds cause any problems in your flight patterns?

Admiral Siler: No, they were right down the runway most of the time.

Paul Stillwell: What was the command arrangement at the air station? Whom did you report to?

Admiral Siler: Well, the district commander was in Seattle, and we had Teletype and telephone between the air station and the district office. Most of the time, we would use the Teletype unless we had something urgent. At night and on the weekends, you could use either one of them; it made no difference, although we would make Teletype messages in order to have a record of them. But lots of people were on that Teletype other than the Coast Guard. It was the State Highway Patrol and the Air Force down at McChord Field.

Paul Stillwell: Kind of like a party line. [Laughter]

Admiral Siler: Yes, it was, so if it only dealt with Coast Guard we frequently would just use the phone. The phones were maintained by Coast Guard people those days. We had the people with a special rating that was maintaining the wires. Used to be something having to do with telephone and Teletype.

Paul Stillwell: Was there an air station commander and then a separate squadron for the planes, or how did that work?

Admiral Siler: The commander of the air station was the commander of the all the planes too.

Paul Stillwell: And who was he?

Admiral Siler: We had a whole bunch of them. When I arrived there we had a William H. Snyder, who had been around for quite some time and was a bit of a politician.* He later was one of the commanders of a search-and-rescue area in the Pacific, in the

---

* Commander William H. Snyder, USCG.

Philippines. The next commanding officer was a man who was a hail-fellow well met. He had been the football player who was next to the exec of the Bayfield when I was on that. The man on the Bayfield had been an aviator also and just decided that there was more activity during the war on a ship than there was on an air station. He went back to aviation and was the CO at San Francisco at one time after that. The commanding officer after that was a man who was known to have a hellacious temper, and he's the one that relieved, and we wrecked the helicopter in three days. [Laughter]

Paul Stillwell: Who was he?

Admiral Siler: His name was R. R. Johnson, Roger Johnson, and he had a charming wife. And I remember that the operations officer lived something like three doors apart from the captain. The wives would get together before it was time for them to get home from the air station, and the operations officer couldn't stand that captain and vice versa. Eventually, the captain recommended that he be assigned to some other duty and the operations officer said, "I'll take any other assignment, aviation or otherwise." He went to sea. [Laughter]

Paul Stillwell: Were there any other ramifications from the Korean War other than these long patrols?

Admiral Siler: Not for us, I don't believe, not for the air people. There were more duties for the marine safety officers, because they would inspect the ships more thoroughly to see if there was cargo that was not supposed to be there and things of that nature. But we didn't have much other than the patrols.

Now, as far as locations were concerned, we had a responsibility to conduct search and rescue all over the Pacific and also a large part of the Atlantic. We established new Coast Guard air stations at Bermuda, increased the size of the one at San Juan, Puerto Rico. We established a much bigger air station in Barbers Point, Hawaii. We established an air station at Midway and Wake and increased the size of the one at Guam and the one at Sangley Point, Philippines.

Paul Stillwell: What was the stimulus for that growth?

Admiral Siler: The entire Pacific was covered by a lot of transport of people going to Korea. The contract with the Military Air Transport Service called for them to use DC-4s and it didn't say how good a DC-4.* They were very frequently tired old airplanes that they'd fill up with troops, and they'd get in those airplanes and fly across the Pacific from San Francisco to Hawaii, and we very frequently would be flying out and intercepting them. I got orders very shortly after that was established to go to Hawaii, and I was stationed in Hawaii, but my first association with the airlift was to go to Wake Island.

The group that was supposedly going to Wake Island was given PBYs instead of the P4Y that they were supposed to get.† They supposedly were going to operate the PBY until the 4Y was available. The first 4Y that we took to Wake Island was a Navy 4Y and it was heavy, slow, not very effective at all. Then we got our own P4Ys, which were stripped of all the guns and the weight in the turrets, and it was a pretty good airplane. It would fly much faster than a DC-4. And so when we went out and intercepted a DC-4, we had to slow it down and put the flaps down a little bit so that we could stay with them.

Paul Stillwell: So this is kind of like a safety escort for those planes?

Admiral Siler: Yes. We'd fly along with them just behind and just 500 feet above them. We'd be there, and if anything went wrong with them, we could cover the ocean with some more life rafts. We carried a lot of rafts in the P4Ys.

Paul Stillwell: How far out did you go on those flights?

---

* R5D Skymaster was the Navy designation for the Douglas-built DC-4 commercial airliner. The four-engine propeller plane had a top speed of 281 miles an hour. It was 118 feet long, wingspan of 94 feet, and gross weight of 65,000 pounds. It first went into Navy service in 1941. The Air Force version was C-54.
† The PB4Y-1B was a land-based Navy Liberator modified for reconnaissance duties. In 1951 it was redesignated as the P4Y-1. The Coast Guard operated a group of PB4Y-2 Privateers that had only a single tail instead of the two that the original PB4Y-1 Liberator had.

Admiral Siler: Well, we'd go as much as halfway from Honolulu to San Francisco. And going the other direction we could also be 1,000 miles from Wake Island toward Tokyo.

Paul Stillwell: So this was kind of a flying counterpart of the ocean station program.

Admiral Siler: Yes. The ocean station program was expanded during that time, too, and we had destroyer escorts that were on the ocean stations. But as far as the aviation part of it was concerned, we found that the Midway detachment didn't work too well, because Midway had so many albatrosses out on the runway that very frequently we would have problems with an engine because the governor on the engines would be hit by a flying bird. The birds didn't know enough to get off the runway. In fact, they rather liked the runways because of the temperature of the runways.

Paul Stillwell: I've heard the term "gooney birds" used also.

Admiral Siler: Yes, indeed, and they're gooney. [Laughter]

Paul Stillwell: What era did the Coast Guard get an airplane called the Albatross?* Was that along in that period?

Admiral Siler: We first got them in '52, I think, but they were not too useful for places in the Pacific because their range was nowhere near as much as the 4Y or the P5M or PBM. They were great for coastal search and rescue. The Albatross was made, I think, under a Department of Defense contract originally, and it was a Grumman airplane. It was two steps above the JRF. One step above was Mallard—I think was what they called it—and we never got any of them at all. But the Albatross is a good airplane, and we kept it for a long time and modified it to change the wing completely, extending the wing and changing the de-icing procedure. Used to be the wings would be like this, and the de-icing would be little bubbles in the wingspan, and that didn't work too well. They

---

* The Grumman-built UF-1 Albatross was a two-engine flying boat that first entered service as an air-sea rescue plane in the late 1940s. The UF-2 model had a wingspan of 97 feet, length of 61 feet, gross weight of 35,700 pounds, and top speed of 236 miles per hour. In 1962 the Albatross became the HU-16.

changed it to when they extended the wing it made the de-icing this way, and if there were changes in the configuration of the wing it didn't affect the airplane as much.

Paul Stillwell: Well, that plane lasted about till the time you became Commandant, and then you had to find a replacement. [Laughter]

Admiral Siler: Well, it was just about then anyway. We used some Convairs for a while and hoped that we'd get a replacement for them, but the Albatross was around a long time. We operated them in Corpus Christi, Miami, and in Alaska when I was there.

Paul Stillwell: Did you get personnel augmentation from the reserves when the Korean War came along?

Admiral Siler: Oh, yes, a good many of those people. In order to find people who were aviators as well as officers, we went to the Navy and found a good many of them. We had them in Hawaii when I was there and in Corpus Christi. There were quite a few of them who had been Coast Guard aviators in World War II and had really not done much of anything having to do with aviation in between, and we got quite a few Navy types. There were still some of them around. When I was in Alaska there were definitely some, and I think some when I was in Miami.

Paul Stillwell: What would be the incentive for a Naval Reserve aviator to come over the Coast Guard?

Admiral Siler: Because the Navy said, "We don't need you." And the Coast Guard said, "And we do." When I was CO in Miami we had at one time under the command there at least one Army officer. There were Marine officers, Navy officers, and Coast Guard officers. The Army officer was a very good pilot and was around for years. And there were a couple of Marine officers that were very good. One very good helicopter pilot and another man whose wife had been a stewardess I know for quite some time, and I'm not sure what his background had been in the Marine Corps. Oh, and one man whose name you would know, Lenny Belk, who was in the Coast Guard Reserve.

Paul Stillwell: No, I don't.

Admiral Siler: You know the department stores, the Belk Company here?

Paul Stillwell: No. Must be a local phenomenon I'm not familiar with.

Admiral Siler: From here south you'll see a Belk store in every city.

Paul Stillwell: I'll look for those now.

Admiral Siler: Lenny Belk got out of the Air Force, where had been a C-82 pilot, a big Flying Boxcar, and he didn't like working in his family stores at all. So he came in the Coast Guard, and he was a good pilot in Miami, qualified in the Albatross with no problems. He was ordered to Hawaii with a stop in between to learn to fly the C-130.* He got to Barbers Point, and they wouldn't let him fly it because he was a new pilot. So he'd go in the airplane and navigate and not fly it at all. He got tired of that rather quickly, so he got out of the Coast Guard again.

That's the second time he'd left the service. He wanted to get back in when I was Commandant, and I checked with our people and they said, "We're just not taking anybody with that rank at all." He was a lieutenant commander at that point, and I don't know that he was very far up on the scale of lieutenant commanders, but he didn't meet the requirements at all. So I guess he's probably selling things today in the stores. [Laughter]

---

* The Lockheed C-130 Hercules is a cargo aircraft powered by four turboprops. It was developed for the Air Force in the 1950s and has since been adapted for use as well by the Navy, Marine Corps, and Coast Guard. The plane has a maximum cruising speed of 357 miles per hour and a maximum takeoff weight of 135,000 pounds.

Paul Stillwell: Was that a problem when you brought in these pilots from other services, that they were rusty?

Admiral Siler: Oh, all of them were, yes, because most of them had had nothing in between. Some of them had flown something, you know, very small, but flying the big airplanes was a little different for them. But we expected that, so it was a matter of giving them an opportunity to get some time and get the feel of the airplanes again. The great majority of those people had not flown multi-engine, or if they had it had to be have been a seaplane.

Paul Stillwell: Now, the reservists who were flying for the airlines, did they go mainly back into the Navy and Air Force?

Admiral Siler: I don't know about that.

Paul Stillwell: Was this retraining program a local thing at Port Angeles, or was there any centralized facility as well?

Admiral Siler: There was no centralized training. But most of the people before they came to a place like Port Angeles were already training someplace, and where I don't know.

Paul Stillwell: By the Coast Guard?

Admiral Siler: It could have been. In those days Elizabeth City would have been one of the places you would have expected that, because it was one of the bigger air stations in those days.* Today if we were looking for a place to train people, Clearwater, Florida, would be a place for C-130s and Mobile, Alabama, for helicopters or the Falcon jets

---

* Coast Guard Air Station Elizabeth City, North Carolina, was commissioned on 15 August 1940. It is located 60 miles north of Cape Hatteras. The site near Elizabeth City was selected by the Coast Guard in 1938 for its potential strategic value as a seaplane base.

Paul Stillwell: You mentioned that you had that material officer job. Any specifics you recall in that?

Admiral Siler: Trying to inventory all that helicopter stuff was just impossible. We had the attic of one building on the reservation absolutely full of helicopter stuff that they'd taken for the helicopter to the South Pole when Byrd made his last expedition.* The Northwind went with the HNS, I guess it was.† Nobody knew what parts were used on that particular helicopter at all. So we had to try to find out what it was and how it could be used on a helicopter, whether it could be used on something as modern, and I use that term loosely, as modern as the HO3S. We probably had the last HO3S in the Coast Guard when we wrecked it. There's one that is now at the Naval Aviation Museum that has a higher number than we did. Ours was the 234, and the 235 is in the museum.

Paul Stillwell: The Army, Navy, and Air Force had their Defense Department supply systems. Where was yours based?

Admiral Siler: Elizabeth City. The Coast Guard had an aviation repair and supply depot in Elizabeth City, and they still have it today.

Paul Stillwell: So they would get the parts from the manufacturers and then parcel them out as needed?

Admiral Siler: Yes, and hopefully they'd get more than were going to be used right away, just so they would have something in supply there at Elizabeth City.

Paul Stillwell: Was fuel supply ever a problem?

---

* Commander Richard E. Byrd, Jr., USN (Ret.), explored Antarctica in 1928, 1933, 1939, 1947, 1955. He was retired for physical disability in 1916 but continued to be promoted, eventually becoming a rear admiral in 1929.
† HNS was the Navy designation for the Army's R-4B helicopter, built by Sikorsky. It first entered Navy service in 1943. The main rotor diameter was 38 feet, length of the aircraft 35 feet, gross weight, 2,600 pounds; maximum speed, 82 miles per hour.

Admiral Siler: Not that I'm aware of. We would order in 5,500-gallon tanks, a truckload, and that would usually last for quite some time on the air station, because we didn't use an awful lot of fuel. Some of the airplanes were pretty conservative on their fuel. The JRF and J4F, for example, hardly used any gas. The PBM and PBY both used a whole lot more, of course, but still we'd keep the supply of fuel in our tanks on the air stations fairly full all the time, and we'd go out and sound them every day so we knew exactly how much was in them.

Paul Stillwell: Any particular recollections on the enlisted men at Port Angeles in that era?

Admiral Siler: They were mighty fine men but no particular memories of them. Interestingly, one of the men, a parachute rigger, married a local girl; I think he was transferred away but later came back and became the mayor of the city. [Laughter] I remember he had a hotrod version of a Chevrolet convertible, and he wanted to test it, see how fast it would go down the runway. We let him do it once or twice but not as often as he'd like.

Paul Stillwell: Well, that would be great. You'd get a long straightaway and no cross traffic.

Admiral Siler: That's right.

Paul Stillwell: Well, anything about Port Angeles that you want to add beyond what we've talked about?

Admiral Siler: There was one interesting rescue operation that was in, I believe, January of 1950. They had ordered some B-36s that had been based at McChord Field in Tacoma to go to Alaska for an operation that they had up there.* These B-36s had ten engines. Four of them were jets and six were reciprocating. Then they were ordered out of Alaska when the operation was completed, and they were going to return to McChord. That meant they'd come the large part of the way just down the coast of Alaska and British Columbia.

One of them ran into trouble, and I think all of his jets failed, so he may have been on six engines. Tough. [Laughter] So he ordered the crew to bail out. Before they bailed out, the navigator gave a position, which was a pretty good position, and they all left the plane by parachute. The only trouble was at least one man put his Mae West over his parachute.† It wouldn't open that way, so he became a bomb. Most of the men got down in the coastal area of British Columbia. We went from Annette Island, off Ketchikan, Alaska, where they had only JRFs, and we went up the coast from Port Angeles in the PBY and JRFs to search for these people once they'd bailed out.

A good many of them got together once they got on the ground so that they were not too hard to find, but we couldn't find all the guys, because, of course, we couldn't find this guy who'd bombed in. I was flying in the JRF when I went up there. There was snow all over the place, and we were flying low enough that we could see footprints in the snow. Of course, you couldn't tell if it was a bear footprint or a man. So we'd circle low enough to try to determine the shape of that footprint.

We spent one interesting night in a little town called Bella Bella. There had been a Canadian Air Force base there at one time, and they had operated the Canso, which is a PBY, Canadian version. There was a hangar that we usually we could put the JRF in with no problem at all. Then I think the next day a Canadian Canso came, and so we couldn't get in. So that night we went to Prince Rupert. Prince Rupert by comparison is a real metropolis, but it's not really. [Laughter] It's kind of a wilderness town. It's

---

* Consolidated Vultee, based in San Diego, built the Air Force's B-36 bomber, known as the Peacemaker. The B-36D model was equipped with four J-47 jet engines in under-wing nacelles and six piston engines that drove propellers. The jet engines enhanced the plane's maximum speed from 376 miles per hour to 435 miles per hour.
† "Mae West" was the nickname for an inflatable life jacket that fit over a man's head and chest. When not in use it was rolled up into a pouch that he carried on his belt. The life jacket was named for a buxom movie actress of the period.

grown a lot since the Alaska ferry system calls in Prince Rupert. But, anyway, we went to Alaska and searched for those people for several days, and I spent one night, as I say, at Bella Bella and one night in Prince Rupert.

We found all of the crew but the one who was known to have made a mistake—a big mistake. When we tried to find him and couldn't, we eventually gave it up. Then, about two days after I left Port Angeles for my next assignment, they found his body. The PBM that I had flown— still remember the number of it, 84740—was going to Prince Rupert, I guess it was, to pick up the body and return it to the States. Unfortunately, the PBM crashed on takeoff. I had left, and I was in San Francisco on my way to Hawaii at that time, but I knew all of the crew who were in that with the exception of the Air Force man who'd been sent along to be the escort for the body. And the copilot or the third pilot, I'm not sure which it was, was killed. Some of the enlisted men were badly wounded. I know that one of the mechanics had his back injured so badly I'm not sure he ever flew again. But that was a disappointing way to end up the tour at Port Angeles.

[Interruption]

Paul Stillwell: Well, we just took a break here, and you showed me a shadowbox that has some of your medals and awards in it and also your father-in-law's wings from being with the Royal Flying Corps. Maybe you could tell me a little more about him, please.

Admiral Siler: Well, he was very active with scouting with Sir Baden-Powell in England, and for some reason he was offered an opportunity to fly airplanes for the Royal Flying Corps.[*] As he put it, someone said, "You think you can take it up, Walfie?"

"But of course." So that was his flight training. It was just take it up, and there he was. [Laughter] I'm not even sure they used seat belts in those days, but he flew for quite some time in France for the Royal Flying Corps, which was the predecessor to the Royal Air Force.

---

[*] Sir Robert Stephenson Smyth, First Baron Baden-Powell of Gilwell (1857-1941) was a British Army career officer who in 1908 founded the Boy Scouts.

Paul Stillwell: Was this in World War I?

Admiral Siler: Yes. When he came back, his businesses had pretty much dried up. He had had a series of theaters where they showed the very early movies, and most of them I guess had gone out of date during the time he was overseas. So at that time he decided maybe opportunity would be better in the United States, so he and his son, who was the oldest child, went to the United States and then sent for his wife and the two girls. They came across the Atlantic and then landed in I guess it was Montreal and took the train across the country. They entered the United States from Vancouver and came down the coast on another steamship. The mother got the two girls up bright and early so that they could see them open the Golden Gate. [Laughter]

Paul Stillwell: And, of course, the bridge wasn't even built then.[*] [Laughter]

Admiral Siler: No. [Laughter]

Paul Stillwell: What was your father-in-law's name?

Admiral Siler: Clarence Walford. And I don't know that he ever accomplished much as an engineer, which he was initially, an electrical engineer, in the United States, because what he had been offered by his brother was a job at either Owens Lake or Tule Lake in the valley of California. By the time he got there, all the business was gone, so he lived south of San Francisco for many years. They lived in the vicinity of Redwood City most of the time. He spent a good deal of his time up in the coastal range mountains, and he had a place he lived in there. Did a little gardening, and half his food he could raise. And that's about it. He tried writing a few times. I've never thought it was anything to be proud of, but I know he did some writing.

Paul Stillwell: Which country was your future wife born in?

---

[*] Construction on the Golden Gate Bridge, one of the largest and most spectacular suspension bridges in the world, began in 1933 and was completed in 1937.

Admiral Siler: She was born in England. In fact, she was born quite near Cheddar, which is where the cheese originated from. We have gone to Cheddar and visited and seen where the home had been, but it is no longer there. We found a man who said that he used to play with my wife's older brother and even remembered the name.

Paul Stillwell: Interesting trip that must have been.

Admiral Siler: Yes.

Paul Stillwell: Well, back to the era that we've been discussing. Any more to follow up on the Port Angeles tour of duty?

Admiral Siler: Well, I think that once the Korean War started, the flying changed its character to checking on shipping offshore more than anything else. Then my orders were delayed, because we all knew that something was going to happen very soon as far as expanding aviation was concerned, and so I was not transferred until—I think I left there in May of 1952.

Paul Stillwell: Well, it says that you had a course from February to May at Corpus Christi.

Admiral Siler: Corpus Christi, yes. My orders came in while I was gone, and they said I was authorized 30 days' leave provided no excess was involved, and I had plenty of leave. But they also said, "And be sure you report to Hawaii by May something or other in 1952," and that would mean that I would report the day after I left Corpus Christi, which was not quite possible. [Laughter]

Paul Stillwell: What do you remember about that instrument training at Corpus Christi?

Admiral Siler: Well, they concentrated on the abilities of navigating when you had to find yourself in the air, and, of course, you did that in old-fashioned method with the A's and the N's.*

Paul Stillwell: These are the Morse code signals.

Admiral Siler: Yes. If you merge A and N, it becomes a constant signal, which is the beam that you listen to, to fly on. If you knew which one of those beams were on, you could fly in to the station. Once you found the station, you knew exactly where you were. And there was a little bit about Omni stations, but the Omni stations were just coming in. They were pretty new at that time. And not any mention at all of tacan, which would also tell you exactly how far you were from the station.† All those things came in later years.

When you finished the course there at Corpus Christi you were qualified for a special instrument card. But you were not issued one, because they felt that if you were to get a special card, the issuing authority had to know enough about that individual to be able to certify him as being the type of individual who was competent enough to have a special instrument card. So they would issue us a regular, a standard instrument card, but not special. But as soon as I got to Hawaii I got the special instrument card.

Paul Stillwell: Did they have any of these tests where they have you out flying with a hood over the canopy or something like that.

Admiral Siler: Oh, yes. Did that all the time, every day.

Paul Stillwell: What plane were you using?

Admiral Siler: We used the twin-engine Beechcraft, SNB, and that was the standard trainer in Corpus Christi. Then when we got to Barbers Point we flew the B-17 and the

---

* The Morse code signal for the letter A is dit-dah; for N it is dah-dit.
† Tacan—tactical aid to navigation, a homing signal broadcast by an aircraft carrier to aid returning aircraft in locating the ship.

DC-4.* Because I wasn't qualified in them as a pilot, I didn't get the special instrument card until I was qualified in the airplanes. Then we got a replacement for the B-17, because it was getting too slow. There were too many commercial DC-6s and -7s. In fact, we could never keep up with a DC-7.† I tried to keep up with a DC-7 one time when it was operating on three engines. It was letting down into Honolulu and still left me in the dust when I was on four engines in a P4Y. And even on high blower at altitude, why—and I've flown at over 200 knots in the P4Y, but the DC-7 on three engines still makes better than that.

Paul Stillwell: Any characteristics you remember from flying the B-17?

Admiral Siler: The B-17 was a very forgiving airplane most of the time, and as far as landing it was concerned it was better to land the tailwheel first rather than on the main landing gear. Although the Air Force landed them on the main landing gear, the Navy and Coast Guard always landed them tailwheel first.

Paul Stillwell: Why was it better tailwheel first?

Admiral Siler: Because it wasn't about to take off and go someplace. [Laughter] Once you got down, you were there. And the Navy in Hawaii at that time used the B-17 as an early warning plane. It had a big radar both on top and underneath, and so it was slower than we were by quite a bit. But when we got the P4Y, we were much, much faster than that because the P4Y that we had had all of the turrets removed. We carried no guns at all and no armor at all. The side blisters on the P4Y had been taken out and smoothed over with Plexiglas there so that there was a seat just inside the Plexiglas. A lookout could look out there and see a good scope, a good part of the air around you. There were two seats there, one on each side. The tail turret was removed, and you could be in there, but by the time you passed it, you really didn't care that much. The nose was completely

---

* Barbers Point is the site of a naval air station at the southwest "corner" of the island of Oahu, Hawaii.
† The DC-7 was the last piston-engine airliner built by Douglas. It was one of the first commercial aircraft able to make nonstop transatlantic crossings between New York and London. The plane, which entered service in the mid-1950s, It had a typical cruising speed of 300 knots.

changed without a chin turret or a nose turret of any kind, and it was all glassed over, and it had a beautiful view from up there too.

Paul Stillwell: What do you remember about the flying characteristics of the P4Y?

Admiral Siler: Well, that one was a tricycle landing gear so that you wanted to land on the main gear again. It had the Davis wing, which meant that you had to have flying capability, or you weren't going to go anyplace. One of the characteristics of it you learned very soon in your breaking in on that airplane was how to fly over a field and look down through a mist or foggy or smoky conditions and dive for the runway. Then you would break the dive just in time and land on the main landing gear. I had done it several times with no trouble, and I was trying to check the commander out who was the commanding officer out at Wake Island. He had graduated from the Coast Guard Academy just before I got there, so he was several years senior to me.

We went out and did several maneuvers, and then we said, "Well, let's try the short-field approach." We went in and got to the point where we said, "Okay, now you can see the runway right down there. Chop the power and dive for the runway." He dove for the runway and got nervous as we got closer, so he pulled it up. We stalled and plunked in on the tailskid, which was back there where there was nothing except a skid, and wiped it off and left it on the runway. So that was his last practice at that—while I was with him anyway. [Laughter]

Paul Stillwell: He sort of fell out of the sky.

Admiral Siler: Yes. And being the responsible pilot, it went in my logbook, not his, and so I have that in my logbook as one of the incidents that is an unfortunate thing. Other than that I loved the airplane. I really enjoyed flying the 4Y.

Paul Stillwell: Was that the main one you flew out of Hawaii?

Admiral Siler: Well, yes, once we got them, that was what we flew almost all the time except the R5D. Now, we supplied logistic support to all of the loran stations in the Pacific. In order to do that we would fly a trip from Barbers Point to Guam and on to the Philippine Islands and Japan once a month. In between we would fly a trip as far as Guam but not the rest of the way with supplies. When we got it as far as Guam they would take supplies to Saipan, Guam itself, Ulithi, which was maintained as a loran station many years after the Navy left it after World War II. I wrote one of those things up in the Naval Institute Proceedings one time when the King gave me a mat, and I still have it upstairs. They would also go down to Anguar, which was down in the—

Paul Stillwell: Palau Islands.

Admiral Siler: Yes. In fact, it was right next to Peleliu. And if we had enough that needed to go on to the Philippines and to Japan, Korea and, well, several stations in Japan, then we'd take it over into Japan. Once it got to Japan, most of the time we would go ahead and deliver it ourselves rather than turning it over to the Air Force for delivery.

Paul Stillwell: Now, were these some kind of special supplies that would go by air rather than by sea.?

Admiral Siler: It was a matter of finding any transportation at that time, so since we had the airplanes we would deliver it as close as we could to the place where it was needed, and usually we'd deliver it right to the station.

Paul Stillwell: So that's a Coast Guard self-sufficiency.

Admiral Siler: Well, usually we called it CATS, Coast Guard Air Transport. [Laughter]

Paul Stillwell: Which was kind of a play on the Military Air Transport Service.

Admiral Siler: Yes. But as far as what we took was concerned, we'd take everything. I remember one time I was not on the flight, but they were taking toilets to one of the stations that was still under construction, and they had very rough air. All those porcelain bowls were broken in the flight. I flew in some pretty rough weather out there, particularly over Japan. There was one time when I took the Commandant during my next assignment. We had known that we were getting into some rough air, and I turned on the seatbelt light. The captain who always served as special assistant to Admiral Richmond didn't pay any attention to it. A minute later he was up on the overhead, because it was very rough. It could get very rough out there.

Paul Stillwell: Was he injured?

Admiral Siler: I don't think injured enough to say anything about it, but he probably had a pretty sore back. [Laughter] Maybe a bump on his head.

Paul Stillwell: From then on he probably fastened his seat belt too.

Admiral Siler: Yes.

Paul Stillwell: Well, you said you went to Wake Island. What do you remember about that? That had been quite a battleground in World War II.

Admiral Siler: Yes, indeed, and it was still a very interesting place to walk through. We had four pilots rotated in, plus the man who was the commanding officer out there. Then later we rotated only one fewer pilot, and one man stayed out there for a year and had credit for his assignment to isolated duty. When we had the day off, which would be every third day, you could wander around the island and see those gun emplacements. The guns that had been taken from Singapore were there. Had English nameplates on them, so it was obvious what they were. It was very interesting to see where the gun emplacements had been and were. Once in a while, you'd still find some Japanese things. It was very interesting location, a very busy location, because this was a stop for all of Pan American's—what do they call them?

Paul Stillwell: The Clippers?*

Admiral Siler: Yes, they were the Boeing Clippers that looked like the Stratocruisers. So they'd come in often in the middle of the night. They were very noisy when they were taxied, because the way you taxied them and a good many other airplanes was you'd keep the brake on but not on hard. You'd just drag them a little bit, and so as you went along the brakes would squeal. If they landed at 1:00 or 2:00 o'clock in the morning and our barracks was right next to the runway, you'd hear this [squealing sound]. [Laughter]

Paul Stillwell: What was the purpose of riding the brakes? Was the runway short?

Admiral Siler: No. The brakes really didn't work well unless they were added to a little bit of drag. In the Martin 404 that we flew later at Coast Guard headquarters it was the same sort of thing, and you always kept the brakes on with that. Part of the reason for that was the wheels would move.

Paul Stillwell: They'd wobble?

Admiral Siler: Sort of. In order to really be effective on the brakes you had to have them dragging a little bit when you put the brakes on. Then, instead of going from here back to here and then apply the brakes, they'd be back here already. And when you applied brakes, it would simply get tight there.

Paul Stillwell: So it was not as abrupt a stop.

Admiral Siler: Well, it wasn't as abrupt as it could have been, yes. So you always had the brakes on.

---

* In the 1930s Pan American initiated transpacific air service with flying boats known as Clippers.

Paul Stillwell: And people went back to sleep afterwards.

Admiral Siler: Well, there weren't too many of us who slept that close to the runway. The Pan American passengers I think were usually taken off and given a snack or some sort of a meal on Wake Island, and we ate there with Pan American for a good many months before a place was finished for us.

Paul Stillwell: Well, there had been a lot of cooperation before the war between the Navy and Pan American in setting up these fueling stops en route to the Far East.

Admiral Siler: They're no longer used because the range is so great now.

Paul Stillwell: What do you remember about going into Japan in that era?

Admiral Siler: Most of the time it was a pretty good location to end up a flight. We'd use the old Haneda Airport, which is closed now, of course, but it was a nice airport, fairly close in.[*] We were able to get into downtown Tokyo without any difficulty, and we always stayed in downtown Tokyo because the office of the Coast Guard was down there.

Paul Stillwell: How well were Americans received in Japan at that time?

Admiral Siler: Very well. If there had been resentment, it was gone by this time. I think most of the everyday Japanese had gotten so used to having Americans around that it was completely a normal thing.

Paul Stillwell: Well, and it was a boost for their economy too.

---

[*] Haneda is the name of the current airport that serves Tokyo.

Admiral Siler: You bet it was. One of the things that we used to hear very frequently was that the younger Japanese women would like to get into the military exchanges because they preferred the kind of underwear that the Americans had. [Laughter] They wanted PX.* [Laughter]

Paul Stillwell: What do you remember about life in Hawaii in that era?

Admiral Siler: Actually, it was far more interesting than it is today. It had a little bit of the odor and the flavor of the older Hawaiian days, and we were so far out of Honolulu that we didn't really see anything except Pearl City and the city where Barbers Point is, Ewa. But we lived initially at Wahiawa, which is where Schofield Barracks is, for a couple of months, and then we moved to the station itself and lived in a Quonset hut for the rest of our time there.† We were happy to be that close to everything that was going on, although it scared my wife to death the first night that I was gone to Wake Island. She heard the airplanes turning up their engines in the middle of the night and didn't know what it was. It was the airplanes that were being readied for instrument training. They had an instrument training facility right there at Barbers Point, and so every morning at about 4:00 o'clock they'd start turning up the Beechcraft for their instrument training. She didn't know what that was and thought the planes were flying over.

Paul Stillwell: And your daughter Marsha had been born by then.

Admiral Siler: Oh, yes. She was born in Port Angeles during the last year that we were in Port Angeles, and so she was toddling around. And our son actually started kindergarten when my wife went to my parents' home in California while I went to all-weather flight training. He couldn't figure out when the birthday cake would be served. [Laughter] But Marsha was too young for school while she was out there, so she didn't start until in Washington, D.C.

---

* PX—post exchange.
† Schofield Barracks is an Army post on Oahu. A Quonset hut is a semi-cylindrical metal building that can be shipped to an advance base area and erected quickly.

Paul Stillwell: Did you get down to Honolulu at all?

Admiral Siler: Oh, yes. We used to go down for evening events. I remember our seeing Brigadoon. I had seen the movie before, but we saw the play Brigadoon out there.

The housing area for the people who were in the district office was just beyond Diamond Head—a very nice facility.* They had their own swimming pool and a tennis court and about four or five houses. It was originally housing for a Coast Guard radio station there, and Wailupe was the name of it. We occasionally would go to parties there. The Coast Guard would also have parties at times at places like the big Army base that's just inland from the Royal Hawaiian Hotel.

Paul Stillwell: Fort DeRussy?

Admiral Siler: No, not DeRussy because it was sort of everybody's place, but there was an Army facility, Fort Ruger. It was inland a little farther than Fort DeRussy. A very nice place.

Paul Stillwell: And Waikiki was much less cluttered than it is now. The Moana and the Royal Hawaiian were there and not much else.

Admiral Siler: That's right, not too much more.

Paul Stillwell: But you said Hawaii was better then. Was there more of the native culture evident then?

Admiral Siler: Yes, much more of the native culture and far less of the Americans making money on the people who went through.

Paul Stillwell: What examples of that did you see?

---

* Diamond Head, the crater of an extinct volcano, forms a headland at the end of Waikiki Beach on Oahu. It is one of Hawaii's most distinctive landmarks.

Admiral Siler: Well, today if you go into Waikiki, there's a big sale place right across the street from the Moana Hotel, and that wasn't there at all. I can't remember what was there. But the park areas have been decreased in size, I think. We just enjoyed more of the Hawaiian atmosphere and less of the American "I'll make the money" routine.

Paul Stillwell: Well, now they have the Polynesian cultural village.

Admiral Siler: Yes, but that's clear around on the other side of the island. I've been there too. [Laughter] But we didn't go there until we went back and the admiral who was there—I guess it was just after I retired—but anyway he made the guest quarters available to us there at Diamond Head. Nice spot.

Paul Stillwell: How much interaction was there between the Navy and the Coast Guard at Barbers Point?

Admiral Siler: We just thought we were part of the base. They knew that we were on the other side of the field, but as far as priority of flights was concerned we were just considered as more airplanes. It didn't make any difference whose airplane it was. We were considered part of the operations there on the base.

Paul Stillwell: So just an integrated operations structure?

Admiral Siler: Completely, yes. And as far as at the club was concerned, my wife was involved with the activities of all the wives. We had some Coast Guard parties that were separate, but we also were included in the parties that were held at the club with no differentiation at all.

Paul Stillwell: What kind of a command structure did you have? Was there a squadron of the Coast Guard planes?

Admiral Siler: We had a Coast Guard air detachment there that was a command of its own. Each command on the air station was a different individual command, and our command instructions and so on would come from the district office, which was downtown.

Paul Stillwell: Who was the senior aviator, Coast Guard aviator, on Barbers Point?

Admiral Siler: The commanding officer of the Coast Guard air detachment then at Barbers Point. When I first went out there, it was Bruce Ing, who is retired and in Florida now.[*] The exec was Ira McMullan, a man that I had known before somewhere.[†] Then Ing was replaced by George Howarth, a man who unfortunately was having cataracts of his eyes, so he really couldn't see very well.[‡] He made a flight with me one night when I was assigned as the third pilot. The first pilot was the man I'd flown with a lot named Jerry McGovern.[§] The first time I'd met him at all he was flying the plane that the Coast Guard operated for the Coast and Geodetic Survey taking photographs of areas around the United States so that they could prepare maps for the Coast and Geodetic.

At this time he was the aircraft commander for a DC-4, and the number-two pilot was the captain who couldn't see. If he concentrated long enough, he could see the instruments on the instrument panel, but once he got to concentrating on that he couldn't see a thing outside. So he took the night flights, and that way all he had to look at was the instruments.

Unfortunately, we arrived in San Francisco after it became light the next morning, and McGovern, thinking that was doing the boss a favor, said, "Go ahead and land it." He couldn't tell when he was close to the runway, and so he landed about 50 feet high and we made a crunch as we went down. McGovern added some power and went around a second time, and that time McGovern landed from the right-hand side, and it was much, much better. But we had had problems we weren't aware of because of the fact that we had taken off about four hours after we had planned and during that time the winds had

---

[*] Commander Edwin B. Ing, USCG.
[†] Commander Ira H. McMullan, USCG.
[‡] Commander George E. Howarth, USCG.
[§] Lieutenant Commander Gerald E. McGovern, USCG.

built up, and we had a very strong headwind crossing the Pacific. So when we landed everything had gone all right except for the fact that we made a standard holding pattern when we were told to make a non-standard pattern, and the captain didn't know the difference. Anyway, we got down all right. Everything was fine, but when the crew members went out the next morning to turn up the engines, there wasn't enough fuel left to start one of the engines, so we were close.

Paul Stillwell: That's scary.

Admiral Siler: That sure is.

Paul Stillwell: Well, I'm surprised he could pass a flight physical in that condition.

Admiral Siler: He didn't take a flight physical. For all of the time he was in Hawaii he never took a flight physical. When he was ordered to something else, I think back at Coast Guard headquarters, he went in right away because he couldn't see anything. Couldn't drive a car, so his wife drove the car all the time. When he finally went in and had a physical and pointed out, "Well, I can't see anything." At that point they put him in the hospital and operated on both eyes for the cataracts. But he was in deep trouble as far as eyesight was concerned.

Paul Stillwell: It's surprising something worse didn't happen.

Admiral Siler: He didn't fly that much. He would usually go up and get a bare minimum to get flight pay and never took a physical.

Paul Stillwell: How could he manage to avoid them?

Admiral Siler: He was the captain and nobody—

Paul Stillwell: Who's going to challenge him?

Admiral Siler: Yes.

Paul Stillwell: Did you see any change in the workload when the Korean War ended? Was there a different pattern of flying after that?

Admiral Siler: Yes, there was somewhat of a different pattern, although it didn't change an awful lot. We left Wake Island, and at the same time a good many of the reserve officers were let go. So much of it didn't change, simply because the airplanes didn't go to Wake Island for the station. They would go through and get fuel, and that's all. Once they'd gotten fuel, they'd go on to Guam and spend the night in Guam. We still had a station in Guam, because it was supplying those stations that were south of Guam and also the one that was up on Saipan, so they still had quite a bit to do. So it really didn't change too much except, as I say, the reserve officers were being released, and some of the supplying of the stations I'm sure went down.

But about that time I was transferred from there anyway to go back to the States. I had orders to Elizabeth City, North Carolina. Then one day a change came, and I was ordered to go to Coast Guard headquarters. While I had been out there, I had my nose operated on, because I had had it bent all over the place in football, and so I went in to have my deviated septum straightened. During the time I was in the hospital, the Assistant Commandant and the chief of personnel came through on a flight from Washington, D.C. The Assistant Commandant was named to be the next Commandant just after they had left Hawaii to go into San Francisco, and the chief of personnel was going to be the Assistant Commandant. Well, I didn't get to that party because I was in the hospital, but my wife went up to this little man who didn't impress her particularly and said, "Where are you stationed?" He was the Assistant Commandant who was going to be the Commandant, and my orders were changed to be his personal aide and pilot.[*]

---

[*] This was Vice Admiral Alfred C. Richmond, USCG, who became Commandant of the Coast Guard on 1 June 1954. He was reappointed to a second four-year term in 1958. On 1 June 1960 he was promoted to four-star admiral. He ended his term as Commandant on 31 May 1962.

Paul Stillwell: Well, was it something that your wife said or did at this party that led you to get that job.

Admiral Siler: [Laughter] I was always curious as to what was said. I still had the orders to Elizabeth City, and I got the change of orders to go to Washington. I called her and realized that she was at the beach. So I called the beach club and had her paged, and when I got her on the phone I said, "Boy, when you impress somebody you really must impress them." [Laughter]

I told her what had happened, and she said, "I don't think I want to come to Washington!" For years she didn't mention this experience to Admiral Richmond. Years later, she asked him if he remembered that he had met her before we came to Washington and he said, "Oh, yes, I remember that." And I should say he was the kind of a person who would have remembered it precisely all those years. So he undoubtedly knew who she was, but he never met me until I walked in and said, "I'm Owen Siler."

Paul Stillwell: He must have warmed up to you fairly quickly, because you were in that job for a long time.

Admiral Siler: Well, the first trip that I ever made with him I made with—you've probably seen the picture—included Walt Disney. We went out to California with the other man who had been my predecessor in that job, Bill Jenkins.[*] After the trip was over, I took over as the pilot. We made a trip to Cleveland, Ohio, and we were on solid instruments right down to the ground. I had forgotten that you'd better go this way with the trim tab just before you touch the ground. So we landed nose wheel first and bounced down the runway. Admiral Richmond always remembered that particular landing. Years later, he came to the Commandant's quarters in Washington, D.C., and reminded me of that landing. It was 1954 when I made that lousy landing, and I guess he was reminding me of it in 1975 or '76, something like that. So he'd remembered it for 30 years.

Paul Stillwell: What was the purpose of the trip involving Walt Disney?

---

[*] Lieutenant Commander William A. Jenkins, USCG.

Admiral Siler: Well, that was just a small part of a visit to the West Coast stations, and we had visited West Coast stations from Seattle all the way down to San Diego. It just happened that when we were in Long Beach, which is where we had the liaison officer assigned to the movie industry, he set up a visit to Walt Disney because at that time they were making a movie of the Eastwind and Westwind when they were making the farthest north trip on an icebreaker at that time. The Eastwind and Northwind both went up that year, and it made an interesting story. At the same time, Walt Disney told us about how he was planning Disneyland in California. We saw some of the models and some of the actual things that would be moved from his studio to Disneyland when it was finished.

Paul Stillwell: Was this film about the icebreakers a documentary?

Admiral Siler: Yes, and I think it got an Academy Award for that type of a film.[*]

Paul Stillwell: So this was mainly a public relations-type visit to his place?

Admiral Siler: Well, yes, but we were doing so many things of public relations type that it didn't happen to be specializing in any particular part of that.

Paul Stillwell: Was the trip mainly to familiarize the new Commandant with the commands on the West Coast?

Admiral Siler: No, I think he'd been there enough that it didn't have anything to do with that except that he felt he needed to see those places again. He was a visitor, and he knew more about many of those stations than the man who officially was in charge.

Paul Stillwell: Well, the other benefit was that the people in those stations got to see the big boss and know that he was interested.

---

[*] Disney Studios' Men Against the Arctic received the 1955 Academy Award for a documentary in the short-film category.

Admiral Siler: Yes.

Paul Stillwell: Any of the other places on that trip that stand out in your mind as highlights?

Admiral Siler: No, I don't think there were any particular ones on that trip. Of course, I was just the number-two pilot on that one.

Paul Stillwell: What plane did you mainly use for trips like that?

Admiral Siler: Martin 404.* It was a wonderful plane for that kind of trip. The only thing was it didn't have high-altitude performance that we would have liked to have when we were crossing the Rockies. But I remember when we left Seattle to come back to the East Coast we got to some altitude like about 12,000 to 14,000 feet, and there was enough tailwind there that we only made one stop across the country to get fuel. Got a pretty nice tailwind.

Paul Stillwell: How high up do you need to be before you need pressurized cabins?

Admiral Siler: Usually we would use the pressurization if we were going above 10,000 feet, and actually we used it for any altitude because we had it. It didn't make that much difference except for comfort of people who had sensitive ears. As far as getting the better wind was concerned, you usually had to be at 12,000 or something like that. But as long as you got to that kind of an altitude you'd usually take a pretty good wind from the west—not always but usually. Of course, sometimes we could never find either smooth air or air with wind going the right direction.

I remember one flight we were going in the Martin to the West Coast, and then we were going to pick up an R5D to fly to Hawaii. We had the Commissioner of

---

* The Martin 404 Skyliner was a two-engine propeller-driven commercial aircraft that went into service in 1950. Its cruise speeds of 280 miles per hour were nearly 100 mph faster than the Douglas DC-3. The Coast Guard acquired two Skyliners in the 1950s as VIP transports.

Customs aboard, and he got airsick and I do mean airsick. He was so sick that when we stopped to refuel in—might have been Reno, Nevada, or something like that—and he was sick enough we made up a bunk for him. That airplane had space for two bunks, one on each side of the airplane. He lay down and didn't move from the time that we landed in—I'm pretty sure it was Reno—until we got to San Francisco. Then he got off and went to a hotel and probably slept the rest of the night there.

Paul Stillwell: Well, I've heard it said that in really severe seasickness and airsickness there are two stages. First you're afraid you're going to die, and then you're afraid you're not. [Laughter]

Admiral Siler: Yes. Well, I think he was in that afraid you're not condition at that point.

Paul Stillwell: Well, please tell me more about Admiral Richmond and what kind of an officer and what kind of a leader and person he was.

Admiral Siler: Well, he was amazing in that I don't think he ever forgot a thing. I don't think that most people have brains that are big enough to keep things with them all the time, but I don't think he ever forgot anything. He gave a speech to a Masonic group one time, and he had been active in the Masonic Lodge at one time years before. And he remembered everything that that lodge did, probably 20 years before. He had made notes or written out the speech ahead of time. I sat there and watched the secretary typing this thing, hour after hour, the same speech. And when he got there to make the speech he probably added 50% more to it. I was sure that most of the audience was thinking, "Ye gods, will it never end?" [Laughter] But he knew that all these things were important as far as he was concerned, and they probably were.

Paul Stillwell: Sounds like he was a person with a lot of enthusiasm.

Admiral Siler: Well, you could hardly tell that, though. He didn't show enthusiasm. In fact, as I said about my wife meeting him at that reception, he was the little man standing all alone and apparently with nothing to do, and so she went over and befriended him. It wasn't until quite some time later that—well, since I wasn't there she had gone with the commanding officer and his wife who lived across the street from us. My wife was going on about, "And where is headquarters?" because he just said, "At headquarters," not "Coast Guard headquarters in Washington" but just "at headquarters."

Paul Stillwell: Was he in civilian clothes?

Admiral Siler: Oh, yes, this was a civilian clothes party. And when he started talking about the Coast Guard headquarters, the captain's wife came up and poked my wife and said, "That's the Commandant-to-be." [Laughter] Well, I don't know that it had been announced yet. But he was the Assistant Commandant anyway. At that point my wife shut up and probably looked for transportation home. [Laughter]

Paul Stillwell: Well, she must have made a good impression.

Admiral Siler: Well, I guess.

Paul Stillwell: What do you remember from working with him on a day-to-day basis? What was his style?

Admiral Siler: Well, again, he remembered the details very easily, and if he had signed something three days ago you'd better not try to fool him with it, because he knew exactly what he'd signed. He was a detailer, and yet at the same time knew the important things like the back of his hand. When he appeared before Congress in congressional testimony I don't know whether he used speeches written out for their benefit or for his own. Probably for their benefit more than his own benefit, because he probably knew exactly what he'd dictated three or four days before and had it backed up.

He would have meetings to review what was going to be said at congressional hearings, but it didn't go into details like his successor at all. Well, I shouldn't say that, because his successor I never was involved with. I knew his successor well, and when I first saw him at an inspection in Miami, his big grin was at me, not at the rest of the people. So I don't know how Admiral Roland prepared for such hearings, but Admiral Smith and Admiral Bender used to spend hours and hours going through every question that they felt could be used during the hearing.*

Admiral Richmond never did that, and I never did it because I felt that I had gotten up to speed already. Unless there was something that I was really suspect on, I would not spend a lot of time with it. So instead of spending all day Saturday for hearings on Tuesday, which was the Smith and Bender style, I'd look at the book that we were supposed to have the information on, and that was usually sufficient for me. And if there was something else, I'd send for the person to look at this particular question but nothing more. And that's the way Admiral Richmond was. I don't think he ever sent for anyone either, because he knew so well what was going on.

There was one policy matter that was taken up when he was the Commandant that had to do with general duty officers. There was an order put out saying that all academy graduates would be considered as general duty officers, and those officers who had formerly been warrant officers would be specialists. There would be so many specialists in the commander rank, so many in lieutenant commander, and I think they went as far as lieutenant. Anyone jaygee or ensign was going to be a general duty officer, whether he liked it or not.

We saw that order that was going to set it up, and it raised a lot of questions in my mind. For one thing, all general duty officers were going to have to take promotion exams. The commanders had to take one or two exams in specialized subjects like military discipline or something like that but not any more. But lieutenant commanders had to take a whole series of exams. I was a lieutenant commander, so I was going to have to take everything that there was. Lieutenants started at lower ranks, and they could only take certain exams until they reached the higher rank.

I think that order had been sent to Admiral Hirshfield, who had been the chief of personnel before he was the Assistant Commandant.† He put a note on for the boss to

---
* Admiral Edwin J. Roland, USCG, was Commandant of the Coast Guard from 1 June 1962 to 1 June 1966. Admiral Willard J. Smith, USCG, from 1 June 1966 to 31 May 1974. Admiral Chester R. Bender, USCG, from 1 June 1970 to 31 May 1974. The oral histories of all three are in the Naval Institute collection.
† Rear Admiral James A. Hirshfield.

say, "A lot of our academy graduates aren't going to like this order," because of the exams that we were going to have to take up in subjects that we had had to show our proficiency in years before. At the same time people who were brought in who had direct commissions, if they were made a lieutenant commander in merchant marine safety and a specialist from then, they only had to take one or two exams, and that was it. But they were going to be promoted, many of them senior to me. So Admiral Hirshfield put this note on saying that, "The academy graduates won't like this."

As it went from his desk to my desk, I was supposed to take it in to the boss to sign. I read it over in my spare time, and then put a note on saying, "We sure won't." [Laughter] Before it was signed he had some spare time, and I went in to announce that there were six admirals in the outer office who wanted to see him, and he said, "Just a minute. I want to talk to you about this order." I stood there for half an hour while I knew all those guys were standing out there waiting. The crux of it, finally, was to take this to Captain Roland, who was going to be shortly afterward Admiral Roland and later the Commandant. Well, I took it to Captain Roland and told him what was wrong, what was my objection to it, and what Admiral Richmond had said about it, and asked him to take a look.

By the time he got back to me, he was now Admiral Roland, and he said, "Si, will this be all right?" And here I was a lieutenant commander. "Will this be all right?"

"You bet." So I don't think I had much input to it except to say, "I don't like it, not to begin with, but it has to be all right now, Admiral."

Paul Stillwell: So did you have to take the exams?

Admiral Siler: You bet. Every one.

Paul Stillwell: Well, did you find that people would come to you sort of to find out what the boss was thinking on certain things?

Admiral Siler: I don't think there was much of that, because I didn't usually get into the questions of policy at all. Once in a while, by sneaking into the back room, I could hear some of the things that were going on, but I tried to make it a point not to hear those things. Once in a while it was interesting to go into the file cabinets, which were just over a very low wall, a wall that you could hear through, and hear the discussions about the next admirals or something like that when no one else knew.

Paul Stillwell: And I'll bet those were quite candid.

Admiral Siler: Oh, yes. There were one or two criticizing the selections once in a while. In fact, they had a system for selecting out aviator captains because they didn't need that many aviator captains, and it stymied the lower-ranking officers if it was all filled with high-ranking aviators who really didn't fly that much if at all. The same week that they held a board to decide what they should do with the aviator captains they held a board on what captains should make admiral. Well, one of the aviator captains was selected out of aviation, and the other board selected him, the same man, to be an admiral. [Laughter] Now, he'd been an aviator all his life, so he had to be considered on his aviation. He was not good enough to be an aviator, but he was good enough to be an aviator admiral.

Paul Stillwell: What was the outcome?

Admiral Siler: He made admiral. He was the district commander in New Orleans when I was commanding officer in Corpus Christi.

Paul Stillwell: What was his name?

Admiral Siler: Olsen, Carl B.

Paul Stillwell: Where was the Coast Guard Headquarters located in that era, the 1950s?

Admiral Siler: Thirteenth and Pennsylvania, right where the Reagan Building is now. It had been the Southern Railway headquarters at the beginning of World War II, and I don't know where the Southern Railway went, but we had that building for a good many years. There were about two suites in the whole building that were air-conditioned. The rest had, perhaps, window air-conditioners. One of those suites was the Commandant's area, and the Assistant Commandant, too, was air-conditioned but not much of the rest of the building. The eighth floor may have had some air-conditioning. I'm not sure, but we were on the seventh floor. And the eighth floor was the Alcohol, Tobacco and Firearms, ATF. I think some of that must have been air-conditioned. I'm not sure. But we went from there. When DoT set things up with everything in one building, we moved to DoT; that was a good many years later.*

Paul Stillwell: Right. How much connection was there between the Coast Guard headquarters and the Treasury Department, to which you belonged at that time?

Admiral Siler: I think there was a lot more than some people thought there was. Admiral Richmond used to go over and see the Assistant Secretary most of the time rather than the Secretary himself.

Paul Stillwell: George Humphrey was the Secretary for part of that time.

Admiral Siler: Yes. When I first went to Washington, Humphrey was the Secretary, and the Assistant Secretary was H. Chapman Rose. Then Rose moved up to being an Under Secretary, and the Assistant Secretary was Gilmore Flues, who still is in the Washington area I think.† At least he was the last time I checked on it, and I think he's still alive there. But Admiral Richmond used to see either Rose or Flues all the time, and that's why the captain that we were speaking of earlier, Walsh, used to see those people a lot too. Messages were going back and forth with Walsh all the time.

Paul Stillwell: What types of issues got discussed with Treasury?

---

* The Department of Transportation was established in 1967, and at that point the Coast Guard shifted to it from its previous home in the Treasury Department.
† Abram Gilmore Flues, who served as Assistant Secretary of the Treasury Department from 1957 to 1961, died 1 March 2003 at Bethesda Naval Medical Command. He was 99 years old at the time of his death. In World War II he served in the Office of Strategic Services.

Admiral Siler: Well, development of what the Coast Guard was going to do from then on, and I think both Rose and Flues were anxious that the Coast Guard do as much as they could to be equal to the other military services. As far as aircraft were concerned, that was a question that was frequently called to the attention of the Secretary. It was not too long after I got to headquarters that there had been a statement put in the congressional budget hearings saying that the requirements for Coast Guard aviation needed to be considered as a whole rather than one of these airplanes and one of those airplanes.

A man named Bob Michaels had been the chief clerk of the appropriations committee, and he was the one who drafted that particular requirement. He asked me at one time, "What did you think of that then?" because he had pride of authorship in it, and I think that it was something that has made the Coast Guard aviation requirements over the years. Unfortunately, there hasn't been a consistent approach to that, and also the Coast Guard budget requirements are handled in a very poor manner today. And I don't know that the Coast Guard can do much about it, because OMB in particular and the congressional committees consider things piecemeal all the time.* And we can't seem to straighten them out.

Paul Stillwell: So this was an exceptional case, really, to have an overall plan.

Admiral Siler: Well, what they did was to look at the overall aviation requirements and say, "Let us know what you need totally rather than what you need for one airplane this year and two airplanes next year," or something like that. That's when the Coast Guard said, "Well, C-130s would be a good solution." Interestingly, my predecessor was one of the members of the board that voted against the C-130.

Paul Stillwell: There's an airplane with a long life.

---

* OMB—Office of Management and Budget. Prior to 1970 it was known as the Bureau of Budget, part of the Executive Office of the President.

Admiral Siler: It sure is. Almost like the DC-3.

Paul Stillwell: Well, I would guess that a lot of the dialog with the Treasury Department had to do with budgetary issues.

Admiral Siler: Well, very frequently, yes.

Paul Stillwell: Did Admiral Richmond use you as sort of a doorkeeper or gatekeeper in who had access?

Admiral Siler: No.

Paul Stillwell: How did that process work?

Admiral Siler: Whoever came first, unless he had given instructions that they were going to have a special meeting and he wouldn't be available for a while.

Paul Stillwell: But normally he was very accessible?

Admiral Siler: Absolutely. First in, first to see him.

Paul Stillwell: Well, and people would learn that very quickly.

Admiral Siler: You bet.

Paul Stillwell: What can you say about his personality and his way of dealing with other people?

Admiral Siler: Well, he wasn't a very outgoing person. Quite a few people, I think, considered him just an old grump, because he didn't smile a lot, and he didn't start conversations very much. He probably started conversations with people from the Bureau of Budget, but I don't think around Coast Guard headquarters he started many conversations ever. People would come to him and say, "Admiral, I've got a problem," and that would be it. But he'd seldom if ever start things in that way.

He had two wonderful boys. The older one became a captain in the Coast Guard, and I don't know where he is now. The younger one was captain of the football team of Lehigh University, and I think he spent two years as the captain of the team. And he was captain of his high school team when he played high school football, so he was a good athlete. I'm not sure how he did in the military. He joined the Marine Corps when he got out of college, and he was on continuing active duty with the Marine Corps for quite some time.

Paul Stillwell: I have a recollection that he retired as a lieutenant colonel in the Marine Corps.

Admiral Siler: That could well be. I think the last time I saw him he was a major, but I sort of expected he would have made lieutenant colonel. I don't think he was destined to go higher.

Paul Stillwell: From what you say about not starting conversations, would it be fair to say that Admiral Richmond didn't bring in a big agenda of his own to accomplish?

Admiral Siler: I'm not sure that's true, because I think he had some ideas about what he wanted to accomplish. I don't think he could have accomplished much more than he did during the time he was Commandant, because he was aware of so much that was going on that if he planned something, the chances were it was going to get done.

Paul Stillwell: What were some of the things that he did bring about?

Admiral Siler: Well, of course, the loran chain was probably started when he was Assistant Commandant, and chains I should say because they were all over the place. And reserve programs were largely his idea.

Paul Stillwell: How robust was the Coast Guard Reserve at that point?

Admiral Siler: It nearly went away at one point, and I think that it was to his credit that it didn't go away.

Paul Stillwell: Well, it was threatened later after that also, wasn't it?

Admiral Siler: Yes. But I think that the first threats were when he was Commandant, and it was largely his action that kept it from being done away with.

Paul Stillwell: What sort of arguments did he use?

Admiral Siler: I wasn't privy to all those, so I can't really say. But the question simply went away as he argued with the individuals who were making the biggest noise about doing away with it.

Paul Stillwell: What other achievements or programs would you ascribe to him?

Admiral Siler: I think there was a much better planning program set up within the Coast Guard during his term of office. Of course, he was in office eight years; he was the last Commandant who ever served more than four. I know that the program for promoting captains and retiring captains and admirals after a limited term was done as one of his ideas, which at the same time he put in wording that said, "And furthermore I can serve as long as I want." [Laughter] It didn't quite say that, but it said, "The Commandant can be reappointed as many times as wanted." It was offered to me, and I said, "No, four years is it."

Paul Stillwell: The Navy in that era was experiencing a problem with the "hump," that is, the large glut of officers that had come in in World War II.[*] How did the Coast Guard manage that issue?

Admiral Siler: Well, a lot of the Coast Guard's was simply that most of them were reserve officers; they released them from the reserve and the hump was gone. Now, some of the people were temporary officers who went back to their original grade, chief warrant officer or something like that, and the hump was partially taken care of with that but only partially. The rest of it had to be taken care of partially with this idea of everyone is a general duty officer and had to take a promotion exam. If you failed a promotion exam twice, you were through being promoted. Then if you didn't get promoted, you did retire involuntarily.

Paul Stillwell: Well, was this business about retiring captains part of that issue also?

Admiral Siler: Probably. I'm not sure how that worked out, because we had so few captains in those days. The total Coast Guard back in the days when he was Commandant was probably only two-thirds of what we have now if that.

Paul Stillwell: And now it's maybe 35,000?

Admiral Siler: About that. I guess we were very close to 20,000 when he was Commandant.

Paul Stillwell: That's really an elite service.

Admiral Siler: Yes.

---

[*] The "hump" was created by the large number of officers who entered the service during World War II. As this cohort of officers moved through the years, there were fewer billets available at each higher rank. To match the available individuals to the billets required attrition, either from those in the hump or those coming along in later year groups.

Paul Stillwell: What role did the Coast Guard Auxiliary play back then?

Admiral Siler: Well, that's something that he set up largely by himself with the proper staff, too, but a lot of it was his idea. The auxiliary initially was established at the beginning of World War II as a reserve, and then they realized that there were actually two aspects of it, and so the reserve was set up, and the auxiliary was a different thing completely. But those two organizations were largely, I think, the result of his work.

Paul Stillwell: What functions did he envision that the auxiliary would perform?

Admiral Siler: I'm not sure he knew exactly what they would do, because if they were started originally as the reserve at that point, they did everything that the reserve could do today. Then they realized that there were problems with law enforcement by auxiliarists, and so that was largely, I think, a reason why the auxiliary was different from the reserve. The reserve was being simply a regular Coast Guard officer but with a different type of mission. The auxiliary can only do certain things and not any law enforcement at all.

Paul Stillwell: What law enforcement functions did the Coast Guard have during the 1950s?

Admiral Siler: Well, it had the marine inspection responsibilities, marine regattas. We had the responsibility for drug enforcement, but there wasn't much to be done.

Paul Stillwell: This was after alcohol Prohibition and before narcotics got big.

Admiral Siler: That's right, yes. So there was quite a lot of law enforcement but of a different nature.

Paul Stillwell: What other programs or interests did he have?

Admiral Siler: Woodworking. He was a very capable cabinetmaker. I think it was '55 when we made a trip with the congressional budget people down where we were considering a loran station in the Caribbean. One of the places that they considered and stopped in at the first part of the trip was Nicaragua. Nicaragua had at one time been a real banana area, I guess it was, and at this point bananas were gone due to a blight. But they had turned now to producing mahogany, because there were huge mahogany forests inland. They could cut them down, put them in the river, float them down the river to the seaport of Puerto Cabezas, Nicaragua, and at that point be put aboard a ship and taken up to New Orleans. And mahogany in New Orleans was going to be that readily available.

When we were there, I flew down in the Martin, and he and the congressional committee had taken the 255-foot cutter out of Mobile, the Sebago. They'd gone down to the Gulf of Mexico and looked at the shrimp boats where they were having problems with the Mexicans seizing shrimpers who were taking Mexican shrimp out of Mexican waters and therefore should be punished. [Laughter] Anyway, I don't know that they accomplished too much on that portion of the trip, but they ended up in Puerto Cabezas. When they got there, they had some time to spare, so the plantation manager who used to manage the banana plantation but now was managing Honduras mahogany took Admiral Richmond to the sawmill. When Admiral Richmond saw these planks that would be about that wide and about that thick—

Paul Stillwell: About a foot wide and four inches thick.

Admiral Siler: Yes. You could see him drool [laughter] because he wanted to have that mahogany for his cabinetmaking. So he said, "I'd like to have some of that. Do you suppose I could?"

The manager said, "How much do you want?"

He said, "I don't know." And so he asked me how much we could take.

I said, "Well, we can fill the belly hatch." The only thing was it was wet mahogany, and wet mahogany smells like somebody took a crap. This wood smelled like someone took a crap on it, and the air-conditioning in the airplane circulated through the cargo compartment as well as through the passenger compartment. [Laughter] We stunk like mad for a few days there till we dried out the mahogany completely, and then it was all right. But the first couple of days were really bad. I don't know whether he ever used it before he died. He moved out of Washington after he retired, and I don't know what he did with his life then.

Paul Stillwell: Did you get to sea any in that job? Did he visit cutters and go out for a day or two?

Admiral Siler: He frequently would go out to ocean station drills and things that we would get the airline people involved with to see exactly what an ocean station ship would do in the event that a plane came down. We had two or three very serious incidents where airplanes came down and ditched alongside one of those ocean stations. There was the one in the Pacific that was well publicized when a Pan American plane came down. There was at least one in the Atlantic that the big seaplane came down alongside, and once it landed it started breaking up almost immediately because it was just too rough. So the Commandant would go out on the cutter sometimes, leaving the port and just going out and doing the exercise. A good many airline people would go out on the ship as well. It was a kind of a fun day for everyone, and yet they'd get some good training out of it.

Paul Stillwell: How much interaction did Admiral Richmond have with the Defense Department?

Admiral Siler: He had some, but I don't think it's nearly as much as it is today. Of course, today we have the NavGuard board, which is the Navy and the Coast Guard meeting regularly on it. Most of the work that was done in those days was done by either a captain who was assigned at lower levels within OpNav or the Commandant himself. Interestingly, in that regard the program that was started back in I guess sometime in the '60s having to do with the merchant vessels reporting their positions, what we call

AMVER, was started during the Korean War so we could keep track of everyone who was not reporting to AMVER.*

Paul Stillwell: That tied in with those patrols you were talking about from Port Angeles.

Admiral Siler: Yes, but it was done to keep track of them particularly, and we at that time tried to keep track of everyone who didn't report to AMVER. Of course, now even the Russians are involved, and we know where they are, but we still can't keep track of everything.

Paul Stillwell: Was the planning or at least advanced thinking coming about in that era for the ships that became the 378s?

Admiral Siler: I couldn't tell you when that started.

Paul Stillwell: But you probably didn't have a lot of new ship programs at that time.

Admiral Siler: Sure didn't. We had some drawings that were put on paper, but I don't think anything ever came of most of them.

Paul Stillwell: What kind of a work schedule did Admiral Richmond maintain?

Admiral Siler: He'd arrive in the morning very close to 9:00 o'clock, I guess, and heaven help when he'd get out of there. If the Treasury called at 4:00 o'clock and said, "I'd like you over here for a meeting in an hour," there was never any question he was going to be there. He was always available to Treasury. Anything that amounted to meetings at the White House always were a must. The Bureau of Budget was always a must. My hours were a whole lot more demanding in those days than they usually were when I was Commandant.

---

* Automated Mutual-assistance VEssel Rescue (AMVER), sponsored by the U.S. Coast Guard, is a voluntary global ship reporting system used worldwide by search and rescue authorities to arrange for assistance to persons in distress at sea.

Paul Stillwell: Why was that?

Admiral Siler: Because I had to lock up everything that was out that was classified when he would leave the office, and if it was something that he wanted to take with him to Treasury or something like that, he'd give it to the duty officer for locking up there when he came back. But I'd stick around at least until he departed the building.

Paul Stillwell: So did you typically put in, say, a 12-hour day?

Admiral Siler: No, I wouldn't say it was that long, but it was a little bit better than most of the people in Coast Guard headquarters. I was very frequently one of the last people out of the building.

Paul Stillwell: The CNO at that time was Admiral Burke, who was a notorious workaholic—probably 12 to 16 hours was his day.[*]

Admiral Siler: I wouldn't say that Admiral Richmond was quite that much, but I don't think he ever turned down an appointment anytime with anybody.

Paul Stillwell: Do you remember any of the visits to the White House?

Admiral Siler: No. I don't think he had as much access to the White House as they do now. I don't think that he went to the White House very much at all.

Paul Stillwell: And from what you've said, he probably didn't have that much contact with Admiral Burke either.

---

[*] Admiral Arleigh A. Burke, USN, served as Chief of Naval Operations from 17 August 1955 to 1 August 1961. His oral history is in the Naval Institute collection.

Admiral Siler: He had a whole lot more with Admiral Burke than he did with, I think, the Secretary of the Treasury.

Paul Stillwell: What sorts of issues would he discuss with Admiral Burke?

Admiral Siler: Well, one thing was there was a proposal during that time for a nuclear icebreaker, and he, I know, met with if it wasn't Admiral Burke it would have been someone high up on his staff. Because there was quite a lot of congressional interest in having a nuclear icebreaker, and I don't think there was that much interest in the Navy at all. So it became a question of how you say "No" without offending a great many people, particularly the congressmen. The chairman of the Coast Guard committee very much wanted to authorize a nuclear icebreaker. In fact, he did introduce the legislation, and I think it was passed, but there was no funding for it.

Paul Stillwell: Any contact with Admiral Rickover?

Admiral Siler: Admiral Rickover was around for such a long time I had contact with him.* [Laughter] The first time I ever met Admiral Rickover we were at a reception in the Senate Caucus Room. I was one of the early arrivers, and Admiral Rickover was there before I was. And I'd never met him before, so I walked up and said, "I'm Owen Siler from the Coast Guard."

He looked me up and down and then he said, "How are the turbines doing on your ships?" Not even a "How do you do?". [Laughter] I didn't know what he had in mind, but, of course, we had the 378s with gas turbines, and that was what he was interested in, this power that they had.†

Paul Stillwell: So that must have been a later meeting.

---

* Hyman G. Rickover was considered the father of the nuclear Navy. He ran the U.S. Navy's nuclear-power program for many years, from 1948 until he eventually left active duty in 1982 with the rank of four-star admiral on the retired list. Rickover Hall at the Naval Academy is named in his honor, as is the nuclear-powered attack submarine Hyman G. Rickover (SSN-709), which was commissioned 21 July 1984.
† USCGC Hamilton (WPG-715, later WHEC-715) was the name ship of a class of 378-foot high-endurance cutters. She was commissioned 20 February 1967.

Admiral Siler: Oh, yes. That would have been probably in the '70s when I first became Commandant. Probably '74 to '75. But he never said "How do you do?"

Paul Stillwell: Typical.

Admiral Siler: Yes, I guess.

Paul Stillwell: Where were you living then, in Northern Virginia?

Admiral Siler: Yes. We lived in Broyhill Park at that time. I can't remember where my son went to high school at all.

Paul Stillwell: How did that tour of duty turn out to be so long? You were five years with Admiral Richmond.

Admiral Siler: Well, the normal tour for people with the Commandant was four years, and when it came time during my fourth year to think of orders I bearded the lion in his den one day and said, "They have been talking about orders over in the aviation section, and I've been here four years now. May I tell them where I'd like to go?"

He said, "I've been meaning to talk to you about that." [Laughter] He said that the chairman of the appropriations committee, J. Vaughan Gary from Richmond, wanted to make a round-the-world trip.* And he said, "He wants to have you as the pilot," and I guess Chris Weitzel was my copilot at that time.† So it was at least the two of us.

I wasn't about to say, "Oh, no, I'm not going to do that." So the condition of making that trip was to have the Navy or the Air Force loan the Coast Guard a DC-6. Because the only way they could justify a round-the-world trip in certain areas where the visit would not meet the requirements for a congressional visit unless they got a congressman whose duties also included foreign aid. That would get them into India and

---

* Julian Vaughan Gary, a Democrat from Virginia, served in the House of Representatives from 6 March 1945 to 3 January 1965.
† Lieutenant Christian A. Weitzel, USCG.

Pakistan and a few places like that. Then it turned out eventually that the Air Force and the Navy each said they didn't have a plane they could lend us, so that flight never was made. However, by that time it was too late for me to go anyplace, so I spent five years there. The last year was a little on the boresome side.

Paul Stillwell: Well, he must have had a lot of confidence in you to keep you that long.

Admiral Siler: Well, it was not Admiral Richmond who was keeping me. It was J. Vaughan Gary who was keeping me at that time.

Paul Stillwell: No, but I mean even to keep you for four years.

Admiral Siler: Well, most of the people who had that assignment stayed for four years. Bill Jenkins before me stayed for four and then stayed on long enough in that fifth year in order to check me out in the Martin 404. I don't know how long Admiral Bender served back before that. I guess he was flying Admiral Farley.[*]

Paul Stillwell: But since he hired you sight unseen he must have liked what he got when you did show up.

Admiral Siler: I think so.

Paul Stillwell: How would you describe the nature of the personal relationship between the two of you?

Admiral Siler: Well, I pretty much knew what he wanted. One interesting aspect of Admiral Richmond was he didn't really care much about a military aide at all. So if I looked out for some of his desires and made certain that we got the transportation to the

---

[*] Admiral Joseph F. Farley, USCG, served as Commandant of the Coast Guard from 1 January 1946 to 31 December 1949. Commander Chester R. Bender, USCG, was pilot and personal aide to the Commandant from 1946 to 1950.

right place and things like that, that was all he was interested in. I frequently did not go with him on trips the way aides in later days I know did.

Paul Stillwell: So it sounds as if he wasn't that demanding.

Admiral Siler: Not at all. One of the things he said when I talked to him the very first day was, "I'm more concerned about your ability as an aviator than I am as an aide." He also said if I said that we shouldn't try that flight, that was it. I only did that once. We were scheduled to go to Elizabeth City, North Carolina, to transfer to automobile transportation and go to the Wright Day observation over on the Outer Banks.* The weather at Elizabeth City was right at GCA minimums, and I said, "I don't think we should try it."† So he got his secretary, Mrs. Strawser, to read his speech over the phone to a secretary in Norfolk and let the admiral there go down from Norfolk to the Outer Banks and make the speech. That was the only time when we didn't arrive at all.

Paul Stillwell: Do you have any other interesting memories of flying with him?

Admiral Siler: I guess I mentioned the R5D that had the hole in the tire.

Paul Stillwell: Well, you told me that when the tape recorder wasn't running.

Admiral Siler: That's right. We took off from Argentia when there was a strong crosswind, and I held the plane on the runway as long as I could and then yanked it off.‡ The airplane had just had a new brake put on the main landing gear. As we broke ground, that wheel locked so that as it just had a tiny bit of weight on it, it was not turning at all, and it wore a huge hole in the tire. I'm happy to say I was smooth enough landing that airplane that when we landed in England the next morning. Nobody knew that there

---

* On 17 December 1903 Orville and Wilbur Wright made the first heavier-than-air powered flight at Kitty Hawk, North Carolina.
† GCA—ground-controlled approach, that is, a landing directed by radio in low visibility.
‡ Argentia, Newfoundland, Canada.

was anything wrong at all until they got out. Even then, I think that if it wasn't pointed out they wouldn't have known of that at all.

There was one other flight to the academy when we scheduled the flight with an alternate to—I think it was someplace in western New York. The superintendent of the academy was not very happy that we were scheduling that as an alternate, but it didn't really make any difference, because we didn't plan to use it and didn't. The flight actually went over Groton, Connecticut, and it really was too bad to make an approach. So then we went to Quonset Point, Rhode Island, and at that time we had a Coast Guard Air Station there. I started a GCA approach and when we got down to minimums and I was still not broken out, I reached for the throttles to put more power on to go around, and the copilot said, "I have the runway in sight." So we went ahead and landed right there. The next day the copilot with a borrowed pilot from Quonset Point flew the airplane back to Groton. So we had some interesting times. [Laughter]

There was one time when we had Mr. Flues, the Assistant Secretary, on the airplane. I think we were coming back from Boston or New London, and we had to make a stop in New York at Floyd Bennett Field.* We were cleared to make an approach downwind. It was on GCA, and we got in without any difficulty except we landed a little longer than usual because of that downwind condition. I'm not sure that Mr. Flues was very impressed with the fact that we'd gotten in that time. [Laughter] Did I mention to you at all the time we held up all the traffic in New York?

Paul Stillwell: No.

Admiral Siler: Admiral Richmond was going to make a speech in New York, and we went up to New York and got in the stack because there was quite a large stack. It was lousy weather. We made our letdown in our turn. Of course, we were the only ones going to Floyd Bennett. Everybody else went to Idlewild that day. When we got into a stack at Floyd Bennett we made the beginning of the approach, and the last point where we knew exactly where we were was the lightship that's outside, Ambrose lightship. At

---

* Floyd Bennett Field was the name for the U.S. naval air station in Brooklyn. It was located near the city's major commercial airport, then known as Idlewild and now as John F. Kennedy.

that point we were cleared for a GCA approach to go into Floyd Bennett. We went in, and eventually we could see the runway that way but not that way.

Paul Stillwell: That is directly down but not ahead.

Admiral Siler: Yes, that's right. The minimum in those days at Floyd Bennett was 100 feet. And the bridge towers were 120 feet over here, so you had to be very careful of where you went. We didn't make our landing the first time. We were cleared up to a higher altitude for another approach like that. We tried that and again had exactly the same experience, and we didn't get in. So then air traffic control said, "Would you like to try an approach to Idlewild?" which is Kennedy today. But we were in a position that we had the Ambrose station to begin an ILS just the same.* So we asked for the weather there, and it was exactly at minimums. I think the minimum there on ILS was 200 feet and a half a mile or something like that. When we started an approach there, they said, "Weather has just gone to 150 feet and the same visibility." Of course, that was under the fog.

So we said, "Roger, we'll continue till we get in there at the inner marker," and figured that would be plenty of time to abort and take something else. So we went in, and by that time it had cleared back up to the minimum, and so we touched down. We spent the rest of the day at Idlewild waiting for it get back up so that we could sneak under all of this weather from Idlewild over to Floyd Bennett. We could see Floyd Bennett from underneath all this stuff if they'd let us take off, pull the wheels up, and stay at this high off the ground. [Laughter]

Paul Stillwell: Sort of hop over.

Admiral Siler: Yes. But they wouldn't let us do that. So we waited until we finally had a clearance. We taxied out to the end of the runway ready for takeoff, and a plane taxied onto the runway, and the fog covered the tail rotating red beacon. We figured it had gone

---

* ILS—instrument landing system.

too low, so we went back to the parking place and stayed overnight at Idlewild. The next day it was no trouble.

Paul Stillwell: Now, what did you mean by holding up traffic?

Admiral Siler: Well, while we were making all those approaches, everybody else was up here circling around waiting for that damned Coast Guard plane to get out of the way. [Laughter]

Paul Stillwell: Anything else to say about that tour of duty at headquarters with Admiral Richmond?

Admiral Siler: We made two trips to Europe during that time. The first one was a very interesting trip. Returning became more of a problem than we thought it was going to be, because on that trip we originally had planned—well, this was the second trip—that we would leave at a time so that we'd get back to Washington, D.C., just about time to have Thanksgiving dinner with our families. We taxied out in London at a time it was getting a little questionable, to say the least. Then later, they gave us a clearance to the wrong place. We had hoped that the winds would be light enough that we could fly directly to Argentia, Newfoundland, and it wasn't that good, so we made our clearance to the Azores. We headed that way and got to the Azores with no problem. We had gotten two box lunches each for Thanksgiving, breakfast, lunch and dinner. [Laughter]

Paul Stillwell: What a disappointment.

Admiral Siler: Yes. But we got to the Azores and refueled, but by this time it was fairly late at night. We had checked wind and weather and decided that we had to at least schedule the flight to Boston rather than to Washington. So we filed a flight plan to Boston, and when we got ready to get our flight clearance they said, "You're cleared to the Bermuda Airport."

We said, "But we're not going to Bermuda."

They said, "Wait a minute." They went back to the control center on a different island in the Azores and came back with a flight clearance to Boston, which we went to. On this flight we also had the Assistant Secretary of the Treasury, Flues, with us. We went ahead and flew to Boston. When I got to Boston, I had all the flight clearance papers and the customs papers and the agriculture clearance. Took them into the customs man, and he looked them over quickly and he said, "You have passengers."

I said, "Yes, we do."

He said, "They've got to come in here." By this time it was something like 6:00 o'clock in the evening, and they'd been on the airplane for 24 hours or something like that.

I responded, "Shall I go out and tell them that they have to come in, or would you like to go out and tell your boss that he's got to come in?" [Laughter] And he looked at me, and I said, "I've got the Assistant Secretary of the Treasury on there, you know."

He said, "I think I'll go out." [Laughter]

But another interesting aspect of that was Boston had a system where if you landed there, government airplanes do not have to pay when they landed at an FAA airport.* This was Logan, but I was trying to think of the airport that's down where young Kennedy took off from.†

Paul Stillwell: Teterboro, New Jersey.

Admiral Siler: Teterboro. Teterboro's a private airport, and they charge you to land there. But, anyway, this place was Logan, and they did not charge you for landing. But they do charge you for using the foreign clearance area, so they got the money out of us one way or the other. They went out and told Mr. Flues, "Welcome to Boston." And that's about all they said, of course, because he had his customs clearance all set. All the papers were set, and we just filed the flight plan, got in the airplane and jumped off again. But instead of having Thanksgiving dinner it was in time to have the day-after-

---

* FAA—Federal Aviation Administration.
† On 16 July 1999 John F. Kennedy, Jr., was piloting a private plane, a Piper Saratoga, en route from Essex County Airport in New Jersey to Martha's Vineyard, Massachusetts. Also on board were his wife, Carolyn Bessette Kennedy, and her sister Lauren. The plane went down at sea, and all on board were killed.

Thanksgiving breakfast. [Laughter] That was the time we went to London, because they were dedicating the American chapel in St. Paul's Cathedral.

Paul Stillwell: Would you say that your time with the Commandant in the '50s helped prepare for your own time as Commandant 20 years later?

Admiral Siler: In one way very much so, because many of the stations in the Coast Guard that Admiral Richmond visited I could have visited a second time, but if I knew that there had not been big changes, many times I just didn't bother to go there, because I'd been there and knew the station well enough that I knew that it had so many airplanes or so many ships. Of course, many of the stations too had been changed quite a lot, and if that was true, I wanted to get there and see. But I think I did not have to do as much traveling as Jack Hayes, simply because I had seen that, been there, done that.[*]

Paul Stillwell: What about the aspect of watching him and his relationship with Congress? Did you pattern yourself any on that?

Admiral Siler: To some extent I'm sure that I did. Most of the people had changed a lot, but a lot of the treatment was still the same, if I have to say that it wasn't always as good as it was with Admiral Richmond. Because of some of the things that went on, the congressmen had built up attitudes toward the Coast Guard over the years. We had some changes in merchant marine safety that made one a little bit aggravated before we were through. We were doing some important things about that time with double hulls and pollution control and marine inspection limitations.

Paul Stillwell: Well, we can get to those in your time as Commandant.

Admiral Siler: Yes.

---

[*] Admiral John B. Hayes, USCG, served as Commandant of the Coast Guard from 1 June 1978 to 28 May 1982.

Paul Stillwell: Anything else about your time with Admiral Richmond?

Admiral Siler: I don't think so offhand.

Paul Stillwell: Well, then you finally got back into Coast Guard aviation per se with the job at Corpus Christi. Was that something you asked for specifically?

Admiral Siler: Well, I had thought that I was leaving after four years, and at that time I had my drooling on going to Puerto Rico. The only trouble was the man who assigned people in aviation wanted to go there, too, and I said, "I'm going to be here another year. That job is filled." So I had my choice of any assignment that was available, and Corpus Christi was a good one at that time.

Paul Stillwell: Please tell me what you did once you got there.

Admiral Siler: Well, it was one of the easiest transfers that we ever had. By that time both of the children were old enough that they were a little easier to travel with, and we stopped in New Orleans. We spent one night at the naval station there, which was a pretty old and pretty musty place to stay and not air-conditioned. It was a lousy night, but at least we had a place to stay. The next night we moved to the Monteleone Hotel and took two rooms, both of them air-conditioned. The children could have a TV each, which made things easier. We started going out with our friends. I had a classmate there, and we spent one night with him. One night we went to the admiral's house, and we were entertained there, so it was a pleasant stop in New Orleans.

Then we went on to Corpus Christi, and in Corpus Christi they had a set of quarters ready for us to move in as soon as we were ready to move there. The only question was where were our household goods at that point. They moved in at the same time as we were ready, so that was about as easy a move as you could possibly have. They treated the Coast Guard there as if we were one more squadron. We had a good relationship on the station, with the exception that my exec had managed to make some friends who were no longer friends with respect to moving to a new location.

We were assigned a place right next to operations and rather liked that location, but we were moved from there over to the seawall area, which was a hangar that was twice as big. So from that point of view we were very happy. That was the development of what we had been working on as compared to a brand-new place that had not ever been used by the Coast Guard. We weren't too happy about that, and we were farther away from the runway. So we had some growing pains, but the new location was really a whole lot better. And the town relationships couldn't have been much better.

Paul Stillwell: In what respect? What sort of relations did you have?

Admiral Siler: Well, we were included in all of the things having to do with Navy League. We got along very well with the shipping people. Our Coast Guard district considered us as the most important people in town, although the marine safety officer there was about five years senior to me. They didn't want to talk to him, because he might be drunk if it was after 7:00 o'clock. [Laughter] So in many regards we were in very favorable positions in Corpus Christi. We lived in Navy quarters there once we got established, and we were considered as one more Navy resident of commander rank, and it all worked very well.

Paul Stillwell: Now, in the work with the community what did that involve? Did you make speeches, get involved in charities?

Admiral Siler: I didn't make many speeches. I did talk to the Coast Guard Auxiliary and things of that sort, but there wasn't too much involved with the community except with the Coast Guard Auxiliary and things of that sort. We put on some festivals that were water festivals, and we would demonstrate low passes with the Coast Guard Grumman Albatrosses, but we had no helicopters then. We always could count on some good attendance if we would make JATO takeoffs with the Grumman Albatross.[*]

---

[*] JATO—jet-assisted takeoff.

Paul Stillwell: I've never seen that in person, but I've seen pictures, and it looks spectacular.

Admiral Siler: It is. We've had at least one case in the Coast Guard where the pilot was killed when he took off. His home station was Salem, Massachusetts. He apparently pulled it up too steeply and stalled and went back in. Killed at least the pilot. I'm not sure whether the others got out or not.

Paul Stillwell: Well, we're right at the end of this tape.

Interview Number 3 with Admiral Owen W. Siler, U.S. Coast Guard (Retired)

Place: Admiral Siler's home in Savannah, Georgia

Date: Tuesday, 12 December 2000

Interviewer: Paul Stillwell

Paul Stillwell: Well, good morning, Admiral, great to see you again. Delighted to be in this warm weather when I see on television about all the blizzards up north. You told me just before we started that you had some more things to recall about Admiral Richmond, please.

Admiral Siler: Yes, and one of the things that I think made his appearances before Congress and also before the Bureau of Budget and the Department of the Treasury then was that he had a law degree, and some of those people had gone through law school with him. There was a Colonel Johnson; he was the Treasury budget officer, and the admiral always addressed him as "Colonel," but they were good buddies. So the relationship between the two of them and trying to justify Coast Guard budgets to the colonel was always a little simpler.

Then the same thing was true with the Bureau of Budget. There was a Sam Something-or-other, and I can't remember his last name, but he was apparently a lawyer or had a law background. He had that kind of relationship with some of the congressmen too. So we always made it a point when elections were over to make a congressional trip, inviting the BoB people and the Treasury people who were the appropriate cohorts to make the trip with us, and they were fun trips but really informative to them. We made trips almost every year after the elections.

The first year that I was in Washington they had planned to make a South American trip, and they were going to take the DC-4 from Elizabeth City. In order to plan for it, they had already made plans to have Bob Adamson, who is an old friend and who was stationed in Elizabeth City, to take the airplane.* They cancelled that, because an important part of it was to go through Bolivia, and it was so high that they had to

---

* Lieutenant Robert Adamson, USCG.

mount JATO racks on the R5D just to take off again once they got into La Paz, Bolivia. At the same time, they made plans for an alternative trip, and they made the alternative, which was in the Martin 404, so I made the trip. The next year, too, we made a trip through the Caribbean. The second year I remember more distinctly than the first. The first one I think we went just to San Juan and St. Thomas and so on.

The second year we went down to Nicaragua, and I mentioned to you earlier the odor of the Honduras mahogany we got there. But we went into Nicaragua and Guatemala, and in Guatemala we made the usual trips for tourists. The official party went to Chichicastenango, which is where they burn incense on the steps of the church. And it's a picturesque place, and then they went to lunch at Lake Atitlan, which is the usual program for tourists. Then we went from there to the city that was the capital of the Dominican Republic, and, of course, it was named after the dictator at that time.* As we flew over Haiti, it was always impressive that you could actually tell where the border was, because the land was so well cultivated on the Dominican Republic side and so poorly cared for on the Haitian side. Then we went to Cuba for just one or two nights.

Paul Stillwell: Any contact with Cuban government officials there?

Admiral Siler: I don't know whether they had contact with them. I wasn't involved in it, because when we made trips like that, Admiral Richmond had made it very clear I was the pilot of the airplane and I was to take care of the airplane, so I didn't get involved with the visits at all.

Paul Stillwell: Did he have a separate aide that performed some of those other normal aide functions?

Admiral Siler: No. He had a captain who was his special assistant, and he performed some of those things. He was Captain I. J. Stephens, who became later a rear admiral.†

---

* Ciudad Trujillo, named for President Rafael Leonidas Trujillo Molina, was the name of the capital of the Dominican Republic from 1936 to 1961. It was renamed Santo Domingo after his assassination in 1961.
† Captain Irvin J. Stephens, USCG.

He was rather expected to be a Commandant or Assistant Commandant at some time, but when he did not make it he retired.

Then other years we would make trips to Hawaii or something like that. But almost always right after the election we would have a big trip with the congressional budget committee, which was chaired by J. Vaughan Gary of Richmond. He used to come up to the cockpit of the airplane and particularly when we flying over the western United States, where it was rather sparsely populated, and he would point out that Richmond, Virginia, had more population than the entire state of Nevada.

Paul Stillwell: Would these trips qualify as boondoggles?

Admiral Siler: You might have called them that, but, of course, as far as they were concerned they were informative congressional trips. [Laughter]

Paul Stillwell: Fact-finding missions. [Laughter]

Admiral Siler: Absolutely. But the relationships between Admiral Richmond and those people were so good because he'd lived a large part of his life in Arlington, Virginia. Until he left Washington after his term was up, he lived in a house that was owned by his mother.

He considered at one time very seriously building the Commandant's quarters at the place which is now the Coast Guard's electronic test center or something like that in the suburbs out on Telegraph Road. At that time it was a radio station for the Coast Guard. They looked at it very seriously for quite some time and discovered that in order to build there with a basement in the house they'd have to build an inverted swimming pool because the water level was so high. [Laughter] They eventually felt that it was just too expensive to live there, and so he never built the house.

Then the next Commandant made arrangements to build a house on the grounds of the Bethesda Medical Center and had made arrangements with the Secretary of the Navy to get a certain amount of land from the Navy. I saw that Secretary years later, and he said, "How did the house work out on the grounds of the Medical Center?"

I said, "We didn't build there." Of course, the place where the quarters were built was by the next Commandant, who realized that the best way to do it was to find a house in the neighborhood and modify it, and that's what happened.

Paul Stillwell: And that was in Kenwood, I think you said.*

Admiral Siler: Yes.

Paul Stillwell: Did his background as a lawyer cause Admiral Richmond to take a kind of legalistic approach to things?

Admiral Siler: No, I don't think so. I think it just made him aware of some of the stumbling blocks that he might find. And I think some of those people in BoB or Treasury had been classmates of his at George Washington University.

Paul Stillwell: So it was more the personal connection than strictly the legal background?

Admiral Siler: Yes.

Paul Stillwell: One thing that you mentioned the other day and we didn't get on tape was your contacts with Quentin Walsh during that time in Washington. What do you remember of him?

Admiral Siler: Well, Quenny was the aide to the Secretary, and he was always available over in Treasury. If we needed a question answered in Treasury, the Commandant could call him and say, "Quenny, I need an answer to such-and-such." Quenny would go and push it to get the answer that was necessary, and it was very convenient that way. At the same time he would always come to Coast Guard headquarters the first thing in the morning, because Treasury went to work later than we did. With his being at Coast

---

* Kenwood is an upscale part of Chevy Chase, Maryland, not far outside Washington, D.C.

Guard headquarters the first thing every morning and again during the day, he was capable of carrying material back and forth for a quick response time.

Quenny was always part of our coffee klatch when we got together. The admiral used to go to the office of what amounted to the chief of staff of the Coast Guard, although he was in those days the assistant chief of staff. When the admirals were in there, we aides would get together and have our cup of coffee in the outer office of the Commandant. So if people came in to see the Commandant between about 8:30 and 9:30, we could offer them a cup of coffee too.

Paul Stillwell: Well, you said you learned a lot of Coast Guard history from Walsh.

Admiral Siler: Well, both Walsh and the other person from whom I learned a great deal was admiral later, at that time Commander Russell Waesche, Jr. Russ knew all these people by their personal histories because he'd heard so much from his father when his father was the Commandant.* And it made little difference whom they spoke of. Walsh and Waesche would talk, and Waesche could almost always say, "Yeah, he's class of '31," and knew where he stood in the class and all that sort of thing.

Walsh kidded him after Russ had been selected for captain but was pretty down on the list, since Russ was not too high in his class. Quenny used to say that he believed that Paul Trimble, who later became Assistant Commandant of the Coast Guard, and Russ Waesche would both study the Coast Guard Register before they went to bed.† They would memorize again where the captains stood on the precedence list and then get down on their knees and say, "Dear Lord, please strike the following people dead to make a vacancy for me." [Laughter]

Paul Stillwell: Did you ever have any encounters with the senior Waesche?

---

* Admiral Russell R. Waesche, USCG, served as Commandant of the Coast Guard from June 1936 to December 1945. Initially in that post he was a rear admiral, promoted to vice admiral in March 1942 and four-star admiral in April 1945.
† Commander Paul E. Trimble, USCG; Commander Russell R. Waesche, Jr., USCG.

Admiral Siler: No. In fact, I think I shook his hand at graduation, and that was it. Our graduation speaker was Forrestal, because he was the Assistant Secretary of the Navy at that time. He spoke, and Admiral Waesche presented our commissions to us; that was the only thing that I ever had to do with him.

Paul Stillwell: Now, some of the aide duties like writing thank-you notes and planning for accommodations in various places. Who handled those?

Admiral Siler: Usually the accommodations would be handled by the aide, but he had a special arrangement with Captain Stephens, and so the accommodations when we went someplace were usually handled by Captain Stephens. And, of course, as far as the travel arrangements were concerned, I usually made them, except when he went to Massanutten Academy as a graduation speaker he'd made the arrangements himself because he was a graduate of Massanutten, and that was the reason they called on him to speak.* He knew more about that area than I ever would learn. I still remember when I drive past Massanutten that that's the place Admiral Richmond went, but I've never seen it. [Laughter]

Paul Stillwell: When you went on these so-called fact-finding tours would there be entertainment laid on at each site?

Admiral Siler: Almost always.

Paul Stillwell: And what might that consist of?

Admiral Siler: Well, usually it was a reception to meet the officials in that location. Then, depending on how long they stayed—sometimes they'd stay an extra night because there would be a special amount of entertainment that was the usual routine for that place—and my copilot and I were usually included in those parties.

---

* Massanutten Military Academy is in Woodstock, Virginia.

Paul Stillwell: Did any business get done on these trips?

Admiral Siler: Oh, I'm sure that it did, because that airplane was a good plane to have a conference at. There were two tables for four people each, and they very frequently would get together and confer at those. Although I never flew in that as the Commandant, I had the same sort of arrangement in the Gulfstream that I did fly in.

Paul Stillwell: Well, the other benefit is that you've met people face to face, so that if something comes up in the future you've got that much stronger a relationship.

Admiral Siler: Oh, yes, very definitely. However, of course, in most cases it was too many years between the time when I was—I was only a lieutenant commander then. And yet there were one or two people who—well, some of them live right here now.

Paul Stillwell: Well, I was thinking more in terms of Admiral Richmond so that he would have met people in these locations.

Admiral Siler: Very definitely. I'm sure he used those contacts.

Paul Stillwell: Anything else to recall from your time with Admiral Richmond?

Admiral Siler: I just wanted to mention the fact that we had those regular trips right after elections, and they were usually made by the people who were reelected so that they were all rather happy about it, and so it made for a very pleasant trip usually.

Paul Stillwell: Some military officers decide not to vote so they're above that. What was your own stance on voting?

Admiral Siler: I don't know that I've ever missed an election. I just voted absentee.

Paul Stillwell: We talked yesterday about your getting down to Corpus Christi, and this was the first time you'd had command. What differences did that make in your approach to things?

Admiral Siler: It was very obvious when I arrived there that most of those people had no idea how the budgetary process went to provide money to an air station like that, and I could give them a firsthand view of how it did work. Although I had not appeared before committees at that time, I was called to appear before the committees after that. I knew for sure exactly how many times Admiral Richmond was going up to The Hill and how his conferences worked with Colonel Johnson and Sam Something-or-other at the Bureau of Budget.* Then they'd spend days at the congressional hearings. So I was able to tell the people at the air station what the process was and let them know a little more how much they could expect to get from a request and how long it would take to get to the front of the book.

Paul Stillwell: Did that knowledge help you get a little extra for Corpus Christi?

Admiral Siler: Not really. [Laughter] I think in most cases we either were scheduled for it long before, such as the different airplane. When I got there we were flying the UF-1, which I believe was the HU-16D, and we were scheduled to get the UF-2 when I arrived.† We did get it eventually. I made it a point to be the ferry pilot on the first airplane. We were to fly up one of the old airplanes to Grumman on Long Island and exchange it for a UF-2. So we waited until a front came through Corpus Christi and then figured we'd follow that front up to Long Island. The only trouble was the front stalled just about at Biloxi, Mississippi.

Paul Stillwell: You didn't get very far. [Laughter]

---

* "The Hill" refers to Capitol Hill in Washington, D.C., that is, the U.S. Congress.
† Among the changes in the upgrade were an increase of 16½ feet in the wingspan, bigger ailerons, and a taller tailfin.

Admiral Siler: No. We flew over to New Orleans then. Had the evening with our friends in the district office, and the next day, the front had moved a little farther, so we said, "Well, it'll probably move some more during the day," so we flew as far as Roanoke, Virginia, and landed there because the front had stalled again. Roanoke rolled up the sidewalks at 4:00 o'clock, so we stayed at the beautiful old hotel there, and there was nothing to do. I don't even know if they had a TV station in those days. Anyway, we spent the night at Roanoke.

The next day we figured by now it's certainly cleared up in New York. We were able to get as far as Fort Belvoir [laughter], and this was the biggest airplane that had landed at Fort Belvoir at that little Army field.[*] Here we were with great big floats hanging down to about four feet above the ground. Fortunately, the fireplugs didn't go more than about two feet to three feet above the ground, so we taxied in and said, "We'll just stay here until the weather improves."

In the meantime, we called for some transportation and spent the morning at Coast Guard headquarters. Then came back, and I think that afternoon we were able to get all the way to Floyd Bennett, the Coast Guard air station there. The next morning we flew it over to the Grumman plant, turned it in, and accepted the airplane that we were going to take back to Corpus Christi. But we couldn't get very far because we had bad weather again, but this airplane was well enough equipped for ice and bad weather that we were not too concerned about flying back. By this time we'd taken enough time that we figured we'd better at least make a respectable start. So we flew from there down to Baltimore and spent the night there. I noticed the crew was anxious to spend a little more time at Floyd Bennett, because they had buddies who were stationed there. So we went to Baltimore, where I'd landed many, many times when I was flying a Martin, and we used to practice landings and practice instrument approaches there. We stopped in Baltimore and went into town, and it just happened that my copilot and I went into town looking for the bright spots, and we went to a place called the Piccadilly Night Club. Now, you could pick a dilly anyplace you could try there, and they were dillies.

---

[*] Fort Belvoir is in northern Virginia, not far from Washington, D.C.

Paul Stillwell: That city was famous in that era for Blaze Starr and the Block.*

Admiral Siler: Well, that's what we were in, whether we knew it or not. [Laughter] Fortunately, we got out the next day, I think, without any difficulties. And by that time we knew the airplane well enough that we just flew all the way from Baltimore to Corpus Christi. I sent my travel voucher in for repayment, and the pay officer said, "According to the airline regulations you can fly from Corpus Christi to New York in one day. Why did you spend four days getting there?" I didn't reply to him at all. I wrote to either the chief of operations or chief of staff at that point, and I sent him a copy of the note from the pay officer. And my response to him I said, "This was a ferry flight. Regulations for ferry flights are that you must have as the primary consideration the safe delivery of the airplane, and we had weather that we had to contend with." The chief of staff, I don't recall which was his position at that time because he had been operations and he later became chief of staff. But he sent a note back to me saying, "It will be taken care of as quickly as possible, but that pay officer doesn't know the difference between ferry, F-E-R-R-Y, and F-A-I-R-Y." [Laughter] So, anyway, I got my money.

Paul Stillwell: What advantages did the new model have over its predecessor?

Admiral Siler: Much better in range and much better in icing conditions and bad weather conditions. It was both supposed to be slower in stalling if you were going into rough water, and yet normally it flew faster. That bigger wing and greater capability.

Paul Stillwell: How large a contingent of aircraft did you have at your station?

Admiral Siler: We had either three or four of the Grumman Albatrosses. We moved from where we had been when I first went there—right next to the operations building—down to the waterfront, and we had lots and lots of room in that hangar. In fact, now they have the whole hangar. Originally we had half of the hangar. We used the central part of

---

* Blaze Starr was a well-known stripper of the era; the Block was noted for its seedy establishments.

the hangar for just storage, because while we had the rest of the hangar empty our lease didn't allow us to use that half. Now the entire place is the Coast Guard.

Paul Stillwell: What was your mission there?

Admiral Siler: Almost completely search and rescue. The shrimp boats that operated out of Port Isabel and Corpus Christi itself, although Corpus was not a port of shrimp boats. It was oil and oil tankers were in there all the time. Port Aransas and several small ports along the coast, and we had the responsibility clear up to Galveston for things that were requiring a Grumman Albatross. There was a helicopter detachment that came to Galveston about the same time, but it couldn't go very far offshore with the helicopters they had then.

Paul Stillwell: What kind of helicopters were they?

Admiral Siler: I think they were the HO4S, which was a reciprocating-engine helicopter, and so its range was not as great as the turbine helicopters that they had later.[*] They only had either two or three of those.

Paul Stillwell: So the H-3 hadn't come in yet?

Admiral Siler: Well, the H-3 was never assigned there, I don't think.[†] They have now; Galveston has the H-52 I'm pretty sure. Corpus Christi has H-3s now.

Paul Stillwell: What was family life like in Texas?

---

[*] HO4S was the Navy-Coast Guard designation for the Sikorsky H-55 helicopter, equivalent to the Army's H-19A. Deliveries to the Navy began in 1950. In 1962 the HO4S helicopters in Coast Guard use were redesignated HH-19G.
[†] The Sikorsky SH-3 Sea King is an antisubmarine helicopter. Deliveries to the Navy began in September 1961 when it was the HSS-2; it was redesignated SH-3 in September 1962. The helo has a rotor diameter of 62 feet; length, 72 feet, 8 inches; gross weight, 18,897 pounds; top speed, 166 miles per hour.

Admiral Siler: Great. Our son loved the fishing. He and his teammates, cohorts, would go fishing on the seawall, and they'd catch fish regularly, but he wasn't very interested in eating it, so he'd usually release them. There were gars that would swim in at the seaplane ramps there, and those things were that long.

Paul Stillwell: Maybe four of five feet long.

Admiral Siler: At least five feet. Looked like alligators. [Laughter] I guess they were alligator gars. And you could see them almost anytime that you went down there.

Paul Stillwell: What did you yourself do for recreation in that area?

Admiral Siler: I built a sailboat.

Paul Stillwell: Well, please tell me about it.

Admiral Siler: Years earlier I had found a set of plans in I think it was <u>Popular Science</u> magazine that were pretty well detailed, and so I carried that around with me for probably ten years or so. Finally I decided that there was a hobby shop that I could find the space to build it in, and they had a supply of marine plywood. So I started to build this 18-foot sailboat. I didn't know where I was going to get the sails when I finished it, and I had a little problem with that when I finally did it. But I built the boat upside down, which is the usual way to construct it. Then before I turned it over I completely coated the underwater part of the entire hull up to the waterline with fiberglass so it wouldn't become saturated with water even though it was kept in the water.

Then when I turned it over I fiber-glassed the deck, too, so it was completely fiber-glassed on the outside of the marine plywood. Then I found a mast from a doctor friend who sailed all over the place, and he had a catamaran. I was able to build a tabernacle, so that I had an elevated place on the deck that stuck up about that far and put the mast into that tabernacle to get the height that I needed for the sail. I found a sail manufacturer in, I guess it was someplace in Mississippi or Louisiana, and sent off and got one sail and one jib, and that's all I ever used. But I sailed it against a medical service officer who was stationed there, and he had a boat that was about two feet shorter than mine. I could sail faster than he could anyway, so I figured that I was successful.

Paul Stillwell: It must be a great deal of satisfaction to make something like that and have it work.

Admiral Siler: Yes, it was. I had some problems with it because the rudder would get saturated with water, and it was not coated with fiberglass the way everything else was. It would twist if you tried to put it over too far when you were in pretty strong winds, and Corpus Christi has some very strong winds. There was one time I wanted to move my boat from where I normally kept it in an old hangar that was not used for airplanes anymore at all; it was used by boat people. I had gotten permission to keep my boat with the boats that were the official boats of the station. I got someone to help me, and we sailed it from where it was normally put in the water and sailed it to the other location. There was such a strong wind that we wrapped the sail a couple of times around the boom to reef the sail, because the wind was too strong to sail the boat with just plain trying to stand the wind.

Paul Stillwell: Did you have an engine in it, or was it pure sail?

Admiral Siler: Pure sail.

Paul Stillwell: What eventually became of the boat?

Admiral Siler: Well, when I was ordered out of there I was ordered to Alaska. My father had died at that point, so I knew my mother had only one car, and I thought I could put the sailboat in the other half of the garage. The only trouble was you couldn't close the door [laughter], so for quite some time my mother was unable to close the door to the garage. Then she died, too, so my sister and my brother tried to sell some of her things. I asked them to move the sailboat from Santa Maria, which is halfway between San

Francisco and Los Angeles, up to San Francisco, because the man who was executive officer there had been my copilot part of the time when I was in Washington. I figured if he were the exec that he'd pay some attention to the boat and would check on the boat.

My brother parked the boat, I should say, out in the magazine area. And it was just parked out in the open for at least a year. My brother may have looked at it once or twice, but he didn't pay too much attention, and that exec that I thought was my good buddy didn't pay too much attention to it either. Someone stole the wheels and tires off of the trailer. So when I came back from Alaska before I could move it I had to buy some new wheels and tires someplace, which I did, and we trailed it from San Francisco all the way to Miami to the next assignment. And I sailed it there for a while.

Paul Stillwell: How large a staff did you have as commanding officer there at Corpus Christi?

Admiral Siler: The administrative staff was mostly aviators down there when they were not flying. One of the officers was the supply officer. Another aviator was the first lieutenant, and he'd look around the station and see what needed to be done. We had, I'd say, something like ten people who were non-aviation personnel.

Paul Stillwell: How many aviators altogether?

Admiral Siler: Just guessing now because it's been too long, but right around 20 aviators. And we had two warrant officers, one who was an electronics officer, and he did some flying as a radioman in the airplanes. And we had one other warrant officer who was, I think, the aviation maintenance officer.

Paul Stillwell: You probably had some enlisted people for aircrews and maintenance and what have you.

Admiral Siler: Oh, yes. The entire number of people assigned there was just under 100. We were able to have at least one airplane ready to fly all the time. When we were moved to the seawall, in order to get to the field we had to taxi across the highway. It made things a little slower on takeoff, but it worked out rather well on the whole because we had a much better hangar. The Navy really helped us in our move there.

In spite of the fact that my executive officer had argued with him, the public works officer really did a good job designing the place and making the alterations to that hangar before we moved in. There were some interesting things there. Right around Christmastime one year the aviator who had really taught me to fly in the Grumman Albatross was sent out on a search that was up near Galveston, and the weather in Corpus Christi was foggy. So he had to watch it so that he knew that he would be able to get in before it got dark. He was checking the fuel frequently and decided it was time to come home.

He came back to Corpus Christi and said he'd like to make a GCA approach, and so GCA fired up and made contact. Got him around so that he was on his final approach. At that point he put the RPMs of the engine up to the landing configuration, and one of the engines quit. Well, I've forgotten one thing. Just before that he had put the wheels down, and he got two of the lights indicating green, but the third one didn't indicate green for "safe." So he said, "We'll make a touch-and-go landing and make sure that the wheels are going to hold when we touch down."

So he had turned on final to make his touch-and-go landing, and that's when the engine quit. So he said, "This won't be a touch-and-go. This will be a final landing." The other engine quit then. So he had a little bit of sputter and put the wheels back up and headed for water instead of the runway. Just to the north of the main field there was a place called the Oso Slough, Oso meaning bear in Spanish. So he headed for that place, because it was closer than the bay and put the wheels back in the up position while he still had a tiny bit of power and landed in the slough.

As he ran out and got off the step, the hull went down and went into the mud in the bottom of the slough. That night and the next morning he left someone on the airplane in case it was full of water, and he had a pump ready to pump if any water came in. Fortunately, no water came in, and the next morning they took out everything we possibly could except for a little bit of fuel so we could fly the airplane out of there. And we flew it, the same guy, and it got back and got the engine started, and he didn't really have enough room to make the normal check of the magnetos. So he took it off and flew it over the telephone wires into the Corpus Christi Bay, which was just over there.

He got about 100 feet off the water and over the telephone wires and put it back into the bay on the other side. Then he put the wheels back down and came up the ramp the normal way that we would make seaplane landings. After he made the landing, he put the wheels back down and made all the checks that you could from inside the airplane and taxied up the ramp and back to the Coast Guard. Apparently it was down all right, but just the electronic indicator was not right. Then to complete that operation I said, "You know, that would make a wonderful story for the safety bulletin of the Coast Guard." So he wrote an article called "A So-So Day on the Oso." It made for a good story, and that was, I think, one of the two incidents when we had endangered an airplane.

We made weekly patrols around the Gulf of Mexico: all the way from the Gulf of Campeche and all the way up to Tampico and back to Corpus Christi. Whenever Biloxi did it, and they did it one week out of the month, they would come around and spend the night in Corpus Christi because it was such a long flight for them. For us it was about ten minutes longer, and we weren't allowed to make a stop anyplace. So we would go around to cover the entire gulf, then back to Corpus Christi, and take from eight to ten hours to make that flight. We were supposed to identify as many of the shrimp boats as we could, American or Mexican, because the Mexicans were claiming infringement on their shrimping area, and we would go and locate those.

Then a patrol vessel that was sent down there. We had two out of Brownsville, one out of Corpus Christi and one out of either New Orleans or Biloxi, Mississippi or someplace like that. The patrol vessels would go into that area so that if there were an incident between Mexican patrol boats and American shrimpers, then we would at least be able to see it and perhaps deter it by being there. So our flight was the basis of the location of the patrol vessel, and we would make those flights once a week. About six times, I guess, during the time I was there, we would have an engine failure and have to enter Mexican ports and park the airplane and get an airplane engine down there and change it in the hot Mexican sun, eating Mexican food, and usually having cases of touristas that just wouldn't quit.

Paul Stillwell: Montezuma's revenge.

Admiral Siler: Yes.

Paul Stillwell: Had the oilrigs started to proliferate in the Gulf of Mexico by then?

Admiral Siler: Not yet. That happened shortly after I left when the one had the huge blowout that was down near Mexico. But there wasn't anything when we were there. They were just starting to move offshore with the rigs. And there was one that was being towed one day when the weather turned bad. They had a huge crane on it, and it started swinging back and forth, and they were afraid it was going to just tear itself apart. I forget how that came out, other than I think they got into some more sheltered water, and then were able to get the people off.

Paul Stillwell: How did you stop the traffic when you had to taxi across the highway?

Admiral Siler: I think the tower would handle that for us.

Paul Stillwell: Did they have gates like they do at railroad crossings?

Admiral Siler: I can't recall that.

Paul Stillwell: How was your relationship with the Navy people at the naval air station there?

Admiral Siler: Excellent. The operations division that had the helicopters and the tower operators and all that sort thing just figured that we were their second cousins, and it was a very good relationship.

Paul Stillwell: Was there swapping back and forth of spare parts or things like that if needed?

Admiral Siler: No one else had Grumman Albatrosses.

Paul Stillwell: Oh, okay. [Laughter] Did it fall to you to handle cases of disciplinary infractions as the skipper? What do you remember about those?

Admiral Siler: Most of the time our men were pretty good. We had an unfortunate automobile accident that killed one of our men, and the other man in the car was badly injured in his hand. His arm was broken, and his hand and wrist were shattered. He was given some sponge rubber to do this with. I remember I gave him a falsie that he could use. [Laughter] It was sponge rubber.

Paul Stillwell: More than one purpose there.

Admiral Siler: That's right. We had one other aspect of the station being way over there in Texas. When people in the Coast Guard had mental difficulties—and if they got to physical survey boards—we would be assigned to be members of the medical survey. We'd have to fly to Fort Worth, Texas, which was where the hospital was, and we would be the board. Of course, now the boards would usually have one medical member, and the medical member was always a member of the hospital staff. We'd never have met the man before, but suddenly we were supposed to work together. And yet we surveyed quite a few people. Quite a few of those young men had really fallen apart mentally, and I don't know how that happened, but we surveyed them. Then to finalize the board would usually take our own yeoman with us so that we could work on the record.

Paul Stillwell: Did you talk to the men themselves or just rely on the doctors' reports?

Admiral Siler: Usually the person was in good enough shape that he would appear before the board. If they weren't in good enough shape there would be just continued hospitalization, but after certain medications and a certain amount of time, they would be well enough off that if they continued their medication they probably would be all right out on the street. You wouldn't want to trust them to be working on an airplane. Of course, these people were not just airframe people. They were very frequently people who had come off of ships.

Paul Stillwell: Was it usually some kind of service-caused trauma?

Admiral Siler: I don't think so. I think in most cases it was something that was just latent all the time and finally had come to the surface.

Paul Stillwell: Well, sometimes being in a new environment can cause that kind of an effect.

Admiral Siler: Yes.

Paul Stillwell: Anything else on Corpus Christi that you'd want to mention?

Admiral Siler: The relations with the city were very, very good too. We had one interesting arrangement with the command. My superior was the district office, the admiral there and the captain who was the chief of staff and the other captain who was chief of operations and yet another one who was chief of engineering. The man who was chief of engineering was a very fine officer, and it turned out later his son was the commanding officer of an 82-footer in Alaska when I went up there. But that was something that developed later. But most of the relationships between our station and the district office were very, very good. Of course, the admiral had been an aviator.

Paul Stillwell: Who was he?

Admiral Siler: That was Carl Olsen, the man who selected out of aviation the day he made admiral. And we had a very good relationship, too, with the man who was chief of operations and then chief of staff. Unfortunately, he developed some disease that made it almost impossible for him to speak. Before that he'd been at the academy just before I went to the academy, and everyone at the academy at that time hated him. I got along with him just fine. [Laughter] Then I got orders to Alaska.

Paul Stillwell: And you're smiling as you tell me that. Why did you enjoy it so much?

Admiral Siler: Well, that wasn't the thing. I knew I was due for orders, and my wife got a letter from the Coast Guard one day. "Dear Madam, You are being ordered to Alaska and so on. And the housing is very difficult there because the World's Fair is in Seattle. So we suggest that you investigate quarters on ships that are being ordered into Seattle just for having quarters there." I hadn't gotten orders. [Laughter]

Paul Stillwell: What a surprise.

Admiral Siler: Next thing was I got a phone call from the chief of operations in Alaska, and I'd known him when I was in Washington. He said, "You've got orders to Alaska."

I said, "No, I don't."

He said, "You will." [Laughter] He said, "Anyway, you're coming to Alaska, and don't think it's the end of the world, because it's a wonderful assignment." He was enjoying Alaska and the outings that you could have fishing and hunting. Of course, I was not a hunter, and I'm not a fisherman.

So I said, "Ye, gods. What did I do?"

He said, "And don't think it's something you did." [Laughter] So a few days later, they called me from the district office and said, "We have orders for you."

I don't know how long they'd been there and sat on them without taking any action. But I did have my orders to Alaska, and, sure enough, they informed me that housing was extremely difficult in Seattle. I made a call on the admiral there in Corpus Christi, because he was changed just then too. I called on the new admiral and said, "I have orders, and I'll be over with my relief in a few days. But then I am a little concerned about quarters in Seattle."

He said, "Well, maybe I can do something about that for you." And he wrote to the commanding officer of the station in Seattle. Of course, I knew Seattle pretty well, because we used to fly into there from Port Angeles all the time delivering people to Seattle. If we were going downtown it was just as convenient there as anyplace else. And there was a nice exchange there, so anyway I knew Seattle.

He said he'd contact the commanding officer of the air station, and I thought that was going to work out just fine. Except the response was, "Well, we can make some of the enlisted housing available, and you can go over to the hospitality house there and draw some sheets and so on, which should be just fine."

Well, it turned out that the greatest conversation at the receptions, that's the usual summer routine there, became the Silers' inability to get quarters in Seattle. One of the people said, "Well my cousin's renting quarters in her house." So we ended up going there and never touching those Navy quarters. While we were there we discovered that the difficulty with apartments in Seattle didn't occur. We could go anyplace we wanted on the waterfront and get an apartment for a day or so with no trouble.

Paul Stillwell: Why Seattle rather than Alaska?

Admiral Siler: Well, we would check into the Seattle district office for transportation to Alaska, and they'd fly us to Alaska, and then in the meantime we had to turn our car in for water transportation. So we were without a car. They did not authorize driving your own car to Alaska. So we worked through the 13th district to get to the 17th. But it turned out to be a very simple operation.

Paul Stillwell: Did you get to go to the fair at all?

Admiral Siler: Oh, yes, and we went to the Space Needle, and my wife is afraid of heights. [Laughter] When we got in the elevator to come down, she turned her back to the door because it was glass and you were supposed to be say, "What a wonderful view." She said, "Turn me around and let me out of here." [Laughter]

So the person who was the elevator operator said, "Turn around and face the door, Ma'am."

And she said, "If you're going to wait for that, we're going to be here all day." [Laughter] So we went down with her back turned to the view. It was a lovely view, but we ate lunch up there in the Space Needle. We had our two kids with us, and they both enjoyed the view.

Paul Stillwell: Well, it's still there.

Admiral Siler: Yes. I've never been back, though I've been back to Seattle several times. In fact, I used to fly out of Alaska down to Seattle. That was almost the only way to conduct the instrument training that we needed and to get GCAs. We could go to Alaska—I mean to Anchorage—if the Air Force happened to be up that day, but you could go to Seattle, and you had NAS Seattle for GCA, and they had McChord Field, which was just a few miles farther. So we almost always went to Seattle when we had to take an instrument check. And everybody liked it. They'd have a shuttle into Seattle, and everybody'd say, "Bring me back such-and-such."

Paul Stillwell: Salmon, right?

Admiral Siler: Well, no, we'd get the salmon in Alaska there. No question about that.

We had not had a dog for many, many years at that point. We had tried having dogs in Washington, D.C., and in Port Angeles, Washington, and they'd either run away or gotten lost. Having a dog in Alaska seemed to me might be a good idea, and I think Betty at that time felt that it would provide a little protection. We lived three and half miles out of Juneau on the road to the airport and the road to a fish hatchery. It was in the countryside. So when I went to Seattle I went to a pet store and brought back a little puppy. It was a black and white dog that they said was a cross between a water spaniel and a cocker spaniel, and just about as cute as it could be. We checked it out at the vet, and Betty realized that you could ask the butcher for scrap bones, and they'd give them to you then. Now they sell them to you, but they gave them to her then.

Unfortunately, one day we—I think we had gone to an Elks picnic or something like that, and the dog went down to a neighbor's house, which was closer to the highway than we were. They frequently fed the dog when it went down there, because they liked it too. Only this time it saw a bird flying out on the road, and it went chasing the bird just as a car came by. So when we got home we didn't have a live dog. So a few days after that Betty went shopping, and the butcher always said, "Would you like some bones, Mrs. Siler?" Only in Juneau it's not Mrs. Siler, it's Betty. Even the governor when he walked down the street would say, "Hi, Si." [Laughter] It wasn't a matter of Mr. Siler or anything like that. When they said, "Would you like some bones?" Betty said, "Well, unfortunately the dog was killed."

The butcher replied, "Well, I know just the place that you can go and see about another dog," and described it in the Indian village which used to be right on the edge of the city. Actually, I should use town, the development there, because it was not very much of a city in those days. He described this place in the Indian village. We went there later in the day, because we had nothing to do particularly except watch the sun go down. As we sat there, we said, "Well, shall we go in and look?" And on the way in Betty said, "Now, let's not commit ourselves to that unless it's a really good dog." It was that long.

Paul Stillwell: About eight or nine inches long?

Admiral Siler: Yes. A little cocker, mostly cocker. And apparently it had some dachshund in there, too, because it stood this way. It came stumbling over the threshold of the house, and they said, "Well, that's the one that we want to get rid of," and Betty said, "Let's take it." [Laughter]

Paul Stillwell: So much for caution and hesitation. [Laughter]

Admiral Siler: Right. So we had her for 14½ years, and she was really part of the family, just like this one is now. But we had almost exactly the same experience with this. We were not going to take this unless it was a really good dog. [Laughter] "Okay, let's take it." [Laughter]

Paul Stillwell: What was your job there at Juneau?

Admiral Siler: Chief of Search and Rescue of the State of Alaska. However, although my responsibility was for the state, as far as the operational control of what went on in the state was concerned, the inland part of it was controlled by the Air Force. The part of it out to the west from Kodiak, all the way out to Shemya and Attu, was controlled out of Kodiak, where our biggest air station was. We had two air stations at that time, the one at Kodiak, which had—when I first arrived it had four Grumman Albatrosses and one C-123.* The air station at Annette Island, near Ketchikan, had three Grumman Albatrosses, and that was how much we had for air assets. So if we had a huge search, we would have to call on the Air Force to see what they had.

When we had the biggest incidents we very frequently would call on the Air Force for assistance. When the Northwest Airlines plane went down in Sitka Harbor we didn't call on the Air Force, because we knew where that airplane was all the time. The Sitka loran station went out in its boat, very small boat, and brought people off, and they got quite a few boats from the people in Sitka. But when we had the second Northwest Airlines plane go down, which was just plain lost, we didn't know where it was initially, and it had never made a report of any trouble. But apparently the propeller oversped and then actually departed the plane and crashed. It became completely uncontrollable and went almost went straight in apparently. The biggest piece of an airplane that they found was parts of seats that would float to the surface and the sponge rubber would provide some flotation. The biggest part of a human body that they found was a thighbone that was approximately a foot long. It was a full airplane, and so they lost probably 100

---

* In 1962 the Coast Guard received eight Fairchild C-123 Provider cargo planes on loan from the Air Force, and they kept their Air Force designation. The plane was powered by two radial engines. It had a wingspan of 110 feet, length of 75 feet, gross weight of 71,000 pounds, and a maximum speed of 245 miles per hour.

people at least. And it was going to Japan eventually and would have stopped either at Elmendorf or the Anchorage airport and refueled, but it never got there.*

Paul Stillwell: What can you do in a case like that where it's all broken up?

Admiral Siler: Not much.

Paul Stillwell: Then I take it you flew out and eventually found where the wreckage was.

Admiral Siler: Well, the Coast Guard didn't. I think the first locating of anything of that sort was a ship that was headed south from Alaska and went through a field of debris, and it became so obvious that this was it. I had been flying to Elmendorf Field that day and was going to practice GCA and that sort of thing so I'd be ready for my instrument check, which I took shortly afterward. I was about abeam of Cordova when they sent us a message saying that a plane was in trouble and had not reported in north of about Sitka. So the district told us go out on the airways and fly at low altitude back toward Seattle, which was where it started and see what we could see there.

In the meantime a C-124 landed at Annette and said, "I'm not on such an urgent mission that I can't do something to help if I can help." A C-124, you know, is a huge airplane and uses a lot of gasoline. But I don't know whether it ever got airborne because that ship discovered the debris. We landed at Annette and operated from there, because we were closer to the place where the crash was than Juneau would have been. And most of the operation was by surface vessels. We sent out ships from Juneau, out from Ketchikan, and they went out and found these pieces of people and the upholstery and so on. There wasn't much to be found.

Paul Stillwell: Did you also have cases of missing boaters and so forth?

---

* Elmendorf Air Force Base, adjacent to the city of Anchorage, is the largest Air Force installation in Alaska.

Admiral Siler: All the time. It's very difficult to navigate in Alaska if you're not quite familiar with the country, and so boats overdue were very common. Most of the time we'd find them after a certain length of search, but there were times when they would get into the places where the glaciers come down and break off the ice, and sometimes the boats were capsized with the ice. In fact, one of the very first incidents that I was involved with was at Tracy Arm, which is quite close to Juneau just a little south. A boat went out and was apparently capsized with ice. We didn't find much of it at all.

Paul Stillwell: Did you have any boating safety courses for the public to try to cut down on this problem?

Admiral Siler: Yes, we had a very active Coast Guard Auxiliary squadron there, and the auxiliary would do some instructing, but an awful lot of Alaskans feel very independent, and so I'm not sure how much good it did.

Paul Stillwell: Did you have any contact with power squadrons? Training is one of its functions as well.

Admiral Siler: I don't recall ever seeing a power squadron in Alaska. We had a close friend that he and I considered buying a boat together, and he finally did buy a boat with my successor. He was the district commander several years later. In fact, Jack Hayes, who was my successor when I became Commandant. He was district commander in Juneau when I was Commandant, and he and this fellow got together, and I'm trying to think. We have a picture that he gave us when I went up to visit when I was Commandant. It's a picture of his place in the valley there in Juneau. We had some very interesting operations in Alaska, and, of course, the earthquake occurred when we were there.*

Paul Stillwell: Well, please tell me about that.

---

* On 27 March 1964 a magnitude 8.4 earthquake hit the southwest coast of Alaska. It lasted three to four minutes and left 131 people dead. It was followed by a number of aftershocks, some of which exceeded 6.0 on the Richter Scale.

Admiral Siler: Well, to begin with it was, of course, Good Friday, and one of the things that happened that morning was the man who had been my yeoman in this search and rescue office had been driving to work on the old Alaska Highway. It's just one lane that way, one lane this way. It was known as the Alaska Highway, though, and it was icy, as it frequently could be. He and a friend of his were in a Volkswagen. This other man had been entertaining kids in particular, anybody who wanted him to do some entertaining, in magic tricks and he dressed as a clown. The man who had been my yeoman was driving, and he lost control of the vehicle and headed into the oncoming lane. They had a head-on collision with another car, and it drove the steering wheel of the Volkswagen up so that it hit his jaw and drove the jaw up into the brain. He lived a couple of hours while they tried to do something about it, but it was just not possible.

Both Betty and I had known his family; he had no children but a very attractive young wife. That afternoon we decided we would go to the big hot spots in town because there were practically no places that were decent entertainment in Juneau except that by the time you'd been there a year and a half, almost anyplace was all right. When we first arrived there, we walked up and down the streets, and we stayed in the Baranof Hotel while our household goods came from Texas. When we walked down the main street, there was a place where there was a piano entertainer, and she had silver dollars making a vest. She played honky-tonk piano for hours every night. When we walked past that, Betty said, "I don't think you'll ever catch me going there." Well, she was there a good many times. [Laughter]

We had been there a few months, and there was one place, a Filipino restaurant, which was nearby. And she said, "I'm sure I'll never go in there." Well, she did. It had good Filipino food. We went into that kind of place. Not exactly what we would have thought of in Corpus Christi, although Corpus Christi's gone down and Juneau's gone up. But, anyway, we went out to dinner several times in that area.

The entire town knew that the Coast Guard man had been killed. The funeral was there in Juneau, which was a very sad thing, because both he and his wife were very young and very attractive. So we thought that evening we'd go out and try to get something else on our minds. We went to the Baranof Hotel, and they had a small combo that would always strike up "I Left My Heart in San Francisco" when they saw us come in. It was the place to go. We had been there dancing a good number of times, and we were there having dinner when they passed the word that there was a phone call for Commander Siler.

I got the call that they had lost communications with everything north of Cordova. I said, "Well, keep trying and see what happens and keep me informed." So I went back in to finish my dinner, and one of the people who was there for dinner also was Milly Banfield, who was the state senator for that district. When I got the word passed about the third time she said, "Some people do anything to get their name on the public address system." Well, after about the third time I said to Betty, "It doesn't look to me as if it's going to be a quiet night, so I'd better get to the district office, and I'll see you later." So I went on to the district office, and shortly afterward we discovered that the governor had no communications north of Juneau and Cordova and even to parts of Anchorage.*

Paul Stillwell: This was as a result of the earthquake?

Admiral Siler: Yes. All of the communications lines were out, because we used military lines north of there. The governor came in and used our comm control center as his control center as well as ours that night. We were able to talk to places north when no one else could. The telephone lines per se were out. The governor and the general in the Air Force thought they would send a KC-135, which was the big jet, down to Juneau, and Juneau weather was not too good that night. I tried to tell them, "Go into Annette. Pick up a Coast Guard pilot there and then come back and make a Sister's Island approach, and you can come in under the weather into Juneau."

They wouldn't do it. They made two or three approaches to Juneau and could not get in using the high-altitude approach and wouldn't use what the Coast Guard used all the time. I'm not sure how well it would have worked with a big C-135 anyway, but anyway they didn't get there night, and they waited till the next day when they could get in in daylight.

---

* William A. Egan, a Democrat served as Governor of Alaska from the beginning of statehood in 1959 until his tenure ended in 1966.

Paul Stillwell: Please proceed with the aftermath of the earthquake.

Admiral Siler: Well, there was only one serviceman killed in Alaska by the earthquake. Very few civilians were killed if any but one serviceman who was a Coast Guardsman, and the reason that he was killed was because he had gone rock climbing at Cape St. Elias Light Station. There was a sail rock of a sort that is away from the lighthouse itself, and he and another man had gone out there to climb the rock. The earthquake actually knocked him off the sail rock and probably broke his leg. Anyway, he didn't believe he could walk, and so the other man went back to the lighthouse. In those days the crew was four, and he got a man who was not on watch at the time and a stretcher and headed out to get him off of the beach where he was. They put him in the stretcher, and then the tidal wave came, and he was drowned. Other than that, I don't think there were very many, if any, casualties from that earthquake.

The water level of Kodiak rose about six feet, and the tidal wave went right into the hangar and inundated the electronics shop and the C-123. The light station at Hinchinbrook was raised about six feet. We had just spent hundreds of thousands of dollars extending the dock at Hinchinbrook, and now it hardly reached the water there. [Laughter]

Paul Stillwell: Were there any fires as a result of the earthquake?

Admiral Siler: Not that I'm aware of. Most of the damage was raising or lowering of the ground in the vicinity of Anchorage, and there's one valley there that has built up over the years by the river bringing in silt there. It obviously was not solid so that it sank quite a lot. There was an officer who had been the chief of staff in Juneau in the Coast Guard; he'd now retired and was the port director of Anchorage. His house was altered in its configuration so that you actually went in upstairs rather than the first floor. And his son would climb in the windows on the second floor.

Paul Stillwell: You said you were on a first-name basis with the governor. How was the relationship with the civilian government there?

Admiral Siler: Well, everyone appreciated the Coast Guard tremendously, and everybody in Alaska is on a first-name basis if you've been there more than a couple of weeks. So the shoe store operator would greet Betty when she'd walk down the street with a, "Hello, Betty. Good to see you." It was everybody knew everyone.

Paul Stillwell: Was there some kind of a civil defense network that you coordinated with, or were you the whole civil defense network?

Admiral Siler: We were a good part of it. Everybody who was in either the federal government or the state government there coordinated with everyone else as closely as they could, because when something went wrong you knew you were going to need some assistance. We got along with the National Guard very well and the Air Force very well. I don't remember many reserve units other than the Air Force per se.

Paul Stillwell: What do you remember of the district commander and how much contact did you have with him?

Admiral Siler: His office was two doors down the hall. [Laughter]

Paul Stillwell: Who was he?

Admiral Siler: When we first went up it was Admiral W. D. Shields who had been an aviator and appreciated the problems of the airplanes greatly.[*] He later became the Assistant Commandant of the Coast Guard. He was very easy to get along with and a very good guy. His wife was an interesting person. We got along with her very well, but she wasn't what you called a gracious lady. Then he was replaced by an admiral whose reputation preceded him. I had known him in Washington. His name was George D.

---

[*] Rear Admiral William D. Shields, USCG.

Synon, and with initials like G. D., everybody thought it stood for something else. But he was, interestingly, on an aviation board that I mentioned earlier when we were looking at the requirements of aviation of the Coast Guard. He had been one of two people who opposed getting the C-130. He was not anti-aviation at all. His daughter married the son of Admiral Harry Felt of the Navy.[*] The daughter married Harry Felt, Jr., when I guess he was about a commander.

Paul Stillwell: Wound up as a rear admiral.

Admiral Siler: The younger one did?

Paul Stillwell: Well, the senior one wound up as four stars.

Admiral Siler: Yes. And the junior one I guess was a rear admiral.

Paul Stillwell: I think so.

Admiral Siler: But the thing that I remember most about George Synon was we lost an airplane in Annette Island one day when the plane had brought some supplies to the district office, so it just went from Annette to Juneau and back again. Later in the day it had another flight, which was a rather short one. Then, right around sunset, it had a third flight, and the same crew flew all three missions. The third time, it was getting too dark to see the fishing vessel they were looking for if it were out there where they were looking. I think the fishing vessel returned to port the next day. But the airplane decided it was going to shortcut the method to get back into its home base. The weather was bad, with low fog, and so when they cut the corner instead of going on the ILS path, they went a little short of it and a little low on it and went into the mountain. It was a rather unfortunate situation, because they didn't have to cut the corner. But the plane was lost and all the crew; they wanted to get home. But when we investigated the accident,

---

[*] Admiral Harry D. Felt, USN, served as Commander in Chief Pacific from 31 July 1958 to 30 June 1964. His oral history is in the Naval Institute collection.

George Synon endorsed the investigation that the crew had flown too much that day. That endorsement, I feel certain, was responsible for the regulation that we have now that says you'll only fly a maximum of eight hours in one day. So that the flight-time limitation came about because of the man who was considered as an enemy of aviation before, and yet he was responsible for that determination.

Paul Stillwell: Well, the saying is that nearly every safety regulation is written in blood.

Admiral Siler: Yes, that one for sure.

Paul Stillwell: Well, you said that you weren't a hunter and you weren't a fisherman. What was it about Alaska that you enjoyed so much?

Admiral Siler: You enjoyed the outdoors there if you got outdoors. There were times when we went hiking up to a reservoir that was several miles up above Juneau. But anytime you went there you took your .30-.30 rifle along with you, because as a good example of why you needed to be careful, there was a young man around town who was blind, and a bear had bitten him in such a way that he lost both his eyes. He was, I think, about a senior in high school when it happened.

I played some badminton. I don't recall that I ever played tennis in Alaska, but as far as golf was concerned, which I didn't play anyway, but the way to play golf was to go out on the tailings of the Juneau, Alaska, gold mine. The fairways were places where the boulders were pretty much removed from the fairway and the greens were sand. If you didn't care about your golf clubs, you could play.

Paul Stillwell: Well, your children certainly were exposed to a variety of environments going from Texas to Alaska.

Admiral Siler: And they loved Alaska. Our son worked one summer, I guess it was the second summer, in packing smelt, and when he came home he smelt. [Laughter] He slept in a basement bedroom, and it had a shower right off the bedroom and it was a good thing, because he would drop the oilskins that he wore in the garage area before he stepped into the bathroom for a shower. Without that shower we couldn't have stood him. [Laughter]

Paul Stillwell: Any other specific search-and-rescue incidents that stand out from that period? You mentioned the two Northwest Airline crashes in particular.

Admiral Siler: Yes, the two Northwest were outstanding, and then, of course, the earthquake was an outstanding incident. We searched for some people who had gone into Tracy Arm, which is just south of Juneau, when I first arrived there, and I didn't know anything about the local territory. But apparently a portion of the glacier broke off in Tracy Arm and rolled the boat. So it made you aware of some of the problems that are unique there.

We had one interesting grounding of a Coast Guard buoy tender when it was headed up in the vicinity of Sitka. She was almost exactly where one of the Alaska ferries had had problems a week or so before. The Alaskan ferries developed a system of piloting the ferry boats immediately afterward where the man who had the conn would stand where he could see up forward, and if he wanted to go left he'd say, "Left so many degrees. Right so many degrees."

Paul Stillwell: You're pointing with your arms as you have these voice commands.

Admiral Siler: Yes, because the man who had the wheel went the wrong direction, and by the time the wheel is over and then you try to reverse it, it's too late. The ship is no longer under control. We had that happen with a buoy tender just about the same time. It made it very clear that this way was the way to go when you were in those channels in Alaska.

Paul Stillwell: That is, with arm signals.

Admiral Siler: Yes.

Paul Stillwell: I know that the williwaws were a concern in the Aleutians. How were flying conditions in general in that area?

Admiral Siler: Well, a lot of the time you'd find that it was very easy flying, because if it became overcast without the wind blowing, it would be very calm, very few bumps. But it was very easy to get lost in Alaska. I was flying with the man who had been the commanding officer at Annette, the place that is no longer there. It used to be pretty much the airport for Ketchikan. He was there when one of the planes at Ketchikan was damaged at least. So he figured if he stayed an extra year with a good record that that would look better on his record, so he stayed there and was very knowledgeable about flying in Alaska.

I had taken the flights that I usually took to get half of my flight time when we had the requirement for flight time. We would fly from Juneau to the loran station that was just north of Juneau at Yakutat, and it would take about an hour each way. So the trip up and back would be two hours, and if I did that twice in a month that was my requirement for flight time. But coming back from that location, we came to Cape Spencer, where the channel led past Glacier Bay and on into Juneau.

The weather was getting a little low, so he told me to stay over to the left in order that I could just follow the shoreline along there. All of a sudden I saw a mountain right ahead. I had gotten into a channel where he had not warned me that there was a little bay there. So I had mountains staring me in the face, but we got out of there and back out to the cape and then climbed to altitude and got an instrument clearance to fly just a short distance in to where you could make the letdown and again make a visual approach to Juneau with no problem. But I was surprised, always have been surprised, that we got into that situation because he knew the area, I thought, very, very well.

Paul Stillwell: What was it that made navigation so difficult, just the rugged terrain?

Admiral Siler: The rugged terrain, and the visibility very frequently was very low.

Paul Stillwell: And how about electronic aids to navigation? Were they more sparse than elsewhere?

Admiral Siler: Not more sparse, but in order to be sure where you were in Alaskan waters you had to have extra. Now, if you flew very high as they do now with the jets, you didn't need that many, but in those days and today when they fly the small airplanes around Alaska the pilots that fly up there very frequently just fly very low. They know the terrain itself well enough that they can get by. Still, I think probably the accident rate in Alaska is about as high as anyplace in the United States anyway.

Paul Stillwell: So the low ceiling would be a prime contributor to that?

Admiral Siler: Yes. Low ceilings and poor visibility.

Paul Stillwell: Anything else about that tour that you want to mention?

Admiral Siler: The kinds of ships we had up there were interesting. During the time I was there, we started out with a fishery requirement that a foreign ship could not fish closer than 12 miles off the coast. And 12 miles was not too bad for the foreign ships, because a lot of Alaskan waters are fairly shallow for the fishing for crab in particular and halibut. Then they changed the law to make it 200 miles offshore, and at that point, we didn't quite know how we were going to enforce it, because it was pretty much everything we could do to go out to 12 miles. When we had gone from three miles to 12 that was pretty rugged, and now that distance out there was a real problem.

Paul Stillwell: That was when you were Commandant that it went to 200.[*]

Admiral Siler: That's right. It went to 12 miles when we were up there, though. In fact, it was called the Bartlett Law because Senator Bartlett was, I guess, the first senator of

---

[*] The Fishery Conservation and Management Act of 1976 claims for the United States exclusive authority over fishing resources in zones extending 200 miles from the country's territorial seas. The territorial seas extend three miles outward from coastlines.

Alaska, and he had been the congressional representative before that, the way they have for Puerto Rico.*

Paul Stillwell: That's right. Alaska was just recently become a state by then.

Admiral Siler: Yes. And we had quite a lot of difficulty just enforcing that, but we kept busy and were able to take care of it fairly well until they started thinking about 200 miles, and then we didn't know what we were going to do about that. There was not much we could do because the ships just couldn't cover that much area, and our airplanes wouldn't cover that much area either. We had the four HU-16s in Kodiak but no C-130s at all. The first time we had C-130s was when we brought them in because of the Cuban Missile Crisis.†

Paul Stillwell: What was the connection? Why would Alaska need them in that case?

Admiral Siler: At the time of the Cuban Missile Crisis we were told to keep track of every Russian vessel in Alaskan waters. They said, "Don't expect the Navy to help you, because they're going to be trying to keep track of all the submarines that are farther offshore, and so they're not going to be looking at fishing vessels." I was called by the duty officer when this highly classified message came in telling us to keep track of everything. I took a look at it and called the chief of operations, and he called the chief of staff and the admiral. So we were all in there thinking about it, and I drafted a message that said, "We need—" I think it was 12 C-130s. After I drafted the message, the admiral cleared it and we sent the message. We all went home figuring, "Well, we'd told them what to start thinking about, and then nothing's going to happen right away."

The next morning we had a C-130 en route, so I got on the phone and told my wife, "Pack a suitcase for me. I'm going on some duty, and I'm not sure when I'll be

---

* Edward L. "Bob" Bartlett, a Democrat, served as delegate from the territory of Alaska from 3 January 1945 to 3 January 1959. Upon Alaska's statehood, he served as a U.S. Senator from 3 January 1959 until his death on 11 December 1968.
† The Cuban Missile Crisis was triggered in mid-October 1962, when a U.S. reconnaissance plane photographed a Soviet nuclear missile site in Cuba and the presence of Soviet bombers.

back." She didn't know quite what to do, except I didn't know how long I'd be gone. I wasn't going to tell her where I was going, because everything so far had been at least top secret. I went out on the way to the airport, stopped by the house and picked up my suitcase, and took the commercial airliner to Cordova. We had sent a message to the C-130 that was coming up from San Francisco to pick me up in Cordova. I got off the commercial flight in Cordova, and just about then the C-130 arrived from San Francisco. I got on that, and we started counting the Russian ships.

Paul Stillwell: So you went on the first patrol?

Admiral Siler: Yes, but it wasn't truly a patrol. It was just the en route flight from San Francisco to Cordova to Kodiak. By this time we'd gotten the second message which said Hawaii was to send a C-130 too. The only trouble was, before it got to Kodiak it had lost an engine, so we had to have a second C-130 from Hawaii come up with an engine to replace it. We got the engine changed on that airplane after the first ships had left Cuba with the missiles aboard. By that time the captain in Kodiak had said, "Come on. Let's go to the club." [Laughter] So we were at the club when the report of the patrol on this first C-130 was completed by that San Francisco airplane.

When he called me with his report, I said, "Well, thank you very much. You can go home." [Laughter] That was all there was to it. But it was a real hot few hours there before we were settled down again.

Paul Stillwell: Well, the speed with which you got those planes indicates the seriousness of the situation.

Admiral Siler: I'm afraid that's right. It certainly didn't indicate with the first one that we would ever get C-130s. And, of course, now they have a large number of C-130s in Kodiak. I really don't know how many they have. All of the HU-16s are gone from Alaska. The only thing they have at Sitka is helicopters.

Paul Stillwell: Well, anything more on Alaska before we move you to sunny Florida?

Admiral Siler: No, I think that's about it.

Paul Stillwell: Well, that was another dramatic change in climate for you.

Admiral Siler: Wasn't it?

Paul Stillwell: You went down there as exec and then became the skipper during that tour.

Admiral Siler: Yes. I was exec for a short period of time, and then Captain Sansbury was ordered out, and I became CO.*

Paul Stillwell: Well, you had been CO of an air station before. Was this a bigger one that it had a captain for a CO?

Admiral Siler: Oh, yes. This was a much bigger air station than Corpus Christi. In fact, when I arrived in Miami we had ten HU-16s, and we would park them with the wingtips that far apart.

Paul Stillwell: Two feet, a foot and a half?

Admiral Siler: Yes. They were parked very carefully and never with the engines running. Of course, they would run up the engines in that position, but to get them into that position they would just be parked and moved with tractors. The first operations in Miami were all water operations. We never had runways. We operated in the bay there in Miami, but the station was at Dinner Key, which had been where the PanAm Clippers operated years before. By this time the recreational boats were very frequently a problem because of the airplane operations, particularly at night when it became a real problem.

---

* Captain Lemuel C. Sansbury, USCG.

But at night we would send out our boats and put down float lights that would mark a runway, and they'd better stay out of that.

Paul Stillwell: What do you remember about the administrative part of the job?

Admiral Siler: The first time that I had a real administrative problem was when a young man came in and said, "I'm gay. I want out." We got him off the station within the next two or three hours and moved him to the Miami base, where they had all of the ability to discharge him within as short a period as possible. Most of the time we had just small disciplinary problems. The administrative part of the station was not a very difficult operation. Most of those people on a bigger air station take care of their own problems and don't get up to the CO and exec very often.

Paul Stillwell: That's what chief petty officers are for.

Admiral Siler: Right. Take him out behind the barn. [Laughter]

Paul Stillwell: You said you had about 100 men in Corpus Christi. About how large a group did you have in Miami?

Admiral Siler: About double that.

Paul Stillwell: What made the difference? Did you have a bigger area to cover?

Admiral Siler: Yes, and the fact that the Cubans were making noises all the time. There were times when we had flown patrols and discovered that ammunition and supplies to support an operation were stored on the Bahama Islands, preparing to make an invasion into Cuba or something of that nature. We would make patrols probably about ten times a week that would be around the Bahama Islands and in sight of Cuba. We patrolled the coast of Cuba all the time.

Paul Stillwell: What were you looking for?

Admiral Siler: Well, for one thing we wanted to make certain that the Cubans who were now in the United States and were the dissidents weren't trying to start an operation against the Cubans which would be identified as American-based. We were also trying to make certain that those people who did that sort of thing weren't based in the Bahamas, because the Bahamas didn't have very much at that time. They have far more than they did then. If they based an operation in the Bahamas, we needed to know about it so that we could get them calmed down before they did anything.

Paul Stillwell: Wanted to avoid another embarrassment like the Bay of Pigs.*

Admiral Siler: That's right. Had that very much in mind then. Coast Guard intelligence was in touch with CIA all the time. The man who bought our house when we left was CIA, and he had orders the week after he bought the house to go to Laos. [Laughter]

Paul Stillwell: So he had a house in Florida. [Laughter]

Admiral Siler: Yes. Fortunately the real estate man bought it from the CIA man.

Paul Stillwell: Were there, in fact, any uprisings that did have to be damped down?

Admiral Siler: Not while I was there, but we very frequently saw CIA boats, never any identification on them. We saw lots of Russian vessels, but I don't think there was anything that ever amounted to anything.

Paul Stillwell: You got a commendation for Cuban exodus operations in October and November of 1965. What do you recall about that operation?

---

* In mid-April 1961 a force of 1,400 Cuban exiles, secretly trained by U.S. personnel in Guatemala, landed in the Bay of Pigs, on the southwestern coast of Cuba, in an attempt to overthrow Fidel Castro, that nation's Communist dictator. The invasion attempt was a disaster. President John Kennedy decided that U.S. naval intervention would worsen the situation, so ships and aircraft offshore were prohibited from taking part.

Admiral Siler: At that time there was an exodus out of Cuban waters, and they were taking any kind of junk they could sort of identify as a boat. Half of them were ready to sink any minute. There was one time when we had an Assistant Secretary of State, the district commander, somebody from USIA, and we outlined the trip we were going to take, which included a stop in Naval Air Station, Key West.* Flying over some of the little islands and keys that the refugees used all the time in the Bahamas, I don't think we made any flight the way it was scheduled. But we satisfied them and then some, because the first thing we did was we had a helicopter from our station, working on a Coast Guard cutter out there, and we worked with them for a little while so that our passengers could see how we worked together on that. The only thing we did that was on the schedule was land at Key West.

Paul Stillwell: What could you do in these leaky boat situations?

Admiral Siler: Usually bring a helicopter in close, and that's about it.

Paul Stillwell: You put swimmers in the water to pull people out?

Admiral Siler: Not in those days.

Paul Stillwell: What was the procedure?

Admiral Siler: They would lower the rescue basket from the helicopter and hope they got in in a safe manner. One of the things that you worried about most was getting too many people in one of those baskets. If three people tried to get in, for example, you probably would overpower the hoist. It was an electric hoist with a wire cable, and you could either part some strands of the cable or actually overpower the winch. It was supposedly rated at 600 pounds, I think, but it was pretty heavy.

---

* USIA—United States Information Agency.

Paul Stillwell: So you flew these patrols fairly steadily just to keep track of the situation?

Admiral Siler: We flew one every day, and then we would fly some of the other ones every two days or every three days. It was possible that we could have as many as three planes on patrol at one time. It was an interesting operation to see that number of planes taxiing out on the water to make the takeoffs and then fly out all the way around the patrol area that we had for the daily patrol.

Paul Stillwell: And then what was the procedure if they did spot somebody in trouble to get a helicopter there?

Admiral Siler: Well, we didn't have helicopters that could operate all the way from Dinner Key out to where they'd see them so usually it was a matter of getting boats there.

Paul Stillwell: I see. So your ops officers was kept pretty busy during this time.

Admiral Siler: Yes, indeed.

Paul Stillwell: What specifically was your role during that period in coordinating these things?

Admiral Siler: Well, I was exec to begin with. I was trying to make certain that everything administratively would operate to make it possible to carry out patrols and the other things that would be necessary. Then, when I became the commanding officer, I was going to the meetings that the admiral had once a week, and they were talking about a request that had come in from the Air Force to operate from our new base at Opa-Locka. And my thought was, "If we get in by that time." I may even have said that.

The admiral or the chief of staff, one of the two, said, "We'd better be in by that time."

So I went back to the air station and said, "We're going to be, I think."

[Laughter]

Paul Stillwell: Just flows downhill.

Admiral Siler: Yes. When we moved to Opa-Locka, I flew the last plane out of Dinner Key, and as we got ready to get in the air we got a message from one of the helicopters that had been operating at Baker's Haulover, which is just at North Miami Beach, and that they had an engine failure and had landed on the water. That didn't mean anything too much, since the helicopter had a boat hull, except that it should have been towed in by that point in the operation, because if it had to be landed on the water the chances were it was getting metal chips in the engine oil. So we knew it was somewhere in the water there, and I figured, "Well, I've got an airborne fixed wing. I'll fly over and see what his position and condition are." I never got over it, because I got an engine oil problem before I got there. So I turned toward the field. I had a questionable engine on that HU-16, but it was a whole lot easier to work on when we were in the much bigger stations at Opa-Locka than at Dinner Key.

Paul Stillwell: Was that the reason for moving to Opa-Locka?

Admiral Siler: Yes. But the other main reason was we didn't have to operate on the water. The corrosion of the airplanes when they were operated off the water all the time was really tremendous. We got one in Corpus Christi that came from Miami, and I'm sure that they thought it was in very good condition. There was corrosion all over the place, because while we operated immediately beside the bay in Corpus Christi we didn't operate on the water all the time and get the spray all the time.

Paul Stillwell: When you were in that job, what was your interaction with the district commander?

Admiral Siler: Well, the district commander was in a downtown building, and he'd come down to the air station at times and particularly when there were social functions. And we had, I guess, the only Coast Guard place that you could have social functions there at the officers' club, at one of the buildings there at the air station. Of course, that went by the wayside when we moved to Opa-Locka, but we fixed it up so we had a place at Opa-Locka.

Paul Stillwell: So then you had to move all the gear and spare parts and everything else to Opa-Locka as well.

Admiral Siler: We started moving pretty well ahead of time so that we finally flew the planes out on the 27th of October, which I remember because that's our wedding anniversary. [Laughter] And which year would that have been?

Paul Stillwell: Well, by August of '66 you were at the National War College.

Admiral Siler: Yes, I was. It would have been '65 that we moved there. It was the end of the operation then in saltwater all the time.

Paul Stillwell: Well, there are all these concerns now about immigration of Cuban refugees. We heard about the Elian Gonzalez case that got so much publicity.* What was the immigration stance at that time for the people that you rescued?

Admiral Siler: I think it was pretty much the same.

Paul Stillwell: They would be taken back to Cuba?

Admiral Siler: I don't think so. The great majority of them would be examined by the immigration, and I'm not sure what they did with them after that. But there were a

---

* In November 1999 a Cuban boy named Elian Gonzalez was rescued near Florida when he survived a boat crossing in which his mother and ten others drowned while trying to escape from Cuba. The incident set off a seven-month international custody battle when the boy's father wanted him to return to Cuba. On 28 June 2000, after a great deal of maneuvering by the U.S. Justice Department, the boy and his father flew from Florida to Cuba.

number of them at some time they were interrogated, and it was determined that Castro had sent his outcasts up to the United States.*

Paul Stillwell: Well, that was particularly the case in 1980 when they had the Mariel boatlift I remember.†

Admiral Siler: Yes. That was just the second. The first one didn't have nearly as much publicity, but we were taking an awful lot of people out of there.

Paul Stillwell: Which says something about the repressive nature of the regime that that many people would try to escape.

Admiral Siler: Yes, very definitely.

Paul Stillwell: What do you remember about other types of search and rescue cases, just the routine things there?

Admiral Siler: We had quite a few helicopter incidents. Some of them were strictly routine, and then there was one that I recall particularly because they had a failure on the windshield wiper. It threw a nut up in a way that it went into the turbine. The helicopter we had at that time, the old H-52, had only one engine so that when it threw the nut from the windshield wiper up in the air and into that engine, they were on the water very quickly.‡

---

* Castro has been Prime Minister of Cuba since 16 February 1959.
† From 1 April to 25 September 1980 the Coast Guard was heavily involved in dealing with a massive migration of Cuban refugees in an operation known as the Mariel boatlift. More than 100,000 Cubans sought to reach the United States in boats that were often poorly equipped for the voyage. In all, the Coast Guard assisted 1,387 vessels. For details, see Alex Larzelere, The 1980 Cuban Boatlift (Washington D.C.: National Defense University Press, 1988).
‡ The HH-52 is the Coast Guard version of the Sikorsky S-62 commercial helicopter. It entered Coast Guard service in January 1963 as a search-and-rescue helo. The aircraft had a rotor diameter of 53 feet; length of 45 feet, gross weight of 8,300 pounds, and top speed of 109 miles per hour.

Paul Stillwell: That was a freak accident.

Admiral Siler: Yes, indeed. But in order to get that out of the water and where it could be worked on, we had to tow it a long distance to get it back to our facilities. They had to make a powerless landing, which is a neat thing to do. Usually there was a lot of rotation, and he had to make a very quick turn into the wind in the area just south of Miami itself. After he made the safe landing, then I think they got it onto the beach somehow. How they did that I'm not quite sure.

Paul Stillwell: There's a lot of recreational boating in that area and fisherman as well, so you probably had some business from them.

Admiral Siler: A lot of recreational boating. Nowhere near as much commercial fishing as some other places like Alaska and Corpus Christi where there's shrimp boats.

Paul Stillwell: But the commercial fishermen are more likely to know what they're doing and avoid getting trouble.

Admiral Siler: That's right.

Paul Stillwell: What else about that place do you want to put on the record?

Admiral Siler: Well, there was one incident that I certainly ought to highlight, and that's the fire on the Yarmouth Castle just about the time that we moved into the station at Opa-Locka.* Before we had an intercom system or a telephone system, I don't think there was an alarm system that was set up in Opa-Locka. We got a telephone call from the district office that the Yarmouth Castle was on fire and that they were going to need some helicopters to cover.

---

* SS Yarmouth Castle was a passenger ship built in 1927. During an overnight cruise on 13 November 1965 from Miami to Nassau, a fire started in a storeroom on the main deck and spread quickly throughout the ship, which sank as a result. In the tragedy 89 people were killed.

The duty officer got the phone call from the district, but there was no PA system and no alarm system so he ran out to the gate into Opa-Locka. Told the gate watch to close the gate and secure it, go to the barracks, and wake up everybody. That was the only way that they could work it at that particular time because of the fact that the captain or the chief of the staff, one of the two had said, "They'd better be there on the date of the Air Force exercise." So we were at Opa-Locka, but we weren't in very good shape. We got, I think, something like three helicopters airborne that night, and they were all the H-52s. They were operating with their rotors about that far from the mainstays on the Yarmouth Castle.

Paul Stillwell: About two feet maybe.

Admiral Siler: Not much more than that if that. And it was hoisting onto the helicopters quite a few people who were burned, and then they were taken into the hospital. And there wasn't much sleep that night for anybody.

Paul Stillwell: Did any cutters go out to the rescue as well?

Admiral Siler: Oh, yes, but the first thing that had to be done was get the helicopters out there to get people who were burned. There were quite a few people on the Yarmouth Castle who were burned badly. I'm not sure if any died, but it was largely because of that that the National Transportation Safety Board for many years had as a member at least one Coast Guard officer. The first one was the admiral there in Miami after he was the investigating officer, the official investigating officer. When it was first investigated it was Admiral L. M. Thayer.[*] He gave speeches for a period of about a year of that incident and the things that led up to the fire. And then he became a member of the National Transportation Safety Board, and he was followed by a Coast Guard aviator who didn't have it very long. Then Admiral Pat Bursley, who was the chief counsel of

---

[*] Rear Admiral Louis M. Thayer, USCG.

the Coast Guard when I was Commandant, became a member of the National Transportation Safety Board.*

Paul Stillwell: So again you have safety regulations growing out of an accident.

Admiral Siler: Oh, yes. In fact many of the rules that have to do with the inspection of passenger vessels in the United States grew out of that Yarmouth Castle fire.

Paul Stillwell: Well, anything else on Miami that you'd want to mention?

Admiral Siler: No, I think that's about it on Miami.

Paul Stillwell: Then you went back to school for a year. The National War College is usually for those who are captains that are expected to be on their way up, so that was a feather in your cap.

Admiral Siler: Well, I'm not sure that was always the case then. Having been on a board to select people to do that, I think sometimes it's a matter of selecting someone who has not been to a whole bunch of other schools, and that was true with me too. I hadn't been to a bunch of schools. I think sometimes the selection to the National War College could be better if they allowed people to go who had been to some other schools, but I'm happy that I made it.

Paul Stillwell: In what ways was it useful professionally for you?

Admiral Siler: The contacts that you make with military officers from the other services were at least an important aspect of the war college. One of my classmates and my roommate on the field trip we made to South America was Tom Hayward, CNO of the

---

* Rear Admiral G. H. Patrick Bursley, USCG (Ret.), was a member of the National Transportation Safety Board in the 1980s. For more on the NTSB in his tenure see the Naval Institute oral history of Vice Admiral Donald D. Engen, USN (Ret.).

Navy.[*] Two of the Chiefs of Staff of the Army were in our class, Shy Meyer and John Wickham.[†] And there was an Army general who was out in the Tacoma area when I was Commandant. We were trying to set up a loran station and a loran chain down the West Coast at that time, because we were about to bring oil out of Alaska, and we wanted to be able to tell exactly where those ships were. In order to get the geography correct we needed to have something pretty much in the location of McChord Air Base or Fort Lewis. Our Coast Guard admiral in Seattle kept trying to call the Army general who was there at Fort Lewis and couldn't even get him to answer the phone. When he told me who it was, I said, "Just a minute," to let me try. I called and he answered the phone immediately. He was a classmate.

Paul Stillwell: Was this when you were Commandant?

Admiral Siler: Yes. And he said, "I'm sure we can find the space and a station location that will work. It may not be right where they had proposed." And, in fact, they eventually went up over the Cascades to find something just on the east side of the Cascades rather than being on the west side, but it worked just fine. Everything was taken care of by the one phone call. That was just one example, and it could work any number of times with that kind of relationship. The relationships at the war college are close enough that it'll always work.

Paul Stillwell: Well, it probably worked the other way too. Some people that you had known back then needed some help from the Coast Guard when you were Commandant.

Admiral Siler: Well, if they did I hope we took care of them. [Laughter]

Paul Stillwell: What do you remember about that trip to South America? Admiral

---

[*] Captain Thomas B. Hayward. As a four-star admiral Hayward later served as Chief of Naval Operations from 1978 to 1982. His Naval Institute oral history includes an account of his time at the National War College and the perils of the trip to South America.

[†] General Edward C. Meyer, USA, served as Army Chief of Staff from 22 June 1979 to 21 June 1983. General John A. Wickham, Jr., USA, was Chief of Staff from 23 July 1983 to 23 June 1987.

Hayward mentioned there was a terrifying bus ride at one point.

Admiral Siler: Oh, yes, indeed. That was in Guatemala, and the place where everyone goes there is Chichicastenago. I think I mentioned that before. But Chichicastenago is the place where they have the burnt incense and burnt offerings on the steps of the Catholic Church. We went there, and then we were going to lunch at Lake Atitlan as everyone did. The bus was a fairly new General Motors engine and chassis, and I don't know what the body was but a fairly comfortable bus. The driver realized that he had problems with the brake system on the bus, and he had brought along a helper, because he thought he was going to have to back and fill several times getting down the valley and back up again to Chichicastenango. He didn't have to do that, but now he was headed toward Lake Atitlan, which is down in a valley, and you have make quite a descent to get there.

He tried to get his helper to grab some of the chocks that he had available in the front part of the bus and leap out and throw those in front of the wheel. And the helper said, "You think I'm crazy?" or words to that effect, because he wasn't about to go out. So the bus driver decided the only thing he could do was to get into the embankment next to the road. He did that, and he just ricocheted off and went back into the road and picked up some more speed. He tried it again and the second time he took enough impact on the left front wheel that he took that wheel completely off. It lodged under the left rear wheel and stopped the bus (slap) like that. Of course, at that point everyone was jerked, but the bus was up about like this. Felt like it was about 45 degrees, but it obviously wasn't.

There was one of the National War College group who had been an Olympic 400-meter runner at one time, but he was now a State Department employee, a black man. I think for his first assignment after the war college he went to be the ambassador to Lesotho, Botswana, and just one other little country like that in there that he was ambassador to at the same time. But at this point he was just one more student. He was at the back door trying to get that back door open. He was thrown backward, and he cracked a vertebra. He didn't know till he started walking down the hill to the place where we were going to have lunch. I think he got a ride before he'd gotten very far, but anyway he was probably the worst injured in the group except for Doc Blanchard, the famous football player.* He got up and grabbed this helper out of the way and leaped out of the front door, and he tore his trousers and skinned his hands and his knee.

Paul Stillwell: He wasn't going to depend on Providence to stop the bus.

Admiral Siler: Well, he was sure not. Most of the rest of us were pretty wide-awake at this point, but we'd sort of drowsed off beforehand because it was a fairly long ride from Chichicastenango to Lake Atitlin. We decided that we were not going to telephone our wives, because they would guess that the thing we weren't telling was that someone was injured. If we just waited until everyone got home and walked in the door then we could tell all we wanted to. [Laughter]

Paul Stillwell: What was the value of that trip? What things did you learn in the various stops you made?

Admiral Siler: I think that that was very valuable to those of us who were not in the State Department in particular, because while the people in the State Department had seen this kind of operation with all of the different commands that are in an embassy, we now knew that this is the way it worked. We were in several places briefed in the classified spaces in the embassy where we knew that anything that we wanted to say was off the record. It gave us an opportunity to see how an embassy works.

Paul Stillwell: How had you gone on that particular trip instead of, say, to Europe or the Far East?

Admiral Siler: There were the five groups divided up approximately equally with each group going to a different area: Europe, the Middle East, the Far East, South America and Africa. Africa was the least popular one. I think some people were drafted to go to

---

* Colonel Felix A. "Doc" Blanchard, USA. While a cadet at the Military Academy, he had won the Heisman Trophy as college football's outstanding player in the 1945 season

Africa. I chose South America because I had studied Spanish before, and I figured I'd have most to do with Latin America anyway. I don't know whether that was necessarily true because the shipping regulations were pretty much worldwide. But at least I knew a little more about Latin America, and I wrote my paper at that time on the efforts of Argentina, Venezuela, and Brazil toward Coast Guard-type operations with their navies or whatever they were. Of course, in Argentina they have pretty much a Coast Guard. Brazil separates out its Coast Guard. But Venezuela just treats them as a part of the Navy. So it was something that fit closer to what I had studied before.

Paul Stillwell: What conclusions did you draw in your paper?

Admiral Siler: That we should have at least some liaison at SouthCom who would know Coast Guard operations and be able to say, "Well, if they have a liaison officer assigned to that embassy they'll make more progress."* When we went to the Panamanian SouthCom I didn't say anything to the general, but there was one of our classmates. In fact he was the man who wrote the op order for the effort to rescue the prisoners from Iran, Jim Vaught.† This guy was known as Springbutt. He always had a question.

Paul Stillwell: That term is not applied approvingly, or it's sort of a condemnation that these are people who are trying to show off by asking so many questions.

Admiral Siler: Yes. This guy did not have a college degree, and so he was showing everyone up by showing how well he paid attention and why he had questions.

Paul Stillwell: Well, as you page through your yearbook do you see any others with whom you developed relationships?

---

* The U.S. Southern Command was then based in Panama.
† In an effort to rescue American hostages held in Iran, on 26 April 1980 six Air Force C-130 cargo planes and eight Navy RH-53D helicopters flew to Iran with a joint-service commando team embarked. The aircraft rendezvoused at Desert One, a site 200 miles from the Iranian capital of Teheran. Because of helicopter problems, the mission was canceled. Several servicemen were killed in the futile rescue attempt. Lieutenant Colonel James B. Vaught, USA, at the time he was at the National War College.

Admiral Siler: No, not very much. Well, there's one who later became the executive secretary for the Panama Canal, and while I was Commandant, he suggested that perhaps I would like to be a member of the Panama Canal Board while it was still American. We still exchange Christmas cards to this day. He left the Panama Canal Board shortly after it became Panamanian. A great majority of these people became flag officers sooner or later, of course the military. I mean, the State Department people didn't become flag officers in the same way. They got higher grades. Jim Vaught was the one responsible for having only one spare helicopter, and that was the problem. They didn't have quite enough helicopters. He made colonel before we finished at the war college, and he was, I think, at least a brigadier general when he was working on the evacuation of the hostages. He retired as a lieutenant general. He now lives in Charleston.

Paul Stillwell: Did pretty well for no college. [Laughter]

Admiral Siler: That's right. Well, he was a thinker, and we didn't always agree with his thoughts, but at least he was busy thinking.

Paul Stillwell: What do you remember about the content of the lectures?

Admiral Siler: Most of them were very, very interesting. At times we'd have Chinese people who spoke of Mao Tse-tung, and at other times we'd be dealing with a different part of the world and talk about the philosophy of life that you'd see in the Far East or something like that, or the Middle East.[*] I thought that the lectures were very good, and I think we had Eisenhower as a lecturer at one time.[†] And we had the head of the old Bureau of Budget. He said that he was one of the few people that one night he said, "Point nine," he meant $900,000.

Paul Stillwell: Vietnam was a hot topic at the time. How much was that discussed?

---

[*] Mao Tse-tung was head of the Communist Party in the People's Republic of China from the time the Communists seized power in 1949 until his death in 1976.
[†] Dwight E. Eisenhower had been President from 1953 to 1961.

Admiral Siler: Very much. A good many of the people who were there had served in Vietnam, and if they had not served at that time a good many of them served afterward. In fact, John Wickham, who was later the Army Chief of Staff, went just afterward and was wounded very severely when they rolled a grenade into his tent wherever he was. It went off, and he was full of shrapnel for some time. There were several of them who had already served in Vietnam.

Paul Stillwell: Did you get lectures in logistics and planning?

Admiral Siler: To some extent, yes.

Paul Stillwell: Was it more geopolitical?

Admiral Siler: It was more political than anything else.

Paul Stillwell: The Middle East Six-Day War occurred right at the end of your time there.* Was that discussed at all?

Admiral Siler: I can't remember now whether it was or not.

Paul Stillwell: Certainly the war college would have a broadening effect for you who had been mostly in straight Coast Guard assignments up to that time.

Admiral Siler: Yes. There was a great deal that was completely new to me. Some of it, the lectures that we had were amusing. We had the man who was at that time the superintendent of education of California; he spoke on the problems of educating young people. He practically said, "We can probably do best in education if we concentrate on reading, writing, and arithmetic." [Laughter]

---

* The Six-Day War of June 1967 grew out of Egypt's action in closing the Gulf of Aqaba and moving troops into the Sinai Peninsula. Israel initiated the war on 5 June with air attacks on airbases in Syria, Jordan, and Egypt. In the days that followed Israeli forces completely defeated their Arab opponents and occupied the Golan Heights, West Bank of the Jordan River, the Sinai, and the east bank of the Suez Canal.

Paul Stillwell: A lot of people are a little short on some of those basics today.

Admiral Siler: Yes. And he spoke in such a convincing way that I think a large number of us would have voted for him for the head of education in Washington, D.C., at that point instead of just California.

Paul Stillwell: Was there a social side of this also, to foster the relationships you've talked about?

Admiral Siler: Oh, yes. We were assigned to study groups in rooms where we would get together in the morning and check the latest in the newspapers and so on. That particular room was supposed to have at least one social function during the time that they were in that room, which was I think usually a month. Whoever was the one whose turn it was would have a social function for that group in his home during that month. So we got to know people socially as well as at the school.

Paul Stillwell: Did the groups change to foster still more of this?

Admiral Siler: Yes. We changed. Every month there would be a change in the organization. I don't know what order they used to do that, but we were with a different group every month.

Paul Stillwell: Then you probably got in with still another group when you went on your South American trip.

Admiral Siler: It didn't make any difference where you'd been before. You were assigned to the group that happened to make it, and since there were five groups some of the people I know did not get their first choice. I got my first, but one of my neighbors was an Air Force man who was largely oriented toward radar and computers and things of determining the impact of atomic explosions around the world. He went to Africa and was not too happy with it.

Paul Stillwell: When you came back from these trips did you have a debriefing so that you could find out what the other groups had discovered?

Admiral Siler: Yes. Each group put on a program that was about an hour in length telling what kind of experiences they'd had and what they'd learned. Some of our experiences were particularly interesting. That case of nearly going over the cliff with us was a very interesting one. One group that went to Yugoslavia was confined to their hotel room while tanks went by out on the street. It was also the same group I guess it was went to Israel and the Israelis showed them movies of an Israeli plane shooting down—I don't know what country it was at that time. But the Israelis were showing how good they were, and there was not much argument about it.

Paul Stillwell: Well, they proved it very soon thereafter in that war against Egypt and Syria.

Admiral Siler: Yes. I think it was a Syrian plane that was shot down.

Paul Stillwell: Any other specific memories that you want to add from the trip to South America?

Admiral Siler: Oh, one thing that I should say about our stop in Panama, which was a rather short stop. We were addressed by the Panamanian foreign office—whatever they called it there. I don't recall whether it was in answer to a question or a simple statement, but he said, "We know that the United States likes to have the Panama Canal. We would like to have it back as a Panamanian stronghold, but we know how you feel about it, so we're not going to push it." Of course, when Jimmy Carter said, "Here it is," why—

Paul Stillwell: They took it.

Admiral Siler: Yes. They said, "Okay. Thank you." *

Paul Stillwell: You also got a master's degree at that time from George Washington University. What was involved in that?

Admiral Siler: Well, I didn't get my degree as soon as the rest of the class did. Most of the class would take classes at GW, which were held after the regular courses were finished at the National War College. Then, during a period of about six weeks at the end, they would take the rest of the courses that they needed to get their master's degree in international affairs. I was not allowed to stay there for the extra weeks. I had to get to Coast Guard headquarters and save the Coast Guard or something like that. [Laughter] But, anyway, I went to the Coast Guard immediately, and so I spent the next year taking courses at GW.

Paul Stillwell: Did you take those at night then?

Admiral Siler: Yes, after the regular workday was over I'd take a bus over either to the Pentagon or sometimes it was a place where other Department of Defense facilities were available.

Paul Stillwell: Did you have to write a separate paper for that course?

Admiral Siler: No. The paper that we wrote for the National War College was accepted. Oh, we had to take courses that were the fulfillment to the international affairs degree. We took one course that I recall particularly was a course in anthropology, and the instructor in that spent about as much time telling us how to make alcoholic beverages as

---

* On 7 September 1977, President Omar Torrijos of Panama and President Jimmy Carter of the United States signed a new Panama Canal Treaty. It specified that the United States would transfer full control of the canal to Panama on 31 December 1999. The treaty did away with the Panama Canal Company, the Canal Zone, and its government as of 1 October 1979. The Panama Canal Commission then operated the canal during the 20-year transition period that began with the treaty.

he did on any other area of anthropology. I think he went to Saudi Arabia and some places in that part of the world where alcoholic beverages were not available, so they made their own. [Laughter]

Paul Stillwell: Well, it sounds as if that was a very useful year for you at the war college.

Admiral Siler: Very much. I was very pleased to have that with me.

Paul Stillwell: Well, we're right near the end of this tape.

Interview Number 4 with Admiral Owen W. Siler, U.S. Coast Guard (Retired)
Place: Admiral Siler's home in Savannah, Georgia
Date: Wednesday, 13 December 2000
Interviewer: Paul Stillwell

Paul Stillwell: Admiral, we wrapped the discussion up yesterday through your time as a student at the National War College. I wonder if you had anything that you've since thought of from that or any previous tours of duty.

Admiral Siler: I just wonder if we've spoken enough of the tour of duty in Corpus Christi, where we flew around the Gulf of Mexico. Unfortunately, several of those planes aborted and went into Mexico and had several days' attacks of Montezuma's revenge. I remember one in particular when the pilot came back looking as if he weighed ten pounds less at least. [Laughter] Then there was one time when the plane made an offshore landing to pick up one of the crew members of one of the shrimp boats, and that plane came back with a good many dents down the side of the airplane. Those offshore landings can be quite stressful, both on the airplanes and the individuals. I think that's the only thing that I've thought of that needed to be added.

Paul Stillwell: Well, you said yesterday you didn't get to complete the full course for your master's degree because you were needed at Coast Guard headquarters. What was the urgency to get you there?

Admiral Siler: Routine. [Laughter] There was nothing that I saw that would have demanded my presence, but it was just the policy that the Coast Guard would not extend you at the additional course at George Washington.

Paul Stillwell: Well, please tell me about the new job you moved into.

Admiral Siler: The job initially was called the administrative management division, and we cleared a good deal of the paperwork that was generated. When it was going out as an all-service notice, it was always cleared by this division. And we maintained the master files of all the paperwork that was done. Then before too long we started a study of how we could lessen the workload of the chief of staff of the Coast Guard. He was a workaholic, and he was trying to get through such an awful lot of paperwork that he couldn't handle it all.

Paul Stillwell: Who was that?

Admiral Siler: Mark Whalen.* He later became the Pacific Area Commander. The solution that we came up with involved not only my division but the other division that the chief of staff supervised, which was the program analysis division headed by my good friend, Ed Scheiderer, who is a retired rear admiral now.† We thought that the responsibility for the divisions that were under the cognizance of the chief of staff could be simplified somewhat by dividing them with the PPB, planning, programming and budgeting in the area of consideration of a captain who would send that material then to the chief of staff with material that was fully reviewed and analyzed by that captain.

The management analysis was under my cognizance and a couple of other areas. One of the things that obviously was a matter of concern was the way the building was run. The captain who was in charge of the building actually had the title of the commanding officer of all the enlisted personnel in the building, and so his division was given a new title and became the headquarters services, I think it was. Then we took all the computer services and put them under the management analysis, and that then was going to be headed by another captain.

When we made the final briefing for the Commandant, who was then Admiral Smith, he knew that we had also been looking at the possibility of if we ever came to the one-star rank for admirals that somehow we needed to have something under the chief of

---

* Rear Admiral Mark A. Whalen, USCG.
† Rear Admiral Edward D. Scheiderer, USCG.

staff who was still rather senior.* He said, "Those people should be considered as one-star billets." We never got the one-star that time, but we came up with a new title of assistant chief of staff, one for PPB and one for management. The man who had been the deputy of chief of staff became the assistant chief of staff for PPB. Then the chief of staff started looking around for someone to head up the other divisions, and I guess the personnel people came up with some suggestions, and he said, "No, I want Siler in that." So I became an assistant chief of staff.

Paul Stillwell: Why do you think you were chosen for that job?

Admiral Siler: I guess he liked me. [Laughter]

Paul Stillwell: Or maybe he didn't like you. [Laughter]

Admiral Siler: Maybe that was true too. But I had responsibility for management analysis, computer services, the building, and I guess that was about it.

Paul Stillwell: Well, these were not areas that you had a lot of experience in, so you had to learn a lot in a hurry.

Admiral Siler: Yes, particularly about the computers. One of the things that we did rather shortly after that was to buy a new computer for the Coast Guard. We had computer services, but they were they were the rather elementary type and we replaced that. And it didn't last too long before the Transportation Department wanted to take over computer services, and so our computers were kept in a rather elementary scale while the department did the greater portion of them.

Paul Stillwell: What computers did you have at that point?

---

* Admiral Willard J. Smith, USCG, served as Commandant of the Coast Guard from 1 June 1966 to 31 May 1970. His oral history is in the Naval Institute collection.

Admiral Siler: I can't remember.

Paul Stillwell: What functions did they perform?

Admiral Siler: Mostly financial services. The one that we had had was an old IBM that was a punch card, and it was well out of date. We replaced it with something that was a lot further up than that, but I can't recall the name of it. It's been too long.

Paul Stillwell: Well, Hewlett-Packard was coming into prominence around that time.

Admiral Siler: We didn't have Hewlett-Packard. It was one of the computer—something computer services.

Paul Stillwell: You mentioned you were in charge of the building. Was the headquarters then where it is now on Second Street, Southwest. It's now down near Fort McNair.

Admiral Siler: It was not there. In fact, the only thing that we had there was a little bit of extra space that was moved into while we were handling special studies.

Paul Stillwell: Was it still on Pennsylvania then as it had been?

Admiral Siler: We moved during that time from the Pennsylvania headquarters to the DoT headquarters at Fourth Street, Southwest. We were given the sixth, seventh, and eighth floors. I think that's right. The ninth floor was the Transportation Department. It was an interesting study for us to determine how much space people really did need. And we outgrew that rather quickly. Much of the reason for outgrowing it was that the department had put new functions in place and wanted to have more reports than we had had before, and at the same time the formation of the Department of Transportation required new functions.

Paul Stillwell: Did bringing in all these computers and so forth lessen the workload for the chief of staff as had been hoped?

Admiral Siler: It was interesting that it functioned about as we had anticipated as long as Admiral Whalen was there. When he was transferred to the Pacific area out in San Francisco, he was replaced by Admiral Tom Sargent, and much of the workload seemed to decrease.* I found before too long after several months with Tom Sargent that I didn't really have enough to do. So one day I walked into the other assistant chief of staff's office and said to him, "Now that we have the situation fairly well in place, how busy are you?"

He said, "Not really busy at all." So we decided that we would propose doing away with the assistant chiefs of staff and have everything under one deputy chief of staff, which we did, and it worked just as well if not better.

Paul Stillwell: And you moved into that new job.

Admiral Siler: Yes. We waited until the other assistant chief of staff retired, which, of course, was the first of July of '69, because he was class of '39.† As soon as he retired, I took over the whole thing, and then we readjusted the offices to handle it that way. At the same time, the department was pushing all the time to take over more and more of our computer functions so that that was reduced.

Oh, one other thing. When I became the deputy chief of staff, there was a requirement for someone in a high level in the Coast Guard to be the supervisor of equal rights. We had a division for equal rights that was reviewing the functions of the Coast Guard to make certain that equal rights were established and carried out in every place. A good many of those people were blacks, of course, because in Washington, D.C., you have so many blacks who are looking for good jobs, and so you have many of the better educated Negroes who look for and take some excellent jobs. The man that was the head of the division in the Coast Guard was a man that I don't think we had any relationship

---

* Rear Admiral Thomas R. Sargent III, USCG.
† This individual was Captain William R. Riedel, USCG.

with at all until we established that organization. But he served for several years, and then he was moved into the Department of Transportation in order to have a higher-level position there.

Paul Stillwell: Do you remember his name?

Admiral Siler: Bill Hudson. I can't tell you the name of the man who has the job now, but he has had it ever since Hudson moved. I became the Civil Rights officer to fill a blank in the organization, but the Civil Rights civilian, a woman, did most of the work.

Paul Stillwell: During the time when you were there, Martin Luther King was assassinated. There was a great racial outburst in Washington, and the National Guard was called out.[*] What are your memories of that experience?

Admiral Siler: Very little. We were not bothered very much by that kind of operation, because we had so many people in positions of importance with the Coast Guard who had worked up because of their abilities. Had some people who probably we'd never tapped their capabilities at all until it became a requirement that we have someone that did this or that and the responsibilities that were assigned to them made the job for them.

Paul Stillwell: Was some of that mandated down from President Johnson and through the Department of Transportation?[†]

Admiral Siler: That could well have been. I was not involved in the initial formation of the department at all, but I came from the National War College to headquarters when the organization had been set, but we still needed to do a lot of smoothing out. I was offered the position once of going to the department and being a division chief in the department, and I turned it down. The man who offered it to me was a Coast Guard rear admiral who had been moved into the position of assistant, I guess, to the administrative assistant

---

[*] Dr. Martin Luther King, Jr., the nation's most prominent civil rights leader, was assassinated in Memphis, Tennessee, on 4 April 1968.
[†] Lyndon B. Johnson served as President of the United States from 22 November 1963 to 20 January 1969.

secretary. He was looking at all of the administrative procedures, and he needed someone that he knew and could trust in one of his divisions and I said, no, I didn't want that. I stayed with the Coast Guard.

Paul Stillwell: Why did you not want to do that?

Admiral Siler: I had some inkling of how it was going to work out, being not a multi-headed person, but you'd have to become a Department of Transportation man rather than Coast Guard officer.

Paul Stillwell: Do you think the change from Treasury to Transportation was beneficial?

Admiral Siler: It was probably beneficial in some ways, but it was very detrimental in other ways. We'd been overshadowed completely by the department. Many of the upper-level people in Transportation were anxious to do their thing. Much of the original organization in the Department of Transportation was FAA-oriented, and there was very little of anything other than FAA.[*] In the second step when once we had thrown these people together and they supposedly formed a Department of Transportation they became a Department of FAA and, oh, yes, Transportation is involving railroads and highways too. The other thing they were very much interested in was urban transportation, and we'd never had anything like that before. So while they were looking for ways to improve urban transportation they very frequently ignored the Coast Guard.

Paul Stillwell: And you said there were a few benefits. What were those?

Admiral Siler: Well, the higher level contacts with the Coast Guard moving into some other contacts with the Office of Management and Budget and things of that sort. And concentration in the multi-organizational setups to have serious looks at how you were going to handle anything that had to do with the oceans. We were contacted and conferred with more frequently than we had been before.

---

[*] FAA—Federal Aviation Administration.

Paul Stillwell: Do you think in the more than 30 years that have passed since then the situation has improved so the Coast Guard's no longer kind of an unwanted stepchild?

Admiral Siler: I don't know whether it's a matter of improvement or what it is. I think the Coast Guard is definitely a part of the Department of Transportation now, simply because, as President Johnson said, "We won't be a department unless we have some big organization like the Coast Guard in it." It was going to be the FAA and, oh, yes, a few other things. I think as long as the Coast Guard is there it balances the FAA's influence in the department.*

Paul Stillwell: What was the impetus to stand that department up in the first place?

Admiral Siler: I think President Johnson wanted to do it right from the first, and he looked for ways to do it. One of the ways was to move big organizations into the department. The Department of Highways used to be just the Federal Roads Organization, and there wasn't a National Highway Traffic Safety Administration. There was no urban transportation organization, and one of the very first things that we were told to do when we were talking with the assistant secretary for administration was that he asked that we write just informal papers on what we believed could be done to improve transportation of all sorts. I remember I wrote about how I had been using the bus for transportation to come to work. Standing out in the weather in Washington, D.C., in all types of weather, very hot at times and very rainy at times, they needed bus shelters for waiting for the buses. And I think a good many of them are in place now. That's something that did take place. The subway system, of course, was still a gleam in somebody's eye, and that was a real step in the right direction as far as I'm concerned.

Paul Stillwell: That really came into being in the mid-'70s. How much interaction did you have with the Commandant while you were in that job?

---

* On 1 March 2003, subsequent to this interview, the Coast Guard transferred from the Department of Transportation to the newly formed Department of Homeland Security.

Admiral Siler: Not a lot. Most of the time it was with the chief of staff, and once in a long while we would make a presentation that we could be involved with the Commandant also. When we set up that organization for the assistant chiefs of staff I was the one who made the presentation to the Commandant, and he said, "I think this makes sense and let's do it." That was one of the few times. It was quite apparent that Admiral Smith didn't like big meetings. He would be briefed, but he would not say, "Let's go that way," or "Let's do that." He'd say when we finished the briefing, "Uh-huh. Thank you," and obviously we were dismissed. Then he would take the briefing material and put a memo at the bottom of the last page with his red ink pen saying what he had decided that we would do. So you wouldn't know for a couple of days how successful you were except that in that particular instance he had said, "We want to do that, and we need to have two assistant chiefs of staff." That didn't last too long either.

Paul Stillwell: What are your memories of working with Admiral Sargent?

Admiral Siler: He was very easy to work with. He was never as busy as Admiral Whalen seemed to be, and so you could get to him and get decisions. It was very easy to work with him. Have you ever heard the story about Admiral Sargent's working in the Pacific?

Paul Stillwell: No.

Admiral Siler: When he was still a captain he was the chief of the civil engineering division, and we were going to put a loran chain in right at the beginning of the Vietnam War. He was ordered to the Pacific to go wherever he needed to to look at the geography and the geometry of loran and see if the stations could be maintained from a logistics point of view. He would check into a BOQ someplace and sign the log as Captain T. R.

Sargent.* The next morning he usually would call for transportation and say, "This is Captain Sargent, and I need a vehicle to go someplace."

Very frequently he would get the answer, "We don't do that for captains," meaning Army or Air Force type. And they would frequently end up with, "What was that name again?" "Captain Sargent."

"Well, we sure don't do it for sergeants." [Laughter] He soon realized that the only way he was going to be successful in getting that transportation was use a false name and have a false rank, [laughter] so he quickly became Colonel Savage. And all through the Pacific he was successful because he was Colonel Savage. [Laughter]

Paul Stillwell: He spoke the language they could understand.

Admiral Siler: That's right.

Paul Stillwell: Do you remember any specific incidents with him when he was the chief of staff?

Admiral Siler: No, I can't remember any particular things because it was so pleasant working with him. When we had problems we'd tell him, and he would work with us to find solutions.

One of the things that happened soon was to talk to him about, "Did we really need this assistant chief of staff organization?"

His response was simply, "Well, let's wait until Bill Riedel retires, and then we'll set it up." One of the reasons for that was that Riedel was just one year junior to him, and it was quite apparent that he was not going to make rear admiral, so when Bill Riedel retired his position was done away with, and I took over the whole thing. The other thing was Bill moved rather quickly into a civilian position in the Coast Guard, a fairly high civilian position, because of his briefings on the same things that he would be concerned with as a civilian. He became, I think, a GS-15, and he was the water resources chairman

---

* BOQ—bachelor officers' quarters.

for the Coast Guard dealing with things like "Will the waterways be blocked by dams?" and things of that nature.*

Paul Stillwell: Was the main effect of that change to get you then into the budgeting part of it?

Admiral Siler: Very largely.

Paul Stillwell: What do you remember about that process?

Admiral Siler: Well, the programs division was very easy to work with, because the man who had it initially was the man that I had worked with in order to establish the division separation of the assistant chiefs of staff. He was Ed Scheiderer, the head of the division having to do with programs. I'd worked with him when we were looking for positions that could possibly be designated as rear admiral lower half or commodore. At that time we called it commodore. We identified some positions that would probably be designated as commodore. Ed became chief of staff when we moved to our own building as part of the department but away from Pennsylvania Avenue, and he was a good chief of staff. But he decided to retire when we were going to give him a district as sort of a stepping-stone to something higher like an area command. He didn't want to go from chief of staff to a district, so that's when he retired.

Paul Stillwell: Were the computers helpful to you in the budgeting process?

Admiral Siler: I think they probably were, but I didn't get involved with that particular aspect of the computers.

Paul Stillwell: Was the budgeting process in that that era—as it has so often been—an allocation of shortages?

---

* GS, for government service, designates a pay grade level within the U.S. Civil Service.

Admiral Siler: Often it was, yes, but that's only partly true, because a very large amount of what the Coast Guard does has to be really programmed years in advance. So it's not too often that it's simply covering shortages. Well, it wasn't then anyway. I think there are few places that it was a matter of covering shortages. When we were required to enforce fisheries out to 200 miles, we talked for a long time about how much we would need in resources, and the Department of Defense was involved very frequently with that. They were concerned that if we went out to 200 miles and had resources to really cover that, there would be confrontations with foreign vessels all the time. We had one or two boardings but never a true confrontation.

Paul Stillwell: Well, the funding is probably going to stay relatively level just because you have an existing infrastructure and existing hardware and existing missions.

Admiral Siler: Yes, but when you extend that mission from 12 miles to 200 miles, there's quite a change in the resources that are necessary to do that. We were immediately given several more C-130s, because they figured that we would be able to locate everything with the C-130s. I don't know how they figured we were going to board those ships to determine what they were doing. [Laughter] And they gave us enough money to reactivate one of the ships that we had put out of commission at the end of Vietnam, and, of course, it was in terrible condition. It made one patrol, but it was a matter of sticking your finger in the dike to keep that thing afloat.

Paul Stillwell: What ship was that?

Admiral Siler: I think it was the Unimak.* It was stationed on the East Coast—I think at New Bedford. After the one patrol they realized that it needed to go in for a major overhaul in the yard. Of course, I'm skipping ahead now because that didn't happen until I was Commandant.

---

* USCGC Unimak (WHEC-379) was the last surviving member of the Casco-class cutters. She had originally been commissioned as a Navy small seaplane tender in 1943. She was decommissioned from the Coast Guard in May 1975, then recommissioned in August 1977 and stationed at New Bedford, Massachusetts, to be used primarily for fisheries patrol.

Paul Stillwell: Right.

Admiral Siler: But in order to get that ship in condition, we had to do a lot of work on it. We proposed building new ships, and there was not any interest in OMB in that at all. Of course, OMB is never interested in anything that costs money.

Paul Stillwell: The 378s had come into the fleet during the 1960s. What's your evaluation of their role and usefulness?

Admiral Siler: Well, they're extremely useful. The armament on them has varied with the ships and with what availability to the yards they had. They're good ships, though.

Paul Stillwell: In the late '60s, when you were deputy chief of staff, what impact on headquarters was there from the Vietnam operations?

Admiral Siler: I think most of those adjustments had been made already. The offer of the 83-footers, 82-footers then, had been accepted, and they had realized how capable those vessels were. Of course, they had been commanded by a chief petty officer, but when they went out there they had a lieutenant and a jaygee. The vessels were quite capable, and, of course, we had some high endurance cutters, too, out there. The 378s put in several tours out there, and the 255s did. We transferred the 255s to the Vietnamese when we knew that we were getting rid of them anyway, and so we didn't need those ships anymore.

Paul Stillwell: Was that done through Admiral Zumwalt's program, the accelerated turnover, the Vietnamization?[*]

---

[*] Vice Admiral Elmo R. Zumwalt, Jr., USN, served as Commander Naval Forces Vietnam/Chief of Naval Advisory Group Vietnam from 30 September 1968 to 14 May 1970. His oral history is in the Naval Institute collection.

Admiral Siler: I think it probably was. It started before I was Commandant, so I really can't say.

Paul Stillwell: Well, the Coast Guard assets over there were essentially working through the Navy structure, so probably so.

Admiral Siler: Oh, yes, always. During the time that that started, I was the district commander out in St. Louis, and we didn't get involved with that sort of thing at all. Our buoy tenders wouldn't do them much good. [Laughter]

Paul Stillwell: How much evidence did you see in Washington of the antiwar protests during that period?

Admiral Siler: Most of the time I didn't see it at all. Occasionally when I was driving to work we would get something on the radio that said, "Avoid this Memorial Bridge crossing," or something of that nature, but most of the time I didn't see it at all.

Paul Stillwell: Well, the mood in the country had certainly changed. Was there any suggestion of lessening the support by the Coast Guard, or was that going to come from some other level?

Admiral Siler: It would have come from some other level. I don't think that there was ever a question in the Coast Guard or with the Coast Guard in any way that we should provide any less support to the operation.

Paul Stillwell: Well, in Vietnam itself Admiral Zumwalt could see the way things were going politically, and that's when he came up with the plan for Vietnamization.
    What do you remember about the personnel management functions when you were in that job?

Admiral Siler: Well, the things that we were looking at were the assignment of X number of people. Nothing having to do with the training of them or anything of that nature, so we were looking more at the organization of how we were going to utilize those people rather than true personnel management.

Paul Stillwell: So you were justifying an end strength.

Admiral Siler: Yes.

Paul Stillwell: What about on the civilian side? Did you get more into the management there? Civil servants?

Admiral Siler: Not much more. There were a good many times when we tried to justify an increase in personnel to the Office of Management and Budget. They were looking for figures more than anything else. They try to justify the smallest government that they possibly can, and they don't care how well you do it or how poorly you do it, and you can go out and contract for it. That's all right. But trying to get it within your end force was very difficult.

Paul Stillwell: I read something when I was in headquarters recently that in 1970 the General Accounting Office was concerned about Coast Guard financial management. Do you remember that issue?

Admiral Siler: No, because most of the time the General Accounting Office has said that the Coast Guard's accounting is the best in the government.

Paul Stillwell: Interesting.

Admiral Siler: So I don't think that it's ever been very much of a concern.

Paul Stillwell: What else do you recall about that tour of duty?

Admiral Siler: There was one time when I was sent out to San Francisco to take a look at some recommendations that had been made by the personnel officer at the—at that time there was an Alameda Training Station. The training officer was a woman officer who had stayed on active duty almost all the time since World War II, which was very unusual that she would be on active duty all that time. But I went out with the special assistant to Admiral Smith, and we visited Admiral Bender who had not particularly favored the changes to the Alameda Center, because he had control of that training center as part of the 12th District.[*] The proposal had been to make it an independent unit reporting directly to headquarters. There were several other aspects of that change of command structure, and not very many of them were adopted because Admiral Bender as the commander of the 12th District opposed them. He felt that it was important that he as an admiral be aware of anything that went on there. So I had a nice trip to San Francisco.

Paul Stillwell: Do you remember any issues with the Coast Guard Academy when you were in that job?

Admiral Siler: I don't recall exactly when it was when they started talking about the marine simulators there, because I worked on some proposals in response to requests for proposals a good many years later. But the academy did not have actual simulators out in the marine operations at that time. They were probably trying to get them.

Paul Stillwell: Anything else? You were, I presume, selected for flag rank when you were in that job.

Admiral Siler: Yes. In '70 there were some admirals selected, and I remember on the weekend just after the board had met we went to a cocktail party at one of my classmates, which was one of those big Coast Guard get-togethers. Someone had said, "I presume you were selected," and I was not. [Laughter] And I said I had not been. We were

---

[*] Rear Admiral Chester R. Bender, USCG, Commander Western Area and Commander 12th Coast Guard District. He later served as Commandant from 1970 to 1974.

standing right next to the chairman of the selection board, and I don't recall exactly what I said, but discussing it in his presence was quite awkward.

Paul Stillwell: Of course. [Laughter] Who was the head of the selection board?

Admiral Siler: Rear Admiral Goehring.[*] But it was a wife who was saying, "I'm sure you were selected." I had known pretty much how the Commandant informed people every time when he had the board, but it had still not been cleared through the Department of Transportation or Treasury as in earlier years. Those people would know individually but know also that they weren't supposed to say anything. And, of course, I had not been notified, so I knew that I had not been selected.

When I was selected the following year, I had an interesting experience there too. I had not been notified of selection, and so my wife and I were discussing the situation, "Probably this is the end of the road." So we were sitting at home in the recreation room before the fireplace, and the phone rang. When I lifted up the receiver, they hung up. I had no idea what it was, but it was Tom Sargent calling to see if I was at home, because he lived in Maryland and we were in Virginia. He didn't want to come all the way over to Virginia, where he knew where our house was, and find out we were not at home. So he did that, and, sure enough, we were at home, so he gave me a rear admiral's Zippo lighter, and that was the beginning of some of the things that are in the other room. But he and his wife and Admiral Perry and his wife, because Admiral Perry at that time was chief of personnel, they came over to let us know that we had been selected.

The next day that woman that had been suggesting that they change the organization out at the Alameda Training Center had come to Washington for something. I don't know whether she was ordered back, or whether it was something having to do with the training center, but anyway she stopped by because we'd known each other clear back to Admiral Richmond's days.

Paul Stillwell: What was her name?

---

[*] Rear Admiral Robert W. Goehring, USCG.

Admiral Siler: Ellen Sorensen.* She said, "Were you selected this time?"

I said, "No, I don't know anything about it, but I would guess that," and I may have tried to name five people who I thought were probably pretty good bets. One of them never made rear admiral, and I have no idea why because he was in my opinion one of the finest officers in the Coast Guard. That was Curt Kelly, who was a classmate.† Among the people who were selected was Thompson, who was just senior to our class; I served with him a couple of times and went through flight training with him.‡ And Joe Steele, who was number-two man in our class, but the number-one man at that point had gotten out because of the physical problems that his wife had after an automobile accident.§ So it was Joe Steele and myself, and there were two others selected at that time.

Paul Stillwell: But you couldn't let on to Ellen Sorensen.

Admiral Siler: Not to anybody, particularly that I had been selected. So that afternoon they announced it [laughter], and she came back and said, "You knew you'd been selected." [Laughter]

Paul Stillwell: What kind of a family celebration followed?

Admiral Siler: I don't know that there was much a family celebration at all. Our son was off to college, so he didn't know about for a couple of days, and our daughter I don't think was concerned one way or the other. [Laughter]

Paul Stillwell: Well, you used the terminology that "we" were selected, and I'm sure Mrs. Siler had a lot to do with that.

---

* Commander Ellen M. Sorensen, USCG (Ret.).
† Captain Curtis J. Kelly, USCG.
‡ Captain Glenn O. Thompson, USCG.
§ Captain Joseph R. Steele, USCG.

Admiral Siler: Yes, I'm sure she did. Then just a day or so after that Admiral Bender called me in and talked about assignment.[*] Interestingly, I went to St. Louis to relieve Russ Waesche, who was the administrative aide when I was the personal aide to Admiral Richmond back in the '50s.[†] Here he was one of the most senior rear admirals, and that was the end of his career, and that was the beginning of my career as a rear admiral. So it was an interesting time to get out there.

Paul Stillwell: Why did you get picked for that particular spot?

Admiral Siler: It was available. [Laughter] I don't recall exactly where the others went, but Joe Steele was assigned to something having to do with engineering at that time, I think because he was an aeronautical engineer. But there's not an aeronautical engineer position. He was assigned as the district commander in Long Beach shortly after that. I think that he may have moved into that directly from being the chief of operations in the district, because he had been in the 11th District, which is Long Beach, before. I think he may just have moved to other quarters.

Paul Stillwell: Well, you said yesterday that when Russell Waesche was selected for captain he was saying prayers about the people on the list above him. Evidently he made it somehow. [Laughter]

Admiral Siler: Yes, he made rear admiral. I think it was just after his assignment to the senior officer in Europe. When we made a trip to Europe in 1957, I guess it was, he wanted to make that trip with his four stripes on, and Admiral Richmond would not give him a yes or a no just to tease him. [Laughter] Finally he said at the last minute, "Well, I guess you can go ahead and put that fourth stripe on." So then he wore his four stripes all the time on that trip, but it wasn't until the first of July that he really had made it for pay purposes. We were in Athens at that time. The next morning Russ had pretty bleary eyes, I must say. [Laughter]

---

[*] Admiral Bender by this time was Commandant.
[†] Rear Admiral Russell R. Waesche, Jr., USCG.

Paul Stillwell: Well, please tell me about moving into the job in St. Louis and what that entailed.

Admiral Siler: Well, the first thing that it entailed was finding a type of entirely new Coast Guard, because there was no search and rescue in the district out there. If someone was lost overboard on a towboat it was usually the same boat that found them if they were ever found. And an awful lot of people in the vicinity of the Mississippi do not know how to swim, so it was a matter of finding the body. So one of the first things that I did was to find a towboat with a good company, one that had a good reputation with the Coast Guard. And I was on the boat for about three days.

I drove up to Iowa, someplace like Burlington, and we were supposed to climb down onto the boat when it was in the lock. Unfortunately, by the time we got there it had gotten through the lock, and it was downstream. There was a recreational boat that was there and said they'd take—I was able to take Betty and our daughter on the towboat also. We took the recreational boat out and caught up with the tow rather quickly. We transferred over and had a very pleasant time for a couple days, and I spent a lot of time in the wheelhouse trying to understand all that went on with a tow on the Mississippi. One of the things that bothered me quite a lot, the first night at least and I don't know how much after that, was anytime you go around a sharp turn in the Mississippi River they do what they call flanking around the turn, which is starting the turn and then backing the towboat, which is at the back end of the tow, to the direction that gets the whole thing turned. On the other hand, when you're on an oceangoing vessel the only time you'd back the engines is when you're coming to anchor or you're in deep trouble.

Paul Stillwell: So this was sort of to twist the tow around the bend?

Admiral Siler: Yes. So I woke up the first night several times as we flanked around turns because I thought we were in deep trouble or about to come to anchor or something like that. I think the second or third nights we did a whole lot better, but it was an interesting experience to find out about that. The whole construction of the towboats is dependent on that. They have Kort nozzles on all those boats, and the propellers are about one-fourth out of the water when they're just parked. But when you're under way, they drive the water through these nozzles, and so the propellers are doing some good all the time. But when reversed, they pull through the other direction is all.

But then that was an interesting thing, and they usually went to Holland to model these Kort nozzles with different configurations. The rear end of most towboats is such that the propellers are a fourth of the way out of the water all the time when they're parked or tied up. Of course, that led to some court cases when I got out of the Coast Guard, so I was available to testify as an expert witness having to do with towboats.

The assignment there in St. Louis was quite different in many regards. No search and rescue. Aids to navigation were very important, because we were putting buoys in to guide the towboats. The buoys had to be in such a location that first they were convenient for the vessels to use the buoys, and second they had to mark the water that was deep enough for the towboats to use. The depth of the water was supposedly nine feet above where the Ohio comes into the Mississippi, and below that the depth was supposed to be 12 feet. If it wasn't that deep, then the Corps of Engineers was supposed to get either a contract dredge, or I think they had two dredges at that time belonging to the Corps of Engineers. They would assign either their own dredge or the contract dredge to deepen it again.

At one time, I guess in the second or it might have been the third year that I was in St. Louis, we went south to go to a meeting of the American Waterways Operators, which was held in Greenville, Mississippi. The owner of a good many towboats was a man named Jesse Brent, and he and his wife did a great deal for the poor, lesser-educated residents of Greenville, including basing his company and the boats there. It was strongly recommended that I not do that on this first tour, because as far as seeing the country is concerned you don't see anything of the country when you get a little bit south of St. Louis because you have levees on each side. If you didn't have the levees, it would flood the entire country. So it was interesting to take that southern trip, but it would not be as helpful in making the trip to see how things were done on the Mississippi, because you couldn't see anything except what's right there in the river itself.

When we did run into low spots in the river south of St. Louis, we did what was really historical as far as operating the towboats was concerned, and that was tie up to a tree on the bank on the side of the river. Once we were tied up there, the towboat left the tow and went and helped with another tow that belonged to the same company. The skipper thought that he could get through a channel that was off to one side, because he'd just been through there. He couldn't get through. We were hard aground. Before too long they had to go back and go through the main channel and be signaled through. But the first trip that we had made was where the water was all right—deep enough. We never went aground that way.

We got into heavy fog and tied off to the shoreline again, because we couldn't see anything at all. You can operate in some places by radar, but in the Mississippi it's so narrow you don't have much leeway in operating north of St. Louis. Now, when you're south of St. Louis, in many cases it's miles wide, but that's because the levees hold it in deeper depth to operate. North of St. Louis, it does get quite narrow, which makes it very interesting too. I've now taken the river all the way up to St. Paul, and there are some areas where the river becomes a lake. One of them was Pepin Lake, rather a large lake. But there are many lakes up there to the north. There's not very much like that in the south because it was sloughs all over the place.

Paul Stillwell: Did you do something to improve that search-and-rescue situation? Did you institute a system?

Admiral Siler: No, because one of the things we did was to establish a system of controlling the traffic near the main lock and dam in Louisville, Kentucky. But as far as search and rescue is concerned, there's not much search and rescue at all. Most of the time you don't get concerned with that except if someone falls overboard near a lock and dam. In that case, that man had better be a good swimmer or he's gone. Like almost everybody who falls overboard near a dam is a goner. Just can't avoid it. So if you're going to fall overboard, choose the stretch that's halfway between the dams.

We had an incident there, and I believe it was just before Easter in 1972. The place in Louisville was involved with a tow that had one barge of liquid chlorine in tanks, and in another barge was sulfuric acid. When he came to what is known as McAlpine Dam, he tried to use the whistle signals, I think, and also a radio call to the operator of the locks. And the man didn't answer. He was probably asleep. It was the middle of the night. The pilot tried to slow it down and stop where he would have been in good condition, but there was too much current involved.

Paul Stillwell: So it was just carrying him along.

Admiral Siler: Yes. He was swept into the channel that went to the power plant, which was over on one side, and the lock was really over in another channel. When he got into the approach to the power plant, he completely lost control of it, because that's where water was going through the dam at great speed. Eventually he broke up the tow, not intentionally, but the current was so strong. The chlorine barge went over the dam and was caught in the spillway of the McAlpine Dam with one of the—they had a series of pillars sort of to break up the current as it went through instead of letting it dig huge holes below the spillway.

The forward end of this barge was impaled on the things to break up the current, and the rear end of the barge was being held up by the current that was coming through the dam. That was the chlorine barge. The sulfuric acid barge came up broadside on the power plant, and eventually some other towboats were able to get it out quickly. We started thinking about that chlorine barge, and it had 1,600 tons of liquid chlorine in it. The Army had someone in the Chemical Engineering Corps at the Army base at Fort Knox, which is right there in Kentucky. He made some computations about how many people that chlorine could kill if it broke loose in that quantity.

Paul Stillwell: I take it that the barge wasn't ruptured when it went over the dam.

Admiral Siler: No, it was not. At least the tanks were not. Now, whether the barge was, I can't say for sure. But they were very worried about what might happen if the tanks were ruptured. He did the computation of what could happen if one of those four tanks was ruptured, and he figured it would kill so many people as it went downwind that it would be very shocking, to say the least. And he never figured it for two, three or four tanks, but we—

Paul Stillwell: But you could multiply.

Admiral Siler: Yes. And I guess there are figures that have to do with how fast it would spread as it was ruptured, but we didn't bother with that either. It was too shocking with one tank. So since the Coast Guard has to do with safety on the waterways, I went over to Louisville, and I worked with the captain of the port of Louisville. And the Corps of Engineers had all sorts of people that they made available. We talked about how we could get it out of there.

We managed to get a salvage organization there, which consisted of two PCs welded together with a series of beams across so that they could move them farther apart or closer together.* This was maneuvered into place over the barge, almost exactly in the spillway but just a little bit back. We secured the barge to that lifting contraption. Both when that was moved into place and when it came out, we alerted the people who were downwind because if they had ruptured anything at that time, it could have been very, very dangerous. That happened to be Easter Day. We got it stabilized with the lifting contraption, because we felt with it in that position it would be too hard to maneuver. Then we let the chlorine come out and put in the water there. It was probably the purest that water has been in centuries, because the Ohio at that point is pretty muddy.

Paul Stillwell: So you just let it out in small quantities at a time?

Admiral Siler: Opened the valve slowly and then go to it. [Laughter] The barge was like this with two tanks on here and two tanks here. The upstream ones were easy to empty because the valves were down in this position so that they could be emptied. These down here couldn't be emptied by gravity, because the outlet was above a large part of the chlorine. So they pumped that out and pumped it through some chemicals so that it would be converted into just Clorox and released that then into the river. The EPA

---

* PCs—patrol craft.

people got in their little boats and ran around all over the place downstream and wanted to make certain that nobody was bothered by the amount of chlorine that was in the river.* When they got it low enough, they pulled the barge out of there and moved it someplace, and I have an idea that they just scrapped that barge.

Paul Stillwell: So the danger would have been if it had been released into the air and vaporized.

Admiral Siler: Yes. And particularly an uncontrolled amount or speed of release so that it could be so much that it would have affected people.

Paul Stillwell: What about the sulfuric acid?

Admiral Siler: It was easy, because it was just on the face the power plant, and it was not in any trouble, but this barge was impaled in the dam itself.

Paul Stillwell: Now, what should the lock operator have done that he didn't as the load was approaching?

Admiral Siler: Should have opened the gates to go into the controlled height of water into the lock. Then they would have probably split the whole tow in half, and the forward part would have been taken through. Then the towboat and the rear part of the tow would have been taken through, and they would make it up again and head downstream.

Paul Stillwell: One of the other things that I've read that you accomplished during that tour was to upgrade the lighting standards on these towboats and barges.

Admiral Siler: One of the very first things we realized was that there was no way for many of the towboats to be recognized as towboats. And, of course, a towboat could not

---

* EPA—Environmental Protection Agency.

maneuver very capably, but we tried several things to indicate that it was a towboat. I don't know who had the idea. It was not mine, but we involved ourselves in the testing of flashing lights on the towboats, which could then be identified as lights on towboats. We were out on the river a good many times looking at flashing lights of various types and ended up with a yellow flashing light. We couldn't make the light truly white if it were a strobe light. It would be yellow or just a plain strobe light. So we would look at the lights from various distances and then try to make certain that this was identifiable as a towboat from a distance where you could do something about that rather than running under the rake of the forward barge.

Paul Stillwell: Did you consult with the towboat operators on what would serve their interests?

Admiral Siler: Oh, yes. We worked with the towboats to run up and down the river, largely in St. Louis, where there's a great deal of industrial lighting in the background, and so we were facing as much competition as we probably would anytime.

Paul Stillwell: How wide a jurisdiction did you have in these boats. Would this apply to Mississippi, Missouri, and Ohio Rivers?

Admiral Siler: And about six others. We could establish rules that would be requirements on those vessels on the inland rivers of the United States. That was it; it would not be effective in Europe, for example. They have different kinds of lights over there.

Paul Stillwell: Did this require legislation, or how did it become enacted?

Admiral Siler: The rules that the Coast Guard publishes are published in the Code of Federal Regulations, and if there are no objections, they could go into effect rather soon. Usually there is a comment period specified in the first publishing of such regulations, so that if it is a real problem or there's nothing available on the market that will fulfill the requirement, they change the effective date on the basis of the comments of the people who are affected by the regulations.

Paul Stillwell: Did you run into any objection on this?

Admiral Siler: I don't recall that there were any objections at all, but there'd been too many cases where people were drowned by collisions with towboats. Very frequently in areas like Pittsburgh or Cincinnati or St. Louis the pleasure boat operators can get run over by commercial operators. Most of those fortunately don't end up with a tragic end, but it's not too unlikely they will.

Paul Stillwell: You said that this wasn't your idea. Where had the impetus come from?

Admiral Siler: I think the collisions that had happened over the years with commercial operators being unable to stop when a pleasure boat operator cut across too close to him, not realizing that the tow was out to hundreds of feet ahead of the towboat itself.

Paul Stillwell: But that situation had probably existed for years. What gave it the push to get it done while you were in St. Louis?

Admiral Siler: I don't know except that it had been developed, and we needed to see if it would work.

Paul Stillwell: Did you have tests to see what would be the best?

Admiral Siler: Yes, we tried several different configurations, and we still didn't feel that this was the ultimate, because there's nothing to indicate how long a tow is. Most of the tows that are in the lower Mississippi are much bigger than those in the upper Mississippi, and sometimes a large tow in the lower Mississippi will be as big as 40 barges. In the upper Mississippi they are almost always a maximum of 12 barges, and the reason for that is because the locks aren't big enough to take any more than six barges at one time, three wide and two long. So the upper Mississippi is limited in that way, while the lower Mississippi has no locks and you can have a huge tow.

Paul Stillwell: Did the Coast Guard have jurisdiction over the locks?

Admiral Siler: No. That's the Corps of Engineers.

Paul Stillwell: What do you remember about buoy tenders and aids to navigation work?

Admiral Siler: Well, the buoy tenders were all the Coast Guard's responsibility, and the towboats themselves that are the pushing part of the buoy tender were either—most of them were 65 or 75 feet long. There were a couple of older ones that were a little bigger than that, but those are decommissioned now, so we used almost completely the 65- and 75-foot buoy tenders. Each one of them would have a barge that it pushed around with a crane on the barge, and it would have its supply of sinkers and actual buoys on that barge.

Paul Stillwell: How far did your jurisdiction extend on putting out aids to navigation?

Admiral Siler: We had up the Mississippi to about Pittsburgh and up the Monongahela and the Allegheny short distances. Then in West Virginia we went right into Charleston and then all the way down the Ohio to, well, to Paducah, Kentucky, and on into the Mississippi. At Paducah, why, we had the Cumberland and—what is the other one? The Kentucky River is not there, but that's another one that we had responsibility for into I think it's Charleston. Cumberland and the Tennessee. Then in the Missouri, we went all the way up to Omaha, Nebraska, and we buoyed it, although it was not a controlled river. There are no dams in the Missouri River at all. The dams that are there are mainly to impound water to use for irrigation. They make lakes in South Dakota that way, which are mainly used for recreational fishing and that nature. Of course, the real reason for those is impound water that can be used for irrigation. When we get into the lower Mississippi the river has tributaries like the Arkansas. That river goes into Tulsa, Oklahoma, and we had aids to navigation all the way to Tulsa.

Paul Stillwell: But then presumably farther out beyond your reach there would be people coming in from the coast to control the navigation aids from there inland.

Admiral Siler: Well, from the Gulf of Mexico up to—we had buoy tenders in Greenville, Mississippi and Vicksburg. In Natchez, Mississippi, we had a buoy tender stationed there, and they would go both directions, both up and down. The river navigation north of Baton Rouge was performed by the Second District; south of Baton Rouge it was handled by the Eighth Coast Guard district, which went down to the Gulf of Mexico.

Paul Stillwell: Well, one of the big things that you dealt with during that tour was the spring flood in 1973. What do you recall about that operation?

Admiral Siler: Lots of water. [Laughter]

Paul Stillwell: I was living there at the time and I remember that water. My wife and I drove over to Alton, Illinois, just to see how high it was.

Admiral Siler: The water was so high that it didn't make any difference what they did with the gates in the locks. They just opened them up and let the water run. It couldn't do a thing, it was that much water.

Paul Stillwell: What was the Coast Guard's role?

Admiral Siler: In that case it was mainly the search and rescue, to try to make certain that the farmers who were out in that area were warned in sufficient time to move their livestock and their valuables to someplace higher. It was not at all unusual to drive along the highway and see the water up over the windows in the houses.

Paul Stillwell: Well, there was a sandbagging operation, wasn't there?

Admiral Siler: A tremendous amount of that, and unfortunately it didn't do much good. It was almost impossible to keep that water out.

Paul Stillwell: You had involuntary recall of Coast Guard reservists. What necessitated that?

Admiral Siler: The height of the water and the strong current, particularly in Louisville, Kentucky. We established the system of control of the traffic. After that incident where the towboat broke up and had the chlorine and the sulfuric acid, we realized that that was one of those locations where it would help us a great deal if we had a traffic system so we knew exactly what was going on. The vessels would be held away from where the dangerous areas were.

    The Eighth District had already established a vessel traffic system at the Atchafalaya Lock and Dam.[*] There's an Atchafalaya River that branches off from the Mississippi and goes to the west there. The vessel traffic system had been determined to be very successful there. So we established this vessel traffic system in the Louisville area to make certain that things coming through there didn't get into trouble, because there is a bad turn at the lock and dam that's right in the city. And we couldn't operate that except by using reserve personnel. We started out by using reserve personnel with their complete agreement, but we couldn't keep them at it too long without their running into problems with their employers. So we felt that the answer was to have the authority to recall them involuntarily. They didn't have objections to that, because they felt that they were protected for their normal employment if they could say, "I have to go. I've been called by the Coast Guard."

Paul Stillwell: Was that something you could do at the district level, or did it have to go higher than that?

---

[*] This is in southeast Louisiana.

Admiral Siler: It had to go higher, all the way to the Secretary. When it was determined by the Secretary that it was necessary, then we could recall whomever we wanted to. And the legislation had to be passed by Congress in order for us to do that.

Paul Stillwell: Did you recall just from within the district, or were you able to go wider than that?

Admiral Siler: I think in most cases we just kept to our own people, because they were the ones who were most familiar with the operation of locks and dams. But now since we've done that, the authority is in existence that the Coast Guard can recall personnel at any time when it's determined to be necessary by the Coast Guard. I think the Commandant has to get the authority from the Secretary, but it doesn't have to go all the way to the President anymore.

Paul Stillwell: How long did you keep those individuals?

Admiral Siler: Usually a week or two would be about it, because that's how long the water stays high.

Paul Stillwell: Well, it was high for a while in that case.

Admiral Siler: Yes, it was. Well, there's been that more recent case where the river flooded up in South Dakota, and it was up for a month or more. And some of the rescues were amazing in that case.

Paul Stillwell: I remember one town up there was flooded, and then the newspaper building burned down and difficult to get any of the fire-fighting equipment to it.

Admiral Siler: Yes, that's been more recent too. It's been since I retired.

Paul Stillwell: Right. So when the situation stabilized and the water went down, then these people could go back to their regular jobs?

Admiral Siler: Yes.

Paul Stillwell: Did you meet any resistance from people being called up?

Admiral Siler: We did until we had that authority, because initially we just used people with their agreement. But when they started saying, "I'm afraid I'll lose my job," then we went ahead and got this legislation through. I don't think there were any disagreements with the people who were involved there. If there were disagreements we could usually find some substitutes anyway. But if people objected too much, they realized that their careers were pretty much through in the Coast Guard.

Paul Stillwell: What was the job like on a day-to-day basis in headquarters when you weren't dealing with these emergencies?

Admiral Siler: At times it was very dead. At other times you could always do some planning for recurrence of those or something similar to that. There were times when our personnel office dealt a great deal with advance planning of how they would get people, plan for those, for the training of those people. And, of course, our reserve office there in the Second District was probably as busy as any other office we had because we were using reserve personnel so much.

Paul Stillwell: Did you also administer the reserves for their regular active duty training and so forth, not just these emergencies?

Admiral Siler: Oh, yes. The reserve over the years has changed quite a lot, because they don't have reserve units anymore. They somehow just have reserve, and somehow they get them to the right places, but I don't know how it works now.

Paul Stillwell: I think the Nixon Administration at that time made a strong effort to get rid of the Coast Guard Reserve.*

Admiral Siler: Oh, yes.

Paul Stillwell: Any specifics you recall on that?

Admiral Siler: Well, they had started thinking about that when I was still in headquarters, before I went to the Second District, and it was a task group that I headed that said, "Let's train the Coast Guard Reserve by having them do the same functions. And somehow when that group of people is trained, send the regulars home and let the reserves do the whole job." The reservists were quite happy about that, because they were doing something that was very obviously worthwhile. I've never quite been able to figure out how different today's Team Coast Guard is from what we proposed back in the '70s.

Paul Stillwell: I read an article that was in the file from when you were in St. Louis, and apparently you were very popular with your driver. He spoke highly of you. [Laughter]

Admiral Siler: That was the big black fellow, and I'd guess that was the one.

Paul Stillwell: Yes.

Admiral Siler: He was probably an inch or two taller than I was, and he was a very good man. He always was right there where I wanted him.

Paul Stillwell: He used the word "cool" to describe you [laughter] in a favorable way.
　　　How much did you get involved with the city of St. Louis and the surrounding area while you were there?

---

* Richard M. Nixon served as President of the United States from 20 January 1969 until his resignation on 9 August 1974.

Admiral Siler: Well, I worked closely with at least two Army commands that were there. Actually, I guess there were three involved, because the Corps of Engineers we worked with very closely. And the district engineer, Corps of Engineers, was right there in St. Louis. Then we had a systems command, which I was never quite sure what they were supposed to be doing, but they had all sorts of equipment out at their depot. The third command was the Aviation Systems Command. And they had some aviators who were assigned there and who were always concerned about flight time. In those days they had to fly at their regular amount regardless of what their orders said.

I used to go to lunch regularly at the Aviation Systems Command, and I contacted the commander there who was an Army major general, and said, "If those people need to get flight time in and I need to go someplace, could I call and say, 'Can you provide an Army airplane?'"

And he said, "Sure. Just let us know." So I started doing that until we had the gasoline shortage.

Paul Stillwell: That was in early '74. It was after the Arab-Israeli War in the fall of '73.*

Admiral Siler: Yes. About the fall of '73, as I recall. Anyway, at that time, we couldn't get the airplanes when we wanted them, but before that it had been very good. At times I would go and visit a whole bunch of units in various cities, and when my predecessor had wanted to do it he would fly to one location and then get a Coast Guard car there and drive to some other place. Then finally get back on a commercial plane when he could, and it would take him three days to visit a certain number of units. While I was able to use the Army airplane I went to Owensboro, Louisville, and Paducah all in one day, and he couldn't have done that in less than three days. I did it in one day and was back in the office again the next day.

---

* The Yom Kippur War started on 6 October 1973. Egyptian and Syrian forces began major coordinated ground offensives against Israeli positions, seeking to improve territorial claims in the wake of the Six-Day War of 1967. Supported in part by weapons supplied by the United States, Israeli forces counterattacked and drove back the Arabs. A cease-fire finally took effect on 25 October.

Another time I went down the Mississippi and visited Greenville, Natchez and Vicksburg. I visited all three of those cities in one day, and that was an interesting day. They called us as we were going by, I guess, Greenville and said, "The weather's turned bad in St. Louis. What are your intentions?" We were flying a Beechcraft Baron, which was pretty small.

I was doing the flying, and the really qualified pilot was sitting in the copilot's seat. He picked up the microphone and said, "Well, we'll continue. Just keep us informed." So we headed on back to St. Louis, and when we got close to St. Louis it got pretty rough. We were in the soup solidly and just flew on toward St. Louis. They flew us around for a while and then made some violent turns and said, "The reason for these turns is we've had a 180-degree wind shift, and you're number ten to land." But all these airplanes were in the stack somewhere. We were probably about a fourth of the speed of most of those airplanes, too, but we got down finally. The only thing was it was so rough that the Beechcraft Baron doesn't handle the rough air as well as a good many of those bigger airplanes do. My chief of staff was an aviator, also, only he had finished his flying. I said to him, "If I'd been taking an instrument check yesterday, I would have failed it." [Laughter] Because we were just all over the sky. I was glad to get down that day.

Paul Stillwell: Did you get involved in civic activities when you were there?

Admiral Siler: Not very much, although I was invited to the Veiled Prophet Ball at least twice.

Paul Stillwell: That's the pinnacle of society there.

Admiral Siler: Yes. Once in a while we'd get invitations to see a ball game. Never invited to see football. Baseball rather common, and there were enough people who had memberships to the restaurant up there.

Paul Stillwell: The Stadium Club.

Admiral Siler: Yes, we very frequently got that included with the baseball game. And there were some other things that we got involved with but not too many. Just shortly before I left I was given an honorary membership to the Missouri Athletic Club, and I still maintain that.

Paul Stillwell: Anything else to remember about your time as Second District Commander?

Admiral Siler: It was a difficult district to cover anyway, and there were in those days at least two units I never got to.

We had a loran station in Dana, Indiana, and I did get to it, but we had an Omega station in La Moure, North Dakota, which just happened to be the residence of the senator from North Dakota. [Laughter] That was a bit of a problem to be able to keep that on the air all the time, because when the precipitation got unusually heavy in North Dakota it would build up ice on the insulators. The electricity would jump over the insulators and to the ground rather than being sent out as the radio signal. So it was a problem to our electronics officer, who was the one who had immediate cognizance of it.

In those days we had boating safety teams, usually about four people. They would operate small boats on a trailer and go along the river wherever they were assigned and patrol and make inspections of boats and so on. We had one in South Dakota that I never got to. It was a big lake, but I don't know what their primary concern was there except that it was a big enough lake people could get lost.

Paul Stillwell: I wonder how much autonomy you had in that job versus how much you had to keep in touch with headquarters.

Admiral Siler: I didn't have to keep in touch with headquarters at all. In fact, my immediate superior was supposedly the Atlantic Area Commander in New York. He never came to St. Louis at all. And I got together with all of the district commanders, I think, once in the three years that I was stationed there. So it was largely a matter of complete autonomy. When we were having a great deal of trouble with that barge that was stuck in the dam, I just went directly to headquarters and said, "I need a helicopter to do some of the things that are here." They sent one from St. Petersburg the next day.

Paul Stillwell: So probably one of the other few occasions would have been when you needed to get that legislation on recalling the reservists.

Admiral Siler: I think most of the time, though, they were well aware of that, and this just gave it a push.

Paul Stillwell: Well, it was while you were in that job that you got selected for Commandant. What do you remember about that process?

Admiral Siler: Well, that happened right around the first of the year in 1974. I was at home, and a phone call came in. My wife answered the phone and recognized Admiral Bender's voice. He asked for me and asked if I would come to headquarters on a certain date. And obviously I said, yes, I would. He said I was to be interviewed by the Secretary about the Commandant's position.

Paul Stillwell: This was Secretary Brinegar?

Admiral Siler: Brinegar, yes.* I flew into Washington, and our son was still there, so I went out to spend the night with him, but my bag didn't come. I made it a practice always to fly in uniform, and I wore one of my oldest blue uniforms, simply because I wanted to have the newly pressed one, which was in the suitcase, available for the interview with the Secretary. When the bag didn't come, I was a little bit disappointed, to say the least. [Laughter] I pressed the uniform at my son's house; it was the uniform that I had been wearing, but it was old. There was no question about it. Finally, at about 4:00 o'clock in the morning it did come, Eastern Airlines in those days. [Laughter] And so from 4:00 o'clock on I slept pretty well, [laughter] not until then. I was interviewed,

---

* Claude S. Brinegar served as Secretary of Transportation from 2 February 1973 to 1 February 1975.

and I was asked several questions that I wasn't really ready to answer. But they didn't tell me ahead of time what I was going to be asked, so I couldn't prepare myself at all.

Paul Stillwell: What sort of questions were they?

Admiral Siler: For one thing, the question was asked, who would I want as Assistant Commandant if I became the Commandant?"

"I don't know."

"What characteristics would you look for in the Assistant Commandant?"

Well, that one was a little easier because I said, "The same things that you would for a Commandant, because he could be serving as Commandant at any time, and particularly if there were illness or if you were just out of town." And we'd just had that with Admiral Bender because Admiral Bender—I don't know if he had heart problems or what it was, but there were several times when he was absent for a period of two or three weeks because he was either at home in bed or in the hospital. So that was not too difficult, but who I would want wasn't something that I had given consideration to before.

But it was interesting in the way that the Secretary did this. I was interviewed first by the Deputy Secretary, not the Secretary. I certainly had the impression that the Secretary really didn't want to do that. He felt if someone was going to make a choice of that sort, that probably John Barnum was as well qualified to make the choice as he was. Brinegar was an oilman or a businessman, and I'm not sure he was properly chosen to be the Secretary of Transportation.* He went back to Union Oil afterward as well, and I don't know what the function was at Unocal.

But I was interviewed, and they gave me no indication at all of whether I'd done well or very poorly or somewhere in between. It wasn't until a week later I was ordered in to headquarters to serve on a board to select rear admirals for the Coast Guard. I wasn't that senior a rear admiral. I'd never made upper half even.† So we worked on the

---
* John W. Barnum was Under Secretary of Transportation from 30 May 1973 to 20 January 1977; he served as Acting Secretary of Transportation from 2 February 1975 to 6 March 1975.
† The rank of rear admiral is divided into upper half, two stars, and lower half, one star. In the 1970s both upper and lower half rear admirals wore the insignia of the two-star rank.

board for I guess half a day, and somewhere around lunchtime a messenger came to the room where our board was working and told Ed Perry that the Secretary would like to see him. And I knew very well that he had been called in to be interviewed. I don't know what told me that, but I had felt that he would have been interviewed.

Now, I figured that he was going to be notified that he was going to be the Commandant. So I figured that the entire pressure was off. About an hour or two later, the messenger came back and said that the Secretary would like to see me at 5:00 o'clock. So we figured we'd be through with our considerations by 5:00, so that was no problem, but I would have gotten back. I was staying at Fort Myer at the guest quarters, and I called my wife there—she'd come in with me—and told her that I was going to be late because I was asked to be at the Secretary's office.[*]

She said at that time that would be all right, but that we were invited to the quarters of General Kornet. This was the same man that was in St. Louis as the head of the Aviation Systems Command, and we'd gotten to know each other rather well. She asked if I would be particularly late, and I said, "I don't think so." So then while I was waiting to go up, I guess between 4:00 and 5:00 o'clock, I was told that the Secretary was tied up, and would I be there at 6:00 o'clock.

Then I called my wife and said, "Yeah, I will be late." I finally got out of being interviewed the second time by Mr. Brinegar and Mr. Barnum. At this meeting they had told me that I would be the Commandant. I headed for Fort Myer then. I couldn't keep everybody quiet, including myself [laughter], so I told the general and his wife that I would be the Commandant. So they knew it before anybody in the Coast Guard. [Laughter]

Paul Stillwell: You mentioned that you were a lower-half rear admiral when you were in St. Louis. Didn't you get an indication why you were the one who was chosen as Commandant?

Admiral Siler: No, never did. I don't know who all was considered at that time. I do know that a couple of others who were considered. One was Joe McClelland, who was

---

[*] Fort Myer, an Army post, is in Northern Virginia, adjacent to Arlington National Cemetery.

the senior man in the class of 1940, and I was the class of '44, so I should have been four years behind.* I was three years, as it turned out. I feel certain that Admiral Perry was considered, and, of course, he was the one I selected for my Assistant Commandant. But other than that I don't know.

Paul Stillwell: Somewhere I read it might have been a desire for a youth movement at that point. You were 52.

Admiral Siler: I feel certain that that was the case, because the two previous commandants, Admiral Smith was definitely an older man, but interestingly he outlived the one who succeeded him, who was Chet Bender. Chet was class of '36, so I think he would have three years junior to Admiral Smith. It was eight years between Admiral Bender and myself. So there was a feeling that some youth was a good idea, and I think Admiral Bender felt that way in particular, because he'd been ill so much of the time. Admiral Smith would not have been involved in my selection at all.

Paul Stillwell: Do you think Admiral Bender had a vote in those discussions?

Admiral Siler: I think he did. The way that the Commandant was selected, I believe still is to some extent, is that the preliminary selection is made by the Commandant and the recommendation made to the Secretary of Transportation, who then selects the final person and then sends it to the White House.

Paul Stillwell: Do you think that your previous service with Admiral Richmond might have been a factor?

Admiral Siler: I doubt it.

---

* Rear Admiral Joseph J. McClelland, USCG.

Paul Stillwell: What about Leonor Sullivan from Missouri being on the House Merchant Marine and Fisheries Committee?*

Admiral Siler: I don't think she was too active at the time that I was selected. She may have been. I just don't know. I don't think she would have influenced it at all, though. Actually, the Congress very seldom has anything to do with it except in one or two cases where the person recommended was not selected at all. That was in the time several years earlier when the recommendations from congressmen came pouring in because of previous relationships with an individual, and, as I say, he was not selected.

Paul Stillwell: Did you ever hear either directly or indirectly any hard feelings on the part of people who weren't selected when you were?

Admiral Siler: I didn't, but my wife heard from the wife of one of the them who was not selected, and her comment was that she had always dreamed of herself being the wife of the Commandant and Betty being the wife of the Assistant Commandant. It didn't work out that way.†

Paul Stillwell: What factors led you to choose Admiral Perry to be your deputy?

Admiral Siler: Well, for one thing I thought that he was perfectly qualified to be the Commandant. Before that he was two years senior to me, and I'd always felt that he was a very well qualified individual, very even as far as temper was concerned or attitude in general. When I started thinking through the people who obviously would have been in the zone, he was the one who stood out most as far as I was concerned. As far as the one that I really anticipated would have obtained a higher rank at some time, he was so senior to me that I couldn't imagine him as being my assistant.

Paul Stillwell: Was that Admiral McClelland?

---

* Leonor K. Sullivan, a Democrat from Missouri, served in the House of Representatives from 3 January 1953 to 3 January 1977. She was chairman of the Committee on Merchant Marine and Fisheries, 1973-76.
† This was Mrs. McClelland; see the beginning of interview number five of this oral history.

Admiral Siler: Yes.

Paul Stillwell: What about the business of being an aviator? There had not been many aviators previously as Commandant. Was there any controversy on that?

Admiral Siler: I don't know that there was any controversy on it, but my two predecessors were both aviators.

Paul Stillwell: Oh, I didn't realize it was two.

Admiral Siler: Both Admiral Smith and Admiral Bender were aviators, and both of them had quit aviation to go back to sea before they were selected to be the Commandant. I always thought that would be interesting, because I felt that the bigger Coast Guard ships would be interesting, but I never got around to asking for it, and I was selected for the higher rank anyway, so it didn't make too much difference.

Paul Stillwell: What do you remember about the business of being confirmed by the Senate for that job?

Admiral Siler: Mostly the senatorial confirmation was very simple. Most of the questions that were asked in the confirmation hearing were very simple to deal with. The one that I had a little problem with was one that was asked by Senator Long of Louisiana.* One question he asked had to do with deepwater ports in the Louisiana waters. And the other one was if we had problems getting a ship into port would it be a problem because the ships drew so much water when they were loaded. Of course, the answer was supposed to be simply that we would off-load the oil before we tried to bring them in. They were obviously built in shallow water, so it was not much of a real problem. I don't think generally there were any problems in the confirmation hearings.

---

* Russell B. Long, a Democrat from Louisiana, served in the U.S. Senate from 31 December 1948 until his retirement on 3 January 1987. He was chairman of the Senate Finance Committee from 1965 to 1980.

Paul Stillwell: So it was relatively smooth process?

Admiral Siler: Yes. Certainly no real controversy of any kind.

Paul Stillwell: Did you get any idea from Secretary Brinegar and Mr. Barnum on what expectations they might have?

Admiral Siler: No, not really. In fact, I got very little in the way of marching orders from anyone basically. The more difficult things came when we were obviously expanding to cover the 200-mile fishery limit, and we didn't get much support in additional ships that we felt we needed.

Paul Stillwell: Did Admiral Bender pass on to you any things that he considered unfinished business that he wanted you to work on?

Admiral Siler: Well, there was one thing very definitely that he passed on, and that had to do with the very large ship that could lift things off the bottom of the ocean. And I was given top-secret briefings about what we would do with the Hughes—

Paul Stillwell: The Glomar Explorer.*

Admiral Siler: The Explorer, yes. Of course, it's generally known all over the place now.

Paul Stillwell: Right.

---

* The Glomar Explorer, a ship with a large concealed opening in the bottom, was built for operation by the Central Intelligence Agency for the purpose of recovering a Soviet submarine. The Golf-class diesel-powered ballistic missile submarine sank 750 miles northwest of Oahu, Hawaii, in 1968. In August 1974 CIA technicians raised the submarine about halfway to the surface from a depth of three miles. The submarine then broke apart and fell back to the ocean floor. Word of the operation became public in February and March 1975 as a result of news media reports. The cover story for the Glomar Explorer was that she was recovering manganese nodules from the seabed.

Admiral Siler: It's really not anything to be concerned about, but in those days it was very definitely top secret.

Paul Stillwell: What might be a Coast Guard connection with that project?

Admiral Siler: Well, we had to inspect the vessel in order to make sure that it was completely safe to go to sea. And we did inspect it and made it continually inspected until it finished its mission. I'm not sure what ever became of it.

Paul Stillwell: I think the Navy eventually took it over and put in mothballs so it really had only one voyage.

Admiral Siler: Probably.

Paul Stillwell: But did you have to get any special clearances for the people who did the actual inspection?

Admiral Siler: I wasn't involved with it, so I'm not sure.

Paul Stillwell: But that was the only pending thing really that he passed on to you, except running the Coast Guard, of course. [Laughter]

Admiral Siler: Well, yes, but I don't think any of those things were classified in any way.

Paul Stillwell: Well, many people think about what they might do if they do get the top job. Did you have any list of agenda items yourself?

Admiral Siler: I really didn't. I was a little nonplussed that I was named to be the Commandant, because I didn't have a plan for the Coast Guard. Today I think they require people who are interested in being the Commandant to write a thesis of sorts that says what they would do if they became Commandant. I didn't have anything like that at all. I was just called in, interviewed, and given the job, and that's it.

Paul Stillwell: Did you then start to develop a plan for things that you wanted to see implemented?

Admiral Siler: Not directly. I had a few things that I wanted to accomplish that had to do with the 200-mile fishery limit, and I certainly wanted to make certain that our replacement program continued, as it actually did. We looked at the cost of the ships and how much it would cost to build other types of ships, but we were less concerned with the class of ships than we were with the individual design. Then once we decided on an individual design we tried to see how many ships we could fit into what we thought we might be given.

Paul Stillwell: What sort of division of labor did you set up with Admiral Perry? What types of issues did you deal with, what did he take?

Admiral Siler: I dealt more with the personnel, and he dealt more with the engineering and budget aspects of it, although we worked together a great deal on the budget aspects of it. He would look at the engineering aspects far more than I did.

Paul Stillwell: How would you describe your working relationship on a day-to-day basis?

Admiral Siler: We'd probably get together three or four times during the day. We worked quite closely. He let me deal almost completely with external relations, and he would work with the Coast Guard itself.

Paul Stillwell: Who else did you have on your immediate staff that you worked with very frequently?

Admiral Siler: Well, Rick Cueroni, who is a retired rear admiral now, was my first speechwriter.* And I remember that first speech that he handed to me as I walked into the office, practically it was. It was a Memorial Day-type speech that was to given at the site of the fort in Baltimore there.

Paul Stillwell: McHenry.

Admiral Siler: Yes. I was to be the—this was the fifth year, so it was the Coast Guard's turn to give the speech on McHenry Day. He had prepared a speech for whoever who was going to be the Commandant, and he sort of handed it to me. "Here, you take it from here." Then he moved up when the administrative aide was transferred, and he became the administrative aide or the special assistant for administrative purposes. At that time he was replaced by Commander Garrett, who had I think just recently graduated from the Naval War College or the Armed Forces Staff College, one of the two, and he was a very capable person too.† And I had the secretary who was knowledgeable about almost everything that went on in the office too. She stayed on until I retired. She had been Admiral Bender's secretary most of that time.

Paul Stillwell: So that's great to have that corporate memory.

Admiral Siler: Yes.

Paul Stillwell: Well, speaking of your actual takeover, I read that it rained on your parade. You were due to have the change of command on board the Ingham, and it had to be moved inside.‡

Admiral Siler: Yes, the Eagle was in port and that took some doing, too, to have the Eagle there because the draft of the Eagle is such that it had to be moved to the Navy

---

* Captain Richard P. Cueroni, USCG.
† Commander Leonard W. Garrett, USCG.
‡ USCGC Ingham (WHEC-35) was a Secretary-class cutter. The change of command was held at the Washington Navy Yard.

yard at high tide, but it had to be a low enough tide that the masts could get under the bridges, so it was quite a task to get the Eagle there.* And we did some things having to do with the bicentennial program and the fact that the national bicentennial commission was in full scale at that time. But it did rain, and so the ceremony was moved to the rigging loft at the Navy Yard. It's nice, but it's not like being outdoors.

Paul Stillwell: Right. What can you say about the role of the Eagle in the Coast Guard overall?

Admiral Siler: Well, I think that having a vessel of that type, whether it's the Eagle or the Atlantic or the Danmark when she was there, is well worthwhile to the Coast Guard. It teaches seamanship faster than a good many other methods might. My sailing experience was on the Atlantic and the Danmark, and I've never really done any sailing on the Eagle. I know that my successor did sail on the Eagle far more than I did. I'll always regret it that I didn't do more sailing.

Paul Stillwell: Well, beyond the practical benefits she also serves as a very widely recognized symbol of the service.

Admiral Siler: Yes, indeed. It's fortunate that we can get it to the West Coast at times and let the people on the West Coast see it. In fact, the year I was retired, at the request of Senator Magnuson and a few others from Seattle and that part of the world, we did have the Eagle go to the West Coast.† It made things quite complicated trying to get the cadets from the academy to the Eagle, wherever it might be. We did change the crews in Seattle at one time, and then there was one time when were going to change crews in San Diego. We thought that we could borrow Air Force time and have them load the people in San Diego and then fly to someplace, I'm not sure where.

---

* USCGC Eagle (WIX-327) is a 295-foot-long, 1,816-ton, three-masted bark used for sail training by the Coast Guard Academy. She was built in Hamburg, Germany, in the mid-1930s as the training ship Horst Wessel for the German Navy. She was transferred to the United States in January 1946 as part of German reparations in the aftermath of World War II and commissioned by the Coast Guard that year.
† Warren G. Magnuson, a Democrat from the state of Washington, served in the Senate from 14 December 1944 to 3 January 1981.

But making the change in San Diego got to be a little bit complicated because the Air Force Chief of Staff and Deputy Chief of Staff said they weren't sure that they wanted to fly a C-141 to San Diego.* I pointed out to them that we would take Coast Guard C-130s in there if he didn't. And we would have to do at least two flights for the number of cadets that were involved, and that was obviously going to attract attention. We would suggest that they land it over at North Island, which is the naval station there, and it wouldn't be as standoutish as if they came to the Coast Guard Air Station.† They saw the justice of that and decided that they could land in San Diego. Before that they were saying, "We're going to land at the Air Force base at San Bernardino, [which is 100 miles east of Los Angeles], and you'll have to bus them from San Bernardino to San Diego." That's when we got into this little contest about how difficult it would be to fly into the Coast Guard Air Station or at North Island. Eventually they went to North Island.

Paul Stillwell: What was the reluctance about flying into San Diego?

Admiral Siler: It wasn't a listed Military Airlift Command place, while the San Bernardino base was, and therefore they could land at San Bernardino without attracting any attention. It wasn't until somehow we moved the people from San Bernardino into San Diego, where the Eagle would be, that it would attract attention.

Paul Stillwell: What was the concern about attracting attention?

Admiral Siler: I don't exactly know. [Laughter] We would have attracted far more attention by stopping the traffic on the highway there in San Diego, because we'd stop the traffic and open a gate and have the airplane taxi across the highway. So it would have been far more interesting to the people and "Why is that happening?" if we had gone into San Diego with the Coast Guard C-130s.

---

* The C-141 Starlifter, built by Lockheed, is a jet-powered Air Force transport plane.
† North Island Naval Air Station is on the end of the Coronado peninsula, across the harbor from San Diego.

Paul Stillwell: What do you remember about the controversy over the racing stripe on the Eagle?*

Admiral Siler: Well, we'd never had the question arise at all until the bicentennial year, and at that point the Eagle was going into overhaul in Curtis Bay.† Ed Perry called my attention to the fact that if we really wanted to put the stripe on, this was the ideal time to do it. I thought about it a while, and we had one or two letters that said, "I'm glad you keep the Eagle in its pristine white." Thinking about it, this was the time to change it to a stripe if we were going to. So I said, "Yes, let's go ahead and do it."

But then we had a whole slough of letters that said, "Don't ruin that beautiful white Eagle with a stripe on it."

Paul Stillwell: I hear that Mr. Barnum and Walter Cronkite were two of the objectors.‡

Admiral Siler: I don't know that they were involved, but I saw most of the letters sooner or later. As far as Barnum was concerned, I wouldn't have paid much attention to him anyway. [Laughter] But we went ahead and put the stripe on, and we got a few negative comments after it was done, but the strongest affirmative letters came after the vessels had all sailed into the harbor at the end of Long Island Sound. They were getting ready to make one more trip to just south of New York, and they were going to lie at anchor there for a few days until the actual sail into New York took place.

Everyone in Newport, Rhode Island, would come down to see the sailing vessels, and they'd look around for a while and frequently ask someone, "Now which one is—?" and they'd give a name. The person would know which vessel was which, and they'd say, "Well, you can identify the Eagle because it has the stripe on it there. And the one you want is this second to the left," or "third to the right," whatever it happened to be, "of

---

* In the early 1960s the industrial design firm of Raymond Loewy/Williams Snaith, Inc., redesigned the exterior and interior of John F. Kennedy's presidential plane. That led to the firm recommending that the Coast Guard adopt a symbol or mark that would be easily distinguished. The resulting design was a wide red bar to the right of a narrow blue bar, both canted at 64 degrees. In the center of the red bar was a Coast Guard emblem. By April 1967 the slash was in use throughout the Coast Guard.
† The Coast Guard Yard is at Curtis Bay, Maryland, near Baltimore.
‡ Walter Cronkite was then the anchorman for the CBS evening news.

the Eagle." So after that was over, everyone said, "The way to find the ships is to look at the Eagle, because you know which it is." When they sailed into New York Harbor on the Fourth of July, everyone knew which was the Eagle and it had the stripe.* I never got anything except favorable comments from then on.

Paul Stillwell: Was the objection from outside the Coast Guard mostly?

Admiral Siler: I'd say 50-50. There were mostly wives who would write in, probably because the husbands wouldn't do it. [Laughter] But there were quite a few letters from Coast Guard wives saying, "We can identify the Eagle without a stripe." Of course, they might not have known how many similar vessels were going to be there, because the Argentines and the Russians both had their vessels there that were identical. And the Eagle was still easy to identify with the stripe.

Paul Stillwell: Do you remember any other aspects of the planning for the bicentennial celebration?

Admiral Siler: Well, that that been going on for several years, so I don't remember any of the specifics.

Paul Stillwell: John Warner was very active in that I remember.

Admiral Siler: Oh, yes. He was the director of the bicentennial commission. The Eagle was in Washington about a month before the bicentennial, and he had said something then about, "When we do the actual thing," and I don't remember any of the specifics, but I just remember he spoke about it at that time. I went to a whole bunch of his speeches, and during the bicentennial itself he gave the same speech twice one day, to a group at lunch, and it turned out that all the same people plus a few others were at dinner. He gave the same speech exactly.

---

* For the nation's Bicentennial celebration on 4 July 1976 tall ships from a number of nations gathered in New York Harbor.

Paul Stillwell: Where were you on July 4, 1976?

Admiral Siler: I was on the Coast Guard 378 in New York Harbor. We had spent the night before over at Governors Island in the admiral's house.* That's a beautiful house. Too bad we don't still have it. Then we went out on the ship, and we had all of the people that we had flown up the day before. We had circled the harbor just to the south, and I can't remember the name of it right now. But all of the tall ships were in this harbor. Then we flew over and made our approach pretty much on the sailing approach to New York Harbor if you were coming down from New England. And there were sailing vessels all over the place.

Paul Stillwell: I've seen pictures of it. It must have been a wonderful day.

Admiral Siler: It was. Of course, that morning was a little bit foggy, and so it was a little hard to see the vessels until they got through the haze and fog, and then all of a sudden you could see again the stripe.

Paul Stillwell: Interestingly, one of the big topics of conversation that day was a raid the Israelis had just pulled off to rescue some hostages from Entebbe, Uganda.

Admiral Siler: Yes.

Paul Stillwell: So a little bit of upstaging in the news. [Laughter]

Admiral Siler: That was an interesting time.

---

* Governors Island comprises 173 acres of land in Upper New York Bay, south of Manhattan Island. Dutch settlers brought it from Native Americans 1637. It later became the residence of the British colonial governor and as a result was named Governors Island in 1698. It served as headquarters for the Coast Guard's Atlantic Area Command from 1966 to 1997.

Paul Stillwell: You talked about Commander Cueroni handing you a speech when you came in. Did you then sit down with him and give him the flavor of things you wanted to talk about generally?

Admiral Siler: Not at that time, because there weren't very many things that had to do with the Coast Guard in that speech, because it was simply a commemorative-type speech that had to do with Fort McHenry. But before we did many more speeches, I would ask for a draft, the outline of what he had planned for me to say, and we'd go over that before he fleshed it out and worked it up. We worked the same way with Commander Garrett when he took over. Many of the things that he put in the draft speech I would either say, "Let's not put it in this speech," but other times there'd be something that I'd want to mention specifically. So I think that while the two of them did an awful lot to shape my speeches, there were some Silerisms there.

Paul Stillwell: What would be a Silerism?

Admiral Siler: I don't know. [Laughter] It's been too long.

Paul Stillwell: Were there any general themes that you tried to get across generally as you made speeches at various places?

Admiral Siler: Well, we tried to make certain that new training programs were mentioned in speeches of that sort. And anything that affected the entire Coast Guard with times at sea or anything of sort, but I can't remember any of those now.

Paul Stillwell: One thing that now Rear Admiral Cueroni suggested I ask you about was getting women more opportunities in the Coast Guard, and he said you were a bit reluctant on that at first.

Admiral Siler: Very definitely. When we decided we'd send women to the academy, the women who went to the academy kept asking, "What will we do after we graduate from the academy?" And I really didn't know. We weren't particularly concerned with it, because we thought the numbers involved were such that we could assimilate all those women in billets that did not go to sea. Yet we had some women who were very well qualified to go to sea, as we learned later. But at first I didn't feel that that was the kind of thing that we ought to dangle before the women, so I said we were not talking about going to sea.

We were talking about general Coast Guard duties. Then we decided we'd send women to sea before any of the academy graduates were graduates yet.[*] So the first two ships that did this, one was on the West Coast and one on the East Coast.[†] The one on the West Coast was assigned one woman who had been in the Coast Guard for some time and was serving in the marine safety office in I think Norfolk. The other woman was fresh out of OCS. The woman who had been in for some time had a history of going to sea with her father, and she was a sea woman if there ever was one.

One of the enlisted personnel who was going on that first ship on the West Coast had been a coxswain of a small boat. Somehow the news people heard about her when we ordered the two women—I think there was only the one who was from Norfolk—into Washington to be interviewed by the press people and to be with the Secretary. They had all sorts of questions to ask about this coxswain going to sea, and then there was a bunch of questions for the woman who had been the boat operator on the West Coast. She had been in charge of a boat that had a complete crew on it, and the male crew wanted to divert from what they were going out to do. They were supposed to be helping someone who was in trouble from swimming out too far, and they wanted to go over here and see this person who obviously was swimming in the nude. She said to the newspaper people, "I just said, 'No,' and that was it. I was in charge of that boat." So they went to the rescue and accomplished the rescue.

Of the woman officers, one was brand new, and we had no idea what her capabilities were. She was seasick as a dog every time she went out in a whaleboat or that kind of a boat to go over and board a foreign fishing vessel. On the other hand, the

---

[*] The first Coast Guard Academy class with women was that of 1980, which began training in July 1976.
[†] On 25 May 1977 Secretary of Transportation Brock Adams announced at the Coast Guard Academy graduation that for the first time in the service's history women would be assigned to cutters, beginning in the autumn of that year.

woman who had been with her father all these times could do it like it was second nature. She came back from that very first cruise to Alaska fully qualified to do everything that someone of her rank could. She was later assigned as the commanding officer of a 95-footer in Maui, and she was nominated to be a White House aide.[*] But she could do anything that a woman or a man with the rank of lieutenant could do. She has been commanding officer of a 270-footer and earlier the navigator of the same sized vessel. She's been to the Industrial College of the Armed Forces, so I expect good things from her. That is, if she doesn't marry and get out of the Coast Guard, which a lot of women do. Vivien Crea, the woman who ended up as the White House aide, was an aviator, and she said it was harder to learn to ride a horse than it was to fly a jet airplane. [Laughter] She had flown the airplanes that are made here in Savannah now.

Paul Stillwell: You came up with the name, and it was Gulfstream.

Admiral Siler: Right. The Coast Guard now has I think the Gulfstream 4 or 5, I'm not sure which it is, but we had a Gulfstream 1, which was a turboprop airplane and a Gulfstream 2. Vivien Crea, who is now Rear Admiral Vivien Crea, had just come from being an airplane pilot at the unit that had the Gulfstreams.[†] She expressed more difficulty learning to ride the horse than to fly the Gulfstream.

Paul Stillwell: What was the basis for your initial reluctance on sending women to the academy?

Admiral Siler: I didn't have any particular reluctance to send women to the academy, because there were women who had been sent to OCS and served very well. But I did wonder about sending women to sea, because the facilities on a ship are quite limited, particularly the head facilities, and so we believed that we would have more difficulty

---

[*] On 1 April 1979 Lieutenant (junior grade) Beverly Kelly became the first woman to command a Coast Guard cutter when she became skipper of the 95-foot patrol boat Cape Newagen (WPB-95318), based in Hawaii.
[†] Rear Admiral Vivien S. Crea, USCG. On 6 May 2002, subsequent to this interview, Rear Admiral Crea became Commander First Coast Guard District. In 2004 Crea is slated to become the service's first female vice admiral and will take command of the Coast Guard's Atlantic Area.

than it turned out that we had. When we did send them to sea, we found that we gained the advantage of much cleaner language on the mess deck. As far as general work requirements were concerned, there was quite obviously a feeling among the women, "I'm not going to let the men show me up," and obviously the other way—the men were not going to let the women show them up. So we accomplished a great deal by sending women to sea. I think almost every vessel larger than the 82-footers have women on them now.

Paul Stillwell: Your entry in the yearbook when you were at the Coast Guard Academy said you had an anti-profanity campaign, so this would fit right in with that.

Admiral Siler: Yes, indeed. I just never learned profanity. My parents didn't use profanity around the house, and I never felt that there was a particular need to use profanity, so if it were used in my presence, why, I might have said a few things about, "We don't really need that here."

Paul Stillwell: Was there some particular person in charge of getting the ships modified so women could serve on board? Did you have a project officer?

Admiral Siler: I think there was someone assigned as the project officer in naval engineering, but I don't recall who it was.

Paul Stillwell: And then I presume as newer ships came out later they were designed that way from the beginning.

Admiral Siler: There might have been some compartments in the 270-foot cutters that were designed that way, and I suppose the 110-foot class of patrol boat might have been modified, but I don't know about that.

Owen W. Siler, Interview #4 (12/13/00) – Page 281

Paul Stillwell: When I was at headquarters I saw a picture of you and George Elsey, the head of the American Red Cross, signing an agreement on disaster preparedness. What is the relationship between the Coast Guard and the Red Cross?

Admiral Siler: I'd say it's a good working agreement, not too specific because you hate to eliminate things simply because you're too specific so that it's more a matter of authorizing the working together of Coast Guard and Red Cross. We tried to cooperate with the Red Cross when they were doing things like hurricane relief and flood relief and things of that nature.

Paul Stillwell: What do you remember about ending the ocean station program and the considerations that went into that?

Admiral Siler: Well it was ended before I became Commandant except for one ship, which was the Taney.* The Taney had a weather shelter on the forward part of the ship, which was a round balloon-type thing, and that was I think taken off before it went to Baltimore to become a display ship. But the entire program had been ended before I became Commandant.

Paul Stillwell: What were the factors that led to ending that?[†]

Admiral Siler: Well, largely it was a matter of greater dependability of the balloon program that the Weather Bureau had and better radar from the coastal stations that reached out farther at sea.

Paul Stillwell: Would satellites be a consideration then?

---
* The program was terminated in June 1974, except for Ocean Station Hotel, which monitored Gulf Stream currents north of Cape Hatteras. See Michael R. Adams, "Ocean Weather Hotel: A Stormy Address," U.S. Naval Institute Proceedings, April 1975, pages 100-102.
† Budgetary considerations were a big factor in ending the program. See the Naval Institute oral history of Admiral James S. Gracey, USCG (Ret.).

Admiral Siler: Oh, yes.

Paul Stillwell: And perhaps another factor would be the greater reliability of the planes that were flying across the ocean.

Admiral Siler: I don't know that that would have entered in as much as the fact that the planes did fly over and could give weather reports as they flew over. In the earlier planes we used to always make hourly weather reports to our controlling station as we flew a DC-4 or a PBY, whatever it was, anyplace across the ocean that had a requirement for weather reporting.

Paul Stillwell: But there probably wasn't as much concern of a plane crashing at sea as there had been earlier.

Admiral Siler: Well, there weren't as many planes at sea, so when a plane went down, it attracted the attention of ships and other aircraft around it too.

Paul Stillwell: Shortly before you became Commandant the country had moved from the conscription system for getting people into the military and leading some to volunteer for the Coast Guard. What adjustments had to be made for the new all-volunteer force?[*]

Admiral Siler: One of the things that we had to work on very hard was to create incentives and have people volunteer for the Coast Guard. I was quite proud of the recruiting efforts that went on down in the Second District. The Second District, which is the inland district in the center of the United States, I think has always provided the greater proportion of the people who go to sea in the Coast Guard.

Paul Stillwell: How would you explain that?

---

[*] In 1972 the Defense Department announced it would end draft calls in mid-1973. Secretary of Defense Melvin Laird announced on 27 January 1973 that the use of the military draft had ended as of then, several months earlier than planned.

Admiral Siler: Well, maybe it's because they don't know what they're getting themselves into. [Laughter] I think that our recruiters may polish the image a little bit each time that they get a Coast Guard possible recruit. But I think it's mainly because those people feel they'll broaden their experience by going to sea, and they think if they're going to sea they'll just stay close to the coast. Little do they know.

Paul Stillwell: Did you have to step up recruiting and retention efforts specifically when going to the all-volunteer force?

Admiral Siler: Well, that happened before I became commandant, so I don't know how much it was stepped up. The Second District out there in the inland area almost always was the most fertile ground for recruits.

Paul Stillwell: What were the main sales tools or recruiting pitches that were used to attract people to the Coast Guard, other than just being close to the coast? [Laughter]

Admiral Siler: I don't know what the answer to that is. We did quite well in recruiting, and I don't think very often we exceeded our quotas, but some areas provided a lot more recruits than other areas.

Paul Stillwell: Well, certainly one of the things I've heard over time is the humanitarian aspect and being able to save lives and contribute to society.

Admiral Siler: I think that enters into the thoughts of quite a few young recruits. When they're teenagers or just getting to be 20 years old, I think the young people would far rather be saving people than thinking only about going out and firing at people from other countries. So there's definitely a humanitarian aspect of the Coast Guard.

Paul Stillwell: Many people are very idealistic at that age.

Admiral Siler: Yes, indeed.

Paul Stillwell: I read that there was a shortage of manning in some of the specific programs, environmental protection, law enforcement, port safety and security, and search and rescue. Did you have to beef up training in those areas?

Admiral Siler: Not that I can recall particularly. We had some very good teams for environmental protection and combating oil spills in particular. I've always felt that some of the oil spill problems we've made for ourselves.

For example, according to the EPA's rulings if a farmer in the middle of Missouri goes out and has an oilcan that he is not sure has enough oil in it and he goes like that just over a dry spot in the yard and it rains the next day that little squirt of oil can be swept into the nearest stream, which then goes downstream to a river that eventually gets into the Mississippi or the Missouri and eventually could get into the Gulf of Mexico. That man, simply because he did that, could be fined $1,000. He can lessen that by saying, "Oops, I spilled some oil." Then it's only $500. [Laughter] Well, I think that's an absurd approach to oil pollution regulation, but that's EPA. I've always thought it should be modified in some way to say that that's not quite what was the intent here. It's what the law says.

Paul Stillwell: One thing I've read also about your time was an emphasis on personal grooming and military smartness. What do you recall in that area?

Admiral Siler: One of the things that I really disliked was the little care for decent haircuts. There was a time when reserve personnel could come on active duty wearing a wig, and I thought that was about as dumb as we could get, but the Navy accepted it, and so we could hardly say, "Forget that." I always felt that we should be smart by ourselves if necessary and impress people with our smartness.

Paul Stillwell: In that same area what factors let into the adoption of a new Coast Guard uniform during that era?

Admiral Siler: Don't look at me. [Laughter]

Paul Stillwell: Well, I'm asking. [Laughter]

Admiral Siler: That happened before I became Commandant, and I can't say I accepted it with enthusiasm.*

Paul Stillwell: Why not?

Admiral Siler: I felt that the appearance like a Navy officer was as good as the appearance like an Air Force officer. And it's pretty much like the Air Force right now.

Paul Stillwell: Yes.

Admiral Siler: In fact, I've stood next to an Air Force officer and been mistaken for Air Force. One of the things that I did very shortly after I became Commandant was that I went to the White House when President Ford was sworn in.† I sat down next to Jimmy Holloway, and, of course, he was wearing his blue uniform, white shirt, and looked like a naval officer.‡ I thought I looked pretty much like a Coast Guard Navy officer too. Sat down next to him, and one of the ushers who was I guess an Air Force or Army officer came over and said, "You'll have to move, sir. Those seats are reserved for the service chiefs." [Laughter]

I was a little taken aback by that. Didn't know quite what to say, and Jimmy Holloway said, "Do you know who you're talking to? That's the Commandant of the Coast Guard."

---

* Up to the early 1970s, Coast Guard blues were really black rather than blue and closely resembled the uniforms worn by Navy officers and chief petty officers. Admiral Bender brought in new uniforms that were essentially royal blue in color and obviously distinct from Navy uniforms. In addition, the blouses for the new uniforms were single-breasted instead of double-breasted, and the shirts worn with Bender Blue were specified as light blue rather than the white shirts worn by Navy personnel.
† After the resignation of President Richard Nixon on 9 August 1974, Gerald R. Ford was sworn in as his replacement and held the office until 20 January 1977.
‡ Admiral James L. Holloway III, USN, served as Chief of Naval Operations, 29 June 1974 to 1 July 1978.

The man said, "I beg your pardon," and backed away. [Laughter]

But I went back to Coast Guard headquarters and immediately prepared an order that any time that you were going to an official ceremonial event of that nature, or any time you were going to an evening event the proper uniform was with a white shirt. Because I was wearing the light blue uniform shirt with the military rank on the distinguishing pins on the collar, that was a little too much like an Air Force officer. But if you wore a white shirt without things on the collar people would look at the sleeve and there might be just the stripes of rank. So ever since then it's been Bender blue and Siler shirt. [Laughter]

Paul Stillwell: Well, I wonder if the Bender blue came about trying to make the Coast Guard more distinctive from the Navy, just as the racing stripe made the Eagle more distinctive.

Admiral Siler: Well, I don't know that the Eagle's stripe had to be used at all to make the vessel distinguished from the Navy, for example. The only thing it would do would make it distinguished from other foreign ships. As far as the Bender blue was concerned, Admiral Bender did not like the fact that he was once in a long while mistaken for a Navy officer, and so we became Air Force officers. It was too expensive to even think of changing it back again. It was very expensive to provide every enlisted man in the Coast Guard with a new uniform that looked like the Air Force. One of his ideas was that that uniform looks more like the old shore station people who were in the Lifesaving Service. In my opinion it still looks too much like the Air Force.

Paul Stillwell: Well, the Air Force a few years ago had a very short-lived uniform that was even closer to the Coast Guard uniform than the one they've had. It had the stripes on the sleeves instead of stars on the collars.

Admiral Siler: That's what they still have, the stripes on the sleeve, don't they?

Paul Stillwell: Oh, I thought they had phased that one out.

Admiral Siler: I'm not sure. I thought that they still had silver stripes.

Paul Stillwell: Right, they were silver. Well, speaking of Presidents, when you got to Washington in 1974 it was really at the height of the Watergate crisis.[*] Did you have any dealings with President Nixon, and were there any concerns growing out of Watergate for the Coast Guard?

Admiral Siler: I met President Nixon once when I was assistant chief of staff, and I was just a captain then. We were told that we could take all of the flag officers and a few other people over to the Department of Transportation so that we could all meet the President. That's the only time I ever met President Nixon, and I was a little embarrassed about it before I got out of the DoT Building, which was really the FAA Building at that time. I was about the last of the Coast Guard people who went up to shake hands with him, and the man just before me was an FAA man, I believe. He might have been rail or highways even, I'm not sure now.

But it was the President and then Mr. Volpe.[†] When he got to Mr. Volpe, the man preceding me started talking to Mr. Volpe about some concerns that someone else had had recently, but he didn't move on so that other people could come up and shake hands with Mr. Volpe. He stood there in front of Mr. Volpe, and there I was eyeball to eyeball with the President. [Laughter] And Mr. Nixon had learned the practice of looking you in the eyeball when you were in the receiving line. Very frequently when you watch someone in the receiving line they will shake hands and then move on with his sight to the next individual. Not President Nixon. He looked at you, and as long as you were standing there he was going to look at you. [Laughter] I didn't know what I was going to do when I was left there, having said my important thing, which was, "Very pleased to meet you, Mr. President." [Laughter] I couldn't move, and I couldn't think of anything that was reasonable to say at that time. So I was very pleased when the man finished his

---

[*] In June 1972 operatives working indirectly for the Committee to Re-elect the President broke into the headquarters of the Democratic National Committee in the Watergate complex in Washington, D.C. The resulting cover-up led to the August 1974 resignation of President Richard Nixon.
[†] John A. Volpe served as Secretary of Transportation from 22 January 1969 to 1 February 1973.

conversation with Mr. Volpe, and I went over and said, "Nice to see you, Mr. Secretary," and went and sat down again and said, "Well, that's over." But that's the only time I ever shook hands with Mr. Nixon.

Paul Stillwell: Well, I've heard he didn't really have a gift for small talk. [Laughter]

Admiral Siler: I guess not, but he never met me when I was nominated for Commandant. I guess everything was handled by the staff, and when my commission was signed my guess is it was signed by machine instead of him. So that was it as far as Mr. Nixon was concerned.

Paul Stillwell: Was there any fallout at all from Watergate as far as the Coast Guard was concerned?

Admiral Siler: No.

Paul Stillwell: What do you remember of President Ford?

Admiral Siler: Well, we got to the swearing in of Mr. Ford and met with him several times. In fact, one of those photographs over there is of the Christmas reception that he had for the service chiefs and a few other people like the Assistant Secretary of Defense. And I guess there were a few others. Well, the people who were in the joint commands were all included as well. One of them was the big black general who was head of the American Defense Command.

Paul Stillwell: Chappie James?

Admiral Siler: Chappie James.[*] He and I were at the same table with Mrs. Ford and the

---

[*] General Daniel "Chappie" James, Jr., USAF, was the nation's first African-American four-star officer. Upon being promoted to full general on 1 September 1975, General James was assigned as Commander in Chief North American Air Defense Command and Aerospace Defense Command, a position he held until his retirement on 1 February 1978.

Assistant Secretary of Defense. Chappie said that he had had the opportunity to brief several high-ranking people from foreign countries, and the question came up, "What are the Fords going to do after Christmas and before New Year's?"

She said, "Well, we had hoped to go out to Vail to go skiing, but there's been no snow this year."

Chappie said, "You let us know which days you want to be there, Mrs. Ford, and we'll have snow for you." I don't know how he planned to do it [laughter] except with a snowmaking machine.

But, anyway, he had said it that way, and the Assistant Secretary of Defense said, "How are you going to do that, Chappie? Why are you saying you'll have snow anytime you want?"

And he said, "Well, we had said something about having other colored snow, but we'll have to have white snow because I understand it's discriminatory if you don't" [Laughter] Coming from him it was hilarious. [Laughter]

Paul Stillwell: What can you say about President Ford's personality. Certainly he's not considered as stiff as Mr. Nixon.

Admiral Siler: No, he wasn't a bit stiff that evening when all of us were there together, and those other pictures show conversation groups when he would carry on conversations with people. He'd done this when he was Vice President, too, and come to several Navy League things, and he'd speak with anybody who was there. Of course, the majority of us were, I guess, higher level in Navy League, but there was nothing that made us outstanding at all. And the great majority were not in uniform, although I usually wore a uniform to those things while I was still on active duty.

Paul Stillwell: Do you have any particular memories of that ceremony when Ford was sworn in as president?

Admiral Siler: Well, the thing that I remember the most is that question about moving to someplace else because the service chiefs would sit there. Other than that, why, I don't remember too much. One other interesting thing with Mr. Ford and his ceremonies was when the man who ran for Vice President with—ran for Vice President, but someone asked him why he was running for Vice President, and he said he didn't know. [Laughter]

Paul Stillwell: Admiral Stockdale?

Admiral Siler: Yes, Stockdale.* When Jim Stockdale got his Medal of Honor, Mrs. Ford did not come to that ceremony at all. But at that time Betty, my wife, wore her hair in the same way as Betty Ford, and from across the room a good many people mistook her for Mrs. Ford. [Laughter]

Paul Stillwell: Same name too.

Admiral Siler: Yes. When we went to that Christmas party, which was sort of a farewell, it was in late December, and he was going out of office in January, and I was going out of office in June. Betty spoke to Betty Ford and said, "You know, you and I have the same first name and you do some dancing and I can do a little singing. Maybe we can have a Betty and Betty act." [Laughter] I don't know how Mrs. Ford took that, and you could never tell how much she was enjoying something, because at that time she was pretty much under the influence of the drugs that she had taken too much.

Paul Stillwell: You mentioned Admiral Holloway. His term as CNO almost exactly coincided with yours as Commandant.

Admiral Siler: Within a month.

---

* Commander James B. Stockdale, USN, eventually a vice admiral, was a prisoner of war in Vietnam from September 1965 to February 1973. He was subsequently awarded the Medal of Honor for his heroism while in prison. His wife Sybil was active in publicizing the plight of prisoners in Vietnam and calling for more humane treatment than they had received from their captors. He was Ross Perot's running mate in the 1992 presidential election.

Paul Stillwell: What sort of relationship did you have with him?

Admiral Siler: Fairly cordial. See the three books there that are exactly the same?

Paul Stillwell: Right.

Admiral Siler: Those were Naval Institute and—

Paul Stillwell: Letters of Alfred Thayer Mahan.

Admiral Siler: Yes. I was invited to lunch at Jimmy Holloway's quarters when I got those, and Lou Wilson was also invited.* We had a very cordial lunch, and those were presented to me. I think a similar type of books, may have been exactly the same, were presented to Lou Wilson. It turned out that Lou Wilson said, "I have a great deal of respect for the Coast Guard. They put me ashore at Bougainville."

I did a double take and said, "Lou, there was only one Coast Guard ship at Bougainville."

He said, "Yes, the Hunter Liggett."

I said, "Yes, and that was the ship all right. I was a junior officer on it." And so he and I were on the same ship back in '43 and had no idea.

Paul Stillwell: Did you have any business with the Marine Corps when you were Commandant?

Admiral Siler: Cordial relations but that's about all.

Paul Stillwell: How much did you have in the way of substantive dealings with Admiral Holloway?

---

* General Louis H. Wilson, Jr., USMC, served as Commandant of the Marine Corps from 1 July 1975 to 30 June 1979.

Admiral Siler: Well, I didn't have a great deal with Admiral Holloway, but when we wanted to negotiate something with the Navy for equipping of ships or anything of that nature, we had no hesitation about going over and doing that. We had a liaison officer assigned all the time to the Navy OpNav, and so it was a good relationship all the time. Of course, whenever we would go to the Capitol to hear joint sessions of Congress, why, I'd see Jimmy again, and after we both retired he took a position with the American merchant marine.

Paul Stillwell: CASO, the Council of American Ship Operators.

Admiral Siler: I'm not sure it was that name initially. It may have changed a little bit. But he did go to that position. We had a Coast Guard officer who retired just about the same time I did, a few months later. Actually, it was a classmate, and you would have thought he would retire quite a little after me because my turn was up because I was the Commandant, but he stayed until July I think it was when he retired. There are awards now for merchant marine shipping rules named after him because he was so outstanding for the furthering of safety on merchant ships.

Paul Stillwell: What was his name?

Admiral Siler: Mike Benkert.[*] But he would have been very closely related to Jimmy Holloway's work.

Paul Stillwell: Anything else you remember about Benkert?

Admiral Siler: Oh, lots. [Laughter]

Paul Stillwell: Admiral Wallace said to ask you about him.[†]

---

[*] Rear Admiral William M. Benkert, USCG.
[†] Rear Admiral Sidney A. Wallace, USCG (Ret.), is a former member of the Naval Institute's board.

Admiral Siler: Well, Mike was a classmate, and when we were both second or third classmen I got tired of working mathematics and engineering problems, and I wasn't quite sure I wanted to stay in the Coast Guard. Mike lived just a few doors down the hall from me and came in and started a conversation, and I told him what my problem was. He said, "Well, to me the Coast Guard is just another job," very offhand. His background before he went to the academy was he'd been a mudhog under New York Harbor working on the subway tunnels. I started thinking about it a little bit more, and I figured, "Boy, if he's in here just because it's another job and I'm here because I can help people, I'd better stay." [Laughter] So I did.

Mike became a rear admiral and was a highly respected merchant marine safety officer. Boy, when he was a lieutenant and had just gotten into the program he was spoken of as an example of how merchant marine safety could be furthered by very practical things, like if you wanted to be sure that a lifejacket would hold up, throw it in the water. See if it sinks. [Laughter] And he'd throw them in. [Laughter]

Paul Stillwell: Sounds as if he had a good sense of humor.

Admiral Siler: He also had a very strong Brooklynese accent, and he would start a conversation with, "What you thinking about, huh? What you thinking, huh?" And he was a character, to be sure.

Paul Stillwell: What do you recall of him in the marine safety capacity?

Admiral Siler: He was the commanding officer of the Eastwind when the Eastwind was ordered to make an attempt to go north of Asia, and leave the Atlantic and end up in the Pacific.* He got partway across and tried to go north of some islands that are north of Russia and couldn't do it. He felt that he probably could go between the two islands where there was some sheltered water and asked for permission to do that. They told him

---

* In the period from August to October 1967 the icebreaker Eastwind (WAGB-279) circumnavigated the North Pole to obtain meteorological and oceanographic data.

that they'd have to get permission from Russia, because it was definitely close enough that the Russians claimed the water in between. While he was killing time, he was fuming at everybody in the Department of State and the Navy Department and everyone else, and then he never did get permission and he had to come back. But he had extended his time on the Eastwind because he wanted to do that so much. He loved going to sea on the icebreakers.

Paul Stillwell: Anything else on him?

Admiral Siler: He would strike you as a diamond in the rough for sure. [Laughter]

Paul Stillwell: Especially with that opening conversational gambit.

Admiral Siler: Yes.

Paul Stillwell: You talked about women on board ships and at the academy. What do you remember about getting them into the flight-training program? The Navy was just getting going on women also in flight training.

Admiral Siler: Yes, I think the Navy was about a year ahead of us. The first woman that we assigned was Vivien Crea, who worked for Sid Wallace. She was a very charming young jaygee at that point. She got into flight training and got through with no trouble at all. There was a second woman who was ordered into flight training very shortly afterward and was assigned to helicopter training, and unfortunately she lost her life in Hawaii. I think she was working with people that were doing some repair work on the loran station. I've been trying for quite some time to get a portrait of that girl into the Naval Aviation Museum. It may be there now. I don't know.

Paul Stillwell: You talked about earlier the slowness of getting minorities into the Coast Guard Academy. Were there any specific minority recruiting efforts on your watch, either for the academy or for the service at large?

Admiral Siler: Yes, about that time we tried a program called I think MITE, Minority Introduction To Engineering, and thinking that would make the entrance to the academy much easier, because they would be ahead of their equals in mathematics in particular. I don't know that that ever worked very well. There are always a few outstanding blacks who have made very good marks at the academy. There's been a commanding officer of one of the Great Lakes icebreakers, the 140-foot tug/icebreakers. We visited the ship one time when I was in Cleveland. It's a very capable little vessel. And he has gone on. He's, I think, commanding officer of a marine safety office now.

We didn't have any specific programs during the time that I was Commandant, but I think there were ongoing programs trying to encourage minorities to go to the academy. Of course, we had a couple of Chinese who have been very capable. We've had a man who was the commanding officer of the Barbers Point Air Station, and I forget where else he was, but he's very capable.

Paul Stillwell: Well, I suppose a drawback would be that there were not a lot of historic role models to point to, Mike Healy being one but not many others.[*]

Admiral Siler: Well, and Mike Healy was only half Negro. If you didn't look closely you wouldn't think he was a Negro. Of course the Healy, we now have a ship named after him, so he's made his mark.

Paul Stillwell: You have a ship named after Haley too.

Admiral Siler: Yes, very definitely.

---

[*] Michael A. Healy was born near Macon, Georgia in 1839. He was the fifth of ten children born to Michael Morris Healy, an Irish plantation owner, and his wife Mary Elisa Smith, a former slave. In 1864 he joined the U.S. Revenue Cutter Service. He rose steadily through the ranks to captain, serving in various cutters stationed on the East Coast. In 1874 he sailed the cutter Rush around Cape Horn to San Francisco. He spent the next 21 years between there and the Arctic Sea of Alaska; included in that time was his command of the cutter Bear. The Coast Guard icebreaker Healy (WAGB-20) is named in his honor.

Paul Stillwell: Roots came out while you were Commandant.* Did you have any contact with Alex Haley during that period?

Admiral Siler: Not during that period, but he was a chief journalist up in New York when we dedicated the monument that was in Battery Park, and it was first I ran into him there. I'm not sure where—I should have Roots there someplace.

Paul Stillwell: It's probably in one of these bookcases.

Admiral Siler: Well, there's Roots.

Paul Stillwell: So it is. It's endorsed, "March 17, 1977. To Admiral and Mrs. Siler, warm wishes from the family of Kunta Kinte from a proud former Coast Guardsman. Alex Haley, JOC, USCG (Retired)."

---

* Alex Haley produced the Pulitzer Prize-winning book Roots that traced his lineage back to the days of slavery and to his ancestors in Africa. The initial telecast of the dramatization of the story was in early 1977 and drew 130 million viewers, making it the most-watched miniseries of all time. The cutter USCGC Alex Haley (WMEC-39) is named in the author's honor.

Interview Number 5 with Admiral Owen W. Siler, U.S. Coast Guard (Retired)
Place: Admiral Siler's home in Savannah, Georgia
Date: Thursday, 14 December 2000
Interviewer: Paul Stillwell

Paul Stillwell: Good morning, Admiral. We've got a couple of items to go back and finish up on from yesterday. One is you were telling about an admiral's wife who envisioned herself as the Commandant's wife. Who was that?

Admiral Siler: That was Mrs. Jane McClelland, Admiral J. J. McClelland's wife. He was a very capable officer and a very good officer. He was not selected the first time that he could have been, but he was number-one man in his class and I guess had always been number-one man. Because he was so capable I'm sure many people thought that he would be selected the first time he possibly could be. That was the time that Bill Rea, whom you may know, was selected from I guess you would say below the zone.* But it was the first time that anyone had ever been selected sooner than they thought they would be selecting them. Joe did not make admiral until the next selection board, and then he was one of the first ones that I made a vice admiral. Then that led to the statement by his wife that she had anticipated that her husband would be the Commandant, and maybe they could do something about me. [Laughter]

Paul Stillwell: Well, another person we talked about yesterday was Mike Benkert, and you wanted to talk a little more about his international role.

Admiral Siler: Yes, he headed the group that went to the IMO meetings in London several times.† Particularly in the earlier days, when he was chief of environmental protection office in the Coast Guard, he would be involved in formulating the international regulations that had to do with pollution by ships at sea. So he became

---

* Captain William F. Rea III, USCG, whom Admiral Siler later chose to be a vice admiral.
† IMO—International Maritime Organization.

highly respected in that role, and many of the people who were involved with IMO thought of the United States Coast Guard as Mike Benkert.

Paul Stillwell: You've talked about Admiral McClelland and becoming a vice admiral. Who were the other vice admirals that served when you were Commandant?

Admiral Siler: The entire group of people who had been vice admirals retired either at the time that I became Commandant or shortly afterward.

Paul Stillwell: Is that standard practice?

Admiral Siler: No. It just happened that their terms in office expired that same time. Bill Rea became the area commander in New York, and Joe McClelland became the admiral out in San Francisco, the Pacific Area Commander. The only other one who served initially was Admiral Perry, who was the Assistant Commandant.[*] Then Joe McClelland had to retire because of his seniority, and so we made Admiral Austin Wagner the vice admiral in San Francisco.[†]

Paul Stillwell: I suspect that when it comes to picking people for that sort of promotion that the whole Coast Guard knows the flag officers pretty well.

Admiral Siler: Yes, indeed.

Paul Stillwell: Did you do any polling to get this kind of nomination, or how did you come to the decision?

Admiral Siler: Admiral Perry and I thought about it and came up with the decisions each time.

---
[*] Vice Admiral Ellis L. Perry, USCG.
[†] Vice Admiral Austin C. Wagner, USCG.

Paul Stillwell: Well, please tell me about your relationships with the area commanders and what roles they carried out and how much contact you had with them.

Admiral Siler: They were the operational commanders in the two areas, the Pacific and the Atlantic. And many of the things in New York from the point of view of the admirals would be merchant marine safety oriented. That was the ideal place to put Admiral Rea, because he had been involved with marine safety. He was the chief of that office in Coast Guard headquarters shortly before that when Admiral Benkert, I believe, replaced him. He was an obvious choice for New York, because that's the headquarters of the American Bureau of Shipping and things like that. Admiral McClelland I also thought was rather an obvious choice. He had been admired by a large number of the Coast Guard officers, and I think they rather expected that he would make the vice admiral position when it was available. The man who was the area commander before him was Admiral Whalen, who had been my boss as the chief of staff of the Coast Guard before that.* He was retiring at that time, so it was a good time to make Joe the vice admiral.

Paul Stillwell: Well, you've talked about the inspections and standards for shipping. Was that upgraded any particularly after the grounding of the Argo Merchant?†

Admiral Siler: Not particularly at that time. It was to some extent, because we felt that the navigation capability of the people on that ship should be improved, and at that time we started looking at ships as they would come into port and seeing if their compliance with regulations was adequate. And it was not in a good many cases. But the Argo Merchant was particularly bad, because I don't think it had been inspected in recent months, if not for several years.

Of course, the way that the ships got around those regulations was to be inspected in a country where the inspection was lax. The inspectors would give them certificates of adequacy, when really if they were looked at in the United States they would not have

---

* Vice Admiral Mark A. Whalen, USCG.
† On 15 December 1976 the Liberian tanker Argo Merchant ran aground on Nantucket Shoals, 29 miles southeast of Nantucket Island, Massachusetts. On 21 December the ship broke apart, and the bow section sank the following day. Much of the ship's cargo of 193,000 barrels of oil spilled into the sea.

been satisfactory to sail the oceans. They didn't have a radio direction finder, they didn't have any ability to navigate near the coast of the United States, because they had no automatic direction finder, they had no loran. So it was not a surprising thing that they went aground.

Paul Stillwell: There was a concern about making double hulls mandatory at that time, which came about later. Was the Coast Guard involved in that?

Admiral Siler: Admiral Benkert and I didn't feel that it was absolutely essential that we have double hulls. We thought that some other methods could be used to avoid spills. One of the things that was of great interest to many people involved with merchant shipping was how you would clean the tanks and what you would do with the slops that were left after they finished cleaning the tanks.

Admiral Benkert was a proponent of using hot crude to wash the tanks, and that would remove most of the slops from the tanks where the oil had been before. He always maintained that that was better than trying to have double hulls, because you'd be carrying around empty tanks so much of the time. Also, if you holed the external hull of a ship you then opened the double bottom or whatever it was, the double side, to the ocean and that would increase the depth of the hull of the vessel. So he didn't feel that double hulls were the answer. And he was rather persuasive on that, in spite of the fact that there were some people, particularly congressmen, who felt that that was right answer.

Paul Stillwell: Speaking of Congress, what can you say about your relationships with the Merchant Marine and Fisheries Committee in the House?

Admiral Siler: Most of the time it was very good. I can't say that was always the case in the Senate, but the House was quite friendly. Mr. Magnuson usually greeted me as his fellow Washingtonian, and I never bothered to tell him that I'd left at the age of six months. But I was stationed in Washington State for over three years when I first went into aviation.

He held some hearings just after the Argo Merchant, I guess. Anyway, there had been an incident of that nature, and I guess it was the Argo Merchant when he heard the Secretary of Transportation, who was still a Republican at that time and was relieved very shortly afterward when Jimmy Carter became the President. But he listened to the Secretary without too many problems. Although there was one time when Mr. Magnuson was asking questions, and I thought that Secretary Coleman and Senator Magnuson were going to come to blows [laughter] if it went on much longer.[*] When he finished with his testimony, which was the early part of the hearing, he was excused.

I felt that the next logical witness would have been myself and Mike Benkert along with me. But when we got ready for the next hearing, which was after lunch one day, he asked if I would mind stepping back and letting some other witnesses appear. Of course, you do what the senator says. Then he left me to sit there and listen to other testimony for three days before he called me. The important part of that was that he wanted me to hear the testimony of the people who were opposed to the Coast Guard regulation. So we went on and on in that way.

Finally, I had to tell the senator that if they were not going to call me that afternoon I would have to do some things back at Coast Guard headquarters. He said, "You mean this isn't the most important thing you have?"

I said, "It's important but not the only thing I have to take care of." So he did call me that afternoon after hearing something like four witnesses, each of whom were saying that the Coast Guard regulation was no good. [Laughter]

Paul Stillwell: And I assume your testimony was just the opposite. [Laughter]

Admiral Siler: Oh, sure.

Paul Stillwell: In general how would you characterize your appearances before the Senate? Friendly?

---

[*] William T. Coleman, Jr., served as Secretary of Transportation from 7 March 1975 to 20 January 1977.

Admiral Siler: Usually it was quite friendly. We rarely had problems with anyone in the Senate except when they got started on that oil pollution.

Paul Stillwell: How were the budget hearings? Did you generally get what you asked for?

Admiral Siler: Not what we hoped for but what we asked for. The Office of Management and Budget would always ask to see our prepared statement ahead of time, and we had to remember that some organizations made their living by cutting your budget. Particularly the OMB staffers always made it a point that we should not ask for more than what they and the President had agreed to and cut us where we could possibly stand it. Usually they were not too severe, and we pretty much knew what we could get away with, and there were some additions to our budget almost every time because of the congressmen who had a pet project that they wanted to get in.

Paul Stillwell: What would be examples of those pet projects?

Admiral Siler: Well, particularly we had moved a ship out of New Bedford, Massachusetts, and the congressman from that area had been the chairman of the Coast Guard committee. He made it a point that that cutter was to be repaired and sent back to New Bedford as fast as possible. It was one that had been in the Coast Guard quite a few years and was really tired and needed some overhaul. It made one patrol of some kind, I don't recall what it was exactly, and we had to put it back into a yard after that to make certain it was safe to go back to sea and not leak oil all over the place.[*] Many of those ships that we were phasing out were riveted construction, and the rivets were old enough that they were beginning to leak all over the place. So there was a lot of oil that was being leaked from those ships, especially when they were at sea and working all the time. Of course, it was far better to have welded construction, which we didn't have much at all until the class of ships that are the 270-foot cutters, which have all-welded construction.

---

[*] This was USCGC Unimak (WHEC-379), as mentioned in the previous interview.

Paul Stillwell: Did New Bedford get its ship back?

Admiral Siler: They did at that time. I'm not sure whether they still do, because that particular ship was definitely phased out shortly afterward.

Paul Stillwell: One of the things that the files at headquarters talked about was the re-capitalization of the Coast Guard on your watch, including the infrastructure, new aircraft, and new cutters. Could you address those programs please?

Admiral Siler: We had planned for quite some time for a new class of cruising cutter, and there was a lot of discussion about what size and what kind of a ship we should have. We ended up building the 270-foot cutter, which was not quite what we had hoped for.* But when we realized the cost of building a new class like the 378 or the 327 we were really replacing the 327 at that time, the Taney class and the Ingham and so on.

    We looked at something that would be along that line, and the first thing that we thought of was how about turbines again? Well, turbines are a good idea, but they're complicated engineering, and you have to have the engineering capability to operate turbines, and you have to be a good enough engineer to operate the reciprocating engines as well. So then we thought of the steam turbines, which the 327s had, and that was really going out of style for oceangoing vessels. We had tried a combined plant with the diesel engines and turbine to kick in when we needed additional speed, as we did in the 210-foot cutter earlier, but I think all those turbines were removed shortly afterward. Even when they had been in the ship, it was possible that water could be coming from astern and go into the exhaust area for the turbine and get it soaked with salt water, and then it was in deep trouble. So we didn't seriously consider a combined plant.

    Then we thought of four diesel engines and started examining what it would take in personnel to maintain those power plants. And there would be the additional weight of the ship, which would have necessitated a rather large hull, and if you had a hull that

---

* The first ship of the 270-foot-long medium-endurance cutters was the USCGC Bear (WMEC-901). The keel laying was 23 August 1979, launching 25 September 1980, and commissioning 4 February 1983. For a description of the class, see Michael R. Adams, "Can the Coast Guard's New Cutter Cut It?" U.S. Naval Institute Proceedings, April 1978, pages 99-101.

large then you had to have people to maintain the engines, which would mean more space for bunk spaces. So we looked around for the biggest diesel engines that we could find, and we put those in the 270-foot cutter. It was, I think, a fairly good compromise, because our plans showed that that class of a ship with the biggest diesel engines we could get would make a speed of just about 20 knots. That would be able to overtake any fishing vessel that we knew of that was either operating or on the drawing boards at that time. So we went ahead with just two engines.

Some of the other things that were improvements in that class of vessels included a CIC that was largely computerized. We called it the command display and control system; the abbreviation is COMDAC. But it got into one of the most complicated contracting fiascoes that I ever thought we would be involved with, because then the Department of Transportation felt that if it were all done by the same organization there would be unfair competition. So there was a contract to build the ships with two power plants, a contract to build the COMDAC with a computerized function in the CIC, but the final computer programs could not be done by the same contractor.

So the initial design was made by Sperry, and they provided the first computer-aided system for the CIC. Then the department insisted that we not truly consider Sperry for the software to operate the equipment. So Sperry did bid on it, and they obviously knew the most about it, because they'd tested it in their shops before they installed it. But the department reviews insisted that someone else get the final chance to prepare all the software. We ended up with another company doing the software design and then yet another company that was going to be doing the verification and validation they call it, the V and V. I just knew that when it was installed and tried the first time they would sit down at a table and have the Coast Guard, the verification and validation company, the Sperry company because they had designed the equipment initially, and the software company whatever it turned out to be, sitting around the table pointing at each other and saying, "You did it. It would have been all right if you'd done such-and-such." So I'm happy to say I was out of the Coast Guard before that came to pass. [Laughter] But it was quite a complicated contracting plan.

Paul Stillwell: What can you say about the process of replacing the Albatross, moving to the Falcon Jet?*

Admiral Siler: Well, they had talked about replacing the Albatross with a jet-propelled aircraft quite a long time before I became Commandant. Admiral Bender had contracted for two aircraft of differing types, jet propelled, that would supposedly replace the Albatross and would prove or disprove the fact that they could do it with a jet airplane. One of them was the Israeli airplane; it had been a Republic aircraft, and they sold the design to the Israelis. This was a high-wing type jet-propelled aircraft, and they'd had pretty much the same design but improved it as they went along to make it a reciprocating engine, a turboprop and then the jet. It was a little small for the Coast Guard's operation, but that led to a very close study of how large an airplane we needed for our purpose.

Because we realized if it were a large jet such as the smaller passenger jets that were being used in the airlines, that would have taken a lot of fuel. An airplane that size would have cost a great deal anyway. The other plane that was leased was a rather small airplane. In fact, it was so small that you couldn't ever stand up in it, and that was pretty much true of the Falcon jet too. But it led to a size study to see really how much size we did need. We ended up saying that the Falcon Jet just had enough space, and at the same time that Israeli airplane was disqualified because of its size. The other one was a Cessna, which was quite small and was very definitely eliminated on size.

We first went out for bids on the Falcon Jet or whatever it turned out to be simply saying, "This is the airplane we propose," and we had a proposal from Lockheed. Lockheed proposed their Thunderjet, which was a commercial passenger plane, but it had one jet on each side of the after part of the hull. In order for it to meet some of the requirements that we said were necessary, they felt that they would have to re-engine it with four engines, two on each side. And the aircraft had been built that way. There's no

---

* The HU-25 Guardian, manufactured by the Falcon Jet Corporation, is a jet-powered, fixed-wing surveillance aircraft. HU-25A, HU-25B, and HU-25C are three variants; the primary difference is in the sensor packages. The aircraft has a wingspan of 54 feet, length of 56 feet, gross weight of 32,000 pounds, and a cruising speed of 350-410 knots. For details, see Howard B. Thorsen, "The Coast Guard's New Medium Range Surveillance Aircraft," U.S. Naval Institute Proceedings, April 1981, pages 112-114.

question about the fact that it could be done. But if they didn't have the four engines, it would stall at the lower speeds that we said we would need when we were actually searching.

The Germans proposed the airplane that is operated quite a lot in Europe and frequently in Switzerland, as I recall, and it was a pretty big airplane. But we had hoped that Germany would be anxious enough to get the contract that perhaps the government would subsidize the company. They didn't. But we had I think it was four airplanes that could qualify. One was the Falcon, and the Falcon had to be re-engined also, because we said that we wanted to be able to operate at a fairly low altitude, and if we didn't have the right engine, there wouldn't be enough power if we lost one engine because of flying through birds or whatever icing conditions. Anyway, we talked to them about the problem, and they said, "Well, we'll re-engine it with a different engine. It's a quite powerful engine, and we'll have a lot of spare power available."

We did it in two phases. That plane was proposed, and so were the German airplane and the Israeli airplane. We eliminated some because of size, and the German plane was not eliminated and the Lockheed plane was going to have to be re-engined. Then the second phase was, "All right, how much does this cost, then having approved the design?" Then Lockheed dropped out, and the Germans dropped out. We had only one plane that qualified, which was the Falcon Jet. So we worked with the Falcon Jet both on the design and the powering. And then they tried the new engine.

One of the things that we required in our specifications was that the aircraft qualify for the FAA certification, which would have been a passenger-carrying certification. The engine had to qualify for not stalling if you flew through bird flocks. The first test that the FAA did was to throw a chicken of a certain size simulating a bird of that size. They'd throw the chicken into the jet engine and see what happened. The engine died every time. So they redesigned the engine until it was still more powerful and it could take care of that size chicken. The next test was two smaller chickens and tried it, and it stalled again. So they re-engined some more, and all that extra power that we had initially was gone. [Laughter] So I'm not sure how it operates at maximum range, but we had only the one aircraft that had qualified initially and it didn't qualify when it got to chickens. [Laughter]

Paul Stillwell: Well there was another concern, too, about buying a foreign-built plane. How did you deal with that?

Admiral Siler: The company had a brilliant idea. It was originally a French airplane. They were going to build it ready to fly in France and have it certified the way that was required by the FAA and by the French FAA. They'd take it up and go through the tests there. The only electronics in it would be the bare minimum electronics of French manufacture. Then they'd come down having been certified and take the wings off and the engines off, take the radios out and roll it into a C-130, which was owned by Pan American, and fly the C-130 to a site in Texas. Then they'd put the wings back on, put new engines on, which would be the American engines, and put in American electronics. By putting in that much of American parts and using American labor in Texas it then became 50-point something [Laughter] percent American.

Everyone was delighted with that, and we called in the TSARC.* But TSARC had approved it, and we were told, "All right, go ahead and sign the contract." I had the president of Falcon Jet, USA, which was a subsidiary of the French Falcon, the vice president I guess of Garrett Engines, which was the new engine and either the vice president or the president of the electronics company all in the outer office ready to come in and see me sign the contract, and they would be signing for their company. I buzzed out to the outer office and said, "Have them come in."

At that point the phone rang, which was the hotline from the Secretary, and he said, "Is there anything else we don't know about that airplane?"

I said, "Not that I'm aware of."

He replied, "Well, I guess you can go ahead and sign the contract." So by this time they were all lined up, and I don't know what I would have said if he'd said, "I'd better think about that a few more days." [Laughter] Then turn them back around, and I don't think they would have come back to sign the contract. But, anyway, he told me to go ahead and sign the contract and we did. But we still had some problems when it came to those engines.

---

* TSARC– Transportation Systems Acquisitions Review Council.

Paul Stillwell: Another major program then were the new polar icebreakers, and your wife had a personal involvement with one of those.

Admiral Siler: Yes, she christened the Polar Sea. Now, the first one, the Polar Star, was christened by the wife of Secretary Brinegar.* But I don't think the Brinegars had any particular attachment for the Coast Guard. Once he left the department, I don't think he ever paid much attention to the ship or anything about the Coast Guard. But we had a very interesting time with christening that ship. My wife said it was almost like having a baby. [Laughter] I'm not sure how she meant that except the thrill. But there was an interesting aspect of that. Most of the time you christen a ship with hitting a bottle over the bow of the ship. In this case the bow sloped back so much because the ship was designed to ride up on the ice and break the ice partially by the weight of the ship. So the bow of the ship was way over there. They built a special structure so she could break the bottle of champagne somewhere that was more convenient to see and to get to.

Paul Stillwell: What can you say about the upgrade in icebreaking capability with those new ships?

Admiral Siler: Oh, it was a huge increase over the wind class, which was one of the most capable at that time. Now, the Glacier, which was at that time still a Navy ship, had a lot more capability than the Wind class but nowhere near as much as was designed to be done by the Polar class. And now the Healy has been commissioned, and it's a step down from the Polar class.† But the Polar class has a great deal of capability for the icebreaking. When it was first finished and it made some trial runs, unfortunately it had such deep draft that it ran aground in the mud near Seattle a couple of times. And there

---

* The icebreaker Polar Star (WAGB-10) was commissioned 17 January 1976 and the Polar Sea (WAGB-11) on 26 September 1976. Each ship is 399 feet long, 84 feet in the beam, and has a full-load displacement of 13,190 tons. For details, see R. G. Moore, "The Polar Icebreakers: Breaking Through at Last," U.S. Naval Institute Proceedings, December 1979, pages 115-119.
† The icebreaker Healy (WAGB-20) was placed in active commission on 21 August 2000. She is 460 feet long, 94 feet in the team, has a maximum draft of 32 feet, and a top speed of 12.5 knots. Her full-load displacement is 17,710 tons.

were questions about whether that CO, Venzke, although he'd been selected for rear admiral, would actually make it because he ran it aground.[*]

Paul Stillwell: Did he make it?

Admiral Siler: Yes, he did. He didn't stay on active duty much after that. He retired and became the president of National Defense Transportation Association, and I don't know what he's doing now.

Paul Stillwell: You indicated that Secretary Brinegar was not all that concerned with the Coast Guard. What can you say about his replacement, Secretary Coleman?

Admiral Siler: Coleman was a fine Secretary. One of the things that he did was have a Coast Guard aide in the outer office, and he participated in things military as much as he could. I think he was one of the Tuskegee airmen but not one who became spectacular in any way at that time. But he was a very fine lawyer, and he dealt with some legal cases that had to do with the transportation mode after he retired. He took a great deal of interest in the Coast Guard.

Paul Stillwell: What can you say about your personal relationship with him?

Admiral Siler: When I wanted to talk to Bill, all I had to do was pick up the phone, call the military aide up there, and say, "When can you get me in to the Secretary?" Usually it was within a half an hour. That wasn't the same with either Brinegar or Brock Adams.

Paul Stillwell: What can you say about Brock Adams as Secretary?[†]

---

[*] Captain Norman C. Venzke, USCG, was the first commanding officer of the Polar Star. See his article, "The Polar Icebreakers: In a Class by Themselves, U.S. Naval Institute Proceedings, January 1976, pages 91-94

[†] Brock Adams served as Secretary of Transportation from 23 January 1977 to 22 July 1979.

Admiral Siler: If you could talk to him, he was pretty reasonable but he was guarded rather well by his aides. He had a Deputy Secretary that we dealt with almost as much as Brock.[*]

Paul Stillwell: Were there any philosophical changes that came in with the Carter Administration after the Republicans had been in office for several years?[†]

Admiral Siler: Well, the biggest change right away was they didn't want anything to do with the military. The very first thing was at the inauguration. Brock Adams was the only cabinet-level official who did not have a military aide that day, and all the others did. He wanted to show right away that he was disassociating himself with the military, and that's the way he always treated it.

Paul Stillwell: Do you think the service suffered any from that aspect of it?

Admiral Siler: Oh, yes.

Paul Stillwell: In what ways?

Admiral Siler: Well, we would hardly get recognition from the Secretary himself. Things were usually handled by the Deputy Secretary if they could possibly be. He did not have lunch with the flag officers when they were in Washington. When we had all of the flag officers in for the annual meeting, we usually borrowed the Secretary's mess in order to have all of the people in the same mess hall and talking on the subjects that we wanted to address. He made himself unavailable at that time, and that was just two years while I was there, but it was very different.

Paul Stillwell: Did funding become more difficult in the Carter administration?

---

[*] Alan A. Butchman was Deputy Secretary of Transportation from 24 January 1977 to 22 July 1979.

[†] James E. Carter, Jr., who had graduated from the Naval Academy in the class of 1947, served as President of the United States from 20 January 1977 to 20 January 1981.

Admiral Siler: Not particularly more difficult. It was always difficult.

Paul Stillwell: Well, I guess one thing if he was not associating himself with the service that much he probably wasn't interfering very much either.

Admiral Siler: No, that's probably true. He just didn't feel that that he needed to address the Coast Guard.

Paul Stillwell: So it sounds of the three you worked with your favorite would be Coleman.

Admiral Siler: Very definitely. He was great.

Paul Stillwell: Anything else on him specifically?

Admiral Siler: He made a couple of flights with me and other Coast Guard people to show his particular interest in things like the 200-mile fishery limit.[*] We went up the day it became effective and saw American fishing vessels in the area that was out beyond 12 miles and noted that they had numbers to identify that vessel right away. We saw some foreign vessels, but they were licensed to fish in certain areas, so that it was not a violation, it was just of interest that that vessel was there still. But we had some seizures of Russian vessels rather soon after that law became effective, and we've always felt it was testing the United States to see whether our concern was that great.

The 200-mile law didn't become effective until when Adams was the Secretary. But some of the enforcement aspects did go into effect sooner in preparing for the time when we did everything with the 200-mile limit. We had to go all the way to President Carter before we could seize a Russian vessel.

---

[*] The Fishery Conservation and Management Act of 1976 claims for the United States exclusive authority over fishing resources in zones extending 200 miles from the country's territorial seas. The territorial seas extend three miles outward from coastlines.

Owen W. Siler, Interview #5 (12/14/00) – Page 312

Paul Stillwell: That was a dramatic increase from 12 miles to 200 obviously. Did you have adequate resources to do that well?

Admiral Siler: No, not at all. We were given money to buy more C-130s, figuring that we would base them in Cape Cod and Kodiak. The aircraft handled that part of the patrolling rather well, but we definitely needed more ships at that time. One of the problems that I had was that I didn't get much support from my district commanders saying we needed more ships if we were going to patrol out to 200 miles, particularly my successor as Commandant.[*]

Paul Stillwell: Why do you think that was?

Admiral Siler: He was in Alaska before he became the Commandant, and he wanted to show that, "We can do it up here."[†]

Paul Stillwell: The can-do spirit.

Admiral Siler: Yes. It was far too much for what we had in Alaska at that time. And as soon as he became Commandant he started yelling, "Help!" [Laughter]

Paul Stillwell: Interesting how one's perspective changes.

Admiral Siler: Yes.

Paul Stillwell: What do you remember about relations with the Coast Guard Academy during your tenure? How much oversight was there?

Admiral Siler: Well, from the Commandant there was very little. Most of the oversight was handled with the Office of Personnel, and they were in touch almost every day.

---
[*] Admiral John B. Hayes, USCG, was Commandant of the Coast Guard from 1 June 1978 to 28 May 1982.
[†] As a rear admiral Hayes was Commander 17th Coast Guard District.

Paul Stillwell: Were you pleased, satisfied with the way it was running?

Admiral Siler: Well, we had to have a lot of confidence in the superintendent himself, because we couldn't give a great deal of oversight to the academy except at arm's length. Of course, we did have visits to the academy on a regular basis like the congressional board of visitors. The congressional board of visitors, though almost all would accept the appointment and not go to the academy. So most of the supervision and the contact with the academy was handled by lower-level Coast Guard people and visits by Coast Guard higher-level people on a rather infrequent basis.

Paul Stillwell: How smoothly did it go bringing women into the group of cadets?

Admiral Siler: I think it went rather poorly in many regards because we quartered the women in the same barracks as the men.[*] I heard later—much later—that some of the women didn't feel that they needed to be pure white, pure lily white. They were making the most of the fact that they lived next door to a man and that sort of thing. Admiral Cueroni, who was the superintendent some years later, used to visit the barracks quite frequently himself, and he caught women in men's rooms and vice versa.[†] I think more frequently it was the girl would go into a man's room. At least in one instance that he told me about, the woman said, "Don't you do things like this with your wife?" Well, a little different situation. [Laughter] I don't think that woman lasted too long. [Laughter]

Paul Stillwell: What do you recall about administration of the Coast Guard Reserve during that period?

Admiral Siler: I didn't think we had any particular problems with the reserve at that time. Earlier, when Admiral Bender had been the Commandant, I was the president of a board that tried to look at ways to use the reserve more than we did and to show a greater

---

[*] The first women cadets entered the Coast Guard Academy in the summer of 1976.
[†] Rear Admiral Richard P. Cueroni, USCG, served as Superintendent of the Coast Guard Academy from June 1986 to June 1989.

need for the reserve, and I didn't think that we had any particular problem. Using the ideas that my board came up with, which was just that we would train a unit with parallel training to a regular unit that was in the same area and they would become well enough qualified that after they were fully trained, the regulars could be told to, "Go on liberty. We'll take care of it." I think it did work rather well. At least that's what the reservists felt. [Laughter] This Team Coast Guard, which they have gone to now, is simply that same program.* I don't know that they admit that it's the same thing, but it is.

Paul Stillwell: And what can you say about the Coast Guard Auxiliary?

Admiral Siler: Well, we had a tremendous problem with the auxiliary, because about that time some congressman decided that the auxiliary was taking commercial jobs away from commercial towers, and the auxiliary would be out beside someone who had trouble and were not allowed to take the boat in tow. While if it had been someone who wasn't in the auxiliary, it would have been perfectly all right to take them in tow. But if he happened to be Coast Guard Auxiliary, the congressmen and competitors had convinced some people that the auxiliary was taking a living out of the mouths of the commercial towers. So there were many restrictions placed on how the auxiliary could assist people, and I thought that was most unfortunate. I think they're getting back a little bit to some amplification that lets the auxiliary do the towing and things of that nature now than when they couldn't.

Paul Stillwell: How much was the Coast Guard involved in setting and enforcing standards for recreational boaters?

Admiral Siler: Very much. The auxiliary in particular would meet with commercial boat builders, and there were people in the Coast Guard who were looking at these regulations as well and would develop regulations. At one time they had teams that visited almost all the commercial builders in the United States. Now, that's a very large job, because there

---

* For more on the changing role of the Coast Guard Reserve see the Naval Institute oral history of Rear Admiral Richard W. Schneider, USCG (Ret.).

are so many commercial factories that build boats of that nature. So they wouldn't be able to visit them as often as they would have liked to. But they were involved to a fairly large degree for several years, and then they were cut back because of the Congress again feeling that we were competing with the commercial interests.

Paul Stillwell: And what about the educational function we talked about earlier, so that you try to help boaters keep from getting into trouble?

Admiral Siler: The educational part of it was very good, and that's always been growing. The auxiliary has developed some texts which are good. I don't know whether the Power Squadron has other texts that they use or whether they use the Coast Guard texts. I just don't know about that.

Paul Stillwell: On the subject of navigation, loran C was coming in. What do you remember about that project?

Admiral Siler: Well, it was here before I became Commandant. Now, some of the locations could have been added to. In fact, when we were talking about getting oil out of Alaska, one of the things we had to do was to develop the West Coast loran chain, but at the same time as the Vietnam requirement was being phased down the loran out there was being decreased. The loran on the West Coast became automated to such an extent that the crews for it, the stations in the United States, were very small by comparison with a crew on Angaur or in Thailand. But the loran C in Thailand was so accurate that you could use it if you had the right receiver as a landing aid in the airfields in Southern Vietnam and in some places in Thailand.

Paul Stillwell: Along that same line, what do you remember about the inauguration of the vessel traffic systems?

Admiral Siler: Well, I always thought the vessel traffic systems were a very good idea, because we had developed such a system in San Francisco, which was radar controlled, and we knew exactly where the vessels were all the time. We did something of that sort in the Atchafalaya River down in the New Orleans area. And we did it something of a simplified nature in Louisville, Kentucky. We had no trouble at all in setting those stations up. Now, we tried to do something of a complicated nature in the area of New Orleans, from Baton Rouge out to the Gulf of Mexico. There were some people in that area who objected very strenuously to it. I think their main reason for objecting was that they were weren't conferred with constantly in the development of it. Then also they didn't like the idea that Coast Guard men would be controlling their activity.

Paul Stillwell: Well, really it's sort of analogous to an air traffic control system for a safety viewpoint.

Admiral Siler: Very much so, but the concern that they had was that people who weren't perfectly qualified to be the operators of the oceangoing ship or a towboat with ten barges out in front would be controlled by a Coast Guard man whose greatest experience in going to sea was operating a buoy tender.

Paul Stillwell: Do you think they have proved successful in practice?

Admiral Siler: I feel certain that they have. New York has moved in that direction in the last few years with a lot of cooperation from the commercial operators. The area in New Orleans has moved ahead also, but they had to get the towboat operators fully involved before it was practical at all. At the same time the place at Atchafalaya was always successful. And the system we set up in Louisville was very successful. We only activated it when there was high water in Louisville.

Paul Stillwell: What do you remember about a step-up in enforcement against drug smuggling?

Admiral Siler: Well, there was very little enforcement until when I was the Commandant. We always had the authority to board those vessels and inspect them, but there just was not very much involved at all. During the time I was Commandant we started greater enforcement and when we'd board ships, we'd look definitely for drugs. It was of such little concern that we really didn't have much to concern us at all until that time.

Paul Stillwell: What made the change?

Admiral Siler: The realization that there was more and more smuggling going on.

Paul Stillwell: Did this require a step-up in training for law enforcement detachments?

Admiral Siler: Very definitely. Up to that time when we went aboard a recreational boat or a commercial boat we did not go aboard armed at all. We went aboard and said, "I'd like to see your documents," and usually it was, "Okay, here," and nothing more. All of a sudden, we realized that that man over there was fooling with a rifle or a pistol. I don't think there was ever a confrontation of that sort, but about that time also we realized that if we said, "Stop your boat. We want to come aboard," and they didn't stop, we needed to do something about that. For years we'd had an understanding that a Coast Guard vessel could stop a commercial vessel by firing across the bow if he didn't have a working radio or something of that sort. They weren't stopping anymore, so we did fire across the bow, one I remember. But it was an unusual thing, and I remember talking to the duty officer who had come into my office to say, "Shall we go ahead and fire across the bow?"

I said, "Yes, go ahead. But make sure they miss." [Laughter] Well, not too long after I retired they had one that did not stop even though they'd fired across the bow. Then the procedure was to fire into the engine room, hopefully to disable the power plant. But I'm happy that didn't happen on my watch.

Paul Stillwell: Were there any vessel seizures during your tenure as Commandant?

Admiral Siler: Yes, there were some, and I'm not sure what the details were now.

Paul Stillwell: But that's good for morale when you see a concrete result like that.

Admiral Siler: I'm sure it is. But I'm not sure whether it's good for morale when they see a stack of marijuana like that and realize they can't have fun with it. [Laughter]

Paul Stillwell: Did you have to devote more resources to that function as it became more important?

Admiral Siler: Probably, but I can't give you details on it now.

Paul Stillwell: What do you remember about working with senior enlisted advisors when you were Commandant?

Admiral Siler: I used to schedule meetings regularly with them, but they as a rule didn't have problems that we had to deal with at that level. They'd give written reports of visits to places on both coasts, and the fact that they were visiting the units regularly made it a routine thing for them to do that.

Paul Stillwell: Did you consult with them regularly, seek advice on issues?

Admiral Siler: No, it was not my seeking advice on things, but I asked them to give me reports regularly on what they had observed.

Paul Stillwell: What kind of avenues of communication did you have both with the officer and enlisted communities in the Coast Guard?

Admiral Siler: Well, with the officer personnel I think they knew what the channel was to call something to my attention.

Paul Stillwell: Commandant's Bulletin certainly would have been a way of getting the word out.

Admiral Siler: Yes, but that has changed. It's now a magazine intended for use outside the service, as well as informing service personnel. A good many of the enlisted personnel always had hesitation of trying to get something to the Commandant, but having the senior enlisted advisor was a way to get the word out and to get the word from enlisted personnel. Also, because of that I felt it was important that we visit once in a while. The senior enlisted advisor is right in the Commandant's complex there so that he's always available to be visiting with the Commandant, and he has a nice office.

Paul Stillwell: How much did you travel as Commandant?

Admiral Siler: Probably not as much as Admiral Hayes by any means, but my traveling with the Commandant back in the '50s had made me a little more familiar with some of those stations than Admiral Hayes would have been, so Admiral Hayes made a real effort to visit every Coast Guard unit while he was Commandant. I didn't feel that was necessary, because I had seen some of the stations before. Well, for example, I didn't go to Japan at all when I was Commandant. I had visited all those stations back when I was stationed in Hawaii and when I was flying the Commandant, and so I didn't feel it was necessary for me to go again and see what the station looked like today. But, as I said, Admiral Hayes hadn't been to those stations, and so he was on the road all the time.

Paul Stillwell: Well, of course, another part of the travel function is to let the troops see you. How much of that did you do?

Admiral Siler: Not an awful lot. I tried to make visits to the field from time to time and again just let them see what the Commandant was about. I always would talk informally to the crews rather than make formal addresses. My staff pointed out that I was more effective anyway if I didn't have prepared remarks. [Laughter]

Paul Stillwell: Why did they say that?

Admiral Siler: I think too often if you have prepared remarks it becomes a little stilted when it's delivered. I just spoke to them off the cuff, and very frequently I would be provided with some information about what people would be particularly concerned with at a location and try to fit that in, but it was almost always an off-the-cuff-type talk.

Paul Stillwell: Did you open yourself up to questions on those occasions?

Admiral Siler: Yes, always.

Paul Stillwell: Did people out in the field have a mechanism for airing grievances and getting them into headquarters?

Admiral Siler: Well, I think they always do have, but I'm not sure they got into headquarters all the time, because usually things of that nature are routed to the lower commands. And I hope that they weren't all cut off, but they could have been.

Paul Stillwell: Well, I'd presume you'd want to know if there was some common pattern, an issue that kept rising over and over.

Admiral Siler: Yes, but we didn't have any of that kind of thing. The concerns of many enlisted personnel had to do with tours of duty, facilities that they had at that location, and that kind of development. I think most of the time we were able to take care of their concerns. The 14th District I know about that time and the years since have developed real ombudsmen systems. That area is so huge that it's very difficult to spend all the time visiting them, but their ombudsman does visit and brings back the reports all the time.

Paul Stillwell: I read one speech that you made up in Boston, and you addressed the issue of making the Merrimack River and Lake Winnipesaukee federal navigable waters. What do you remember of that case?

Admiral Siler: That was a very interesting situation. Of course, the New Hampshire people and particularly the publisher of the newspaper The Manchester Union Leader—

Paul Stillwell: William Loeb.

Admiral Siler: Yes, was very much for "Live Free or Die," and when we went into Lake Winnipesaukee—and I don't know how we got into it initially—but we realized that there was a passenger vessel that carried more than 1,000 people, and it had never been inspected by the Coast Guard.[*] In fact, today I'm not sure it's inspected. But we thought that it was probably desirable that at least that vessel be inspected, and the only way we could see to do that was to consider Lake Winnipesaukee as navigable waters, because then the Coast Guard would inspect it. New Hampshire for many years did not consider the lake as navigable waters, and they didn't license the boats there. They didn't expect the Coast Guard to look at their boats, but when we did look at them almost always boats met the requirements of the Coast Guard with no trouble.

The only thing was this 1,000-passenger vessel was not trying to meet Coast Guard regulations, and we said, "We think it had better be done before the vessel has problems, and then the people could say, 'Well why didn't Coast Guard look at this?'"

That was a pretty flimsy thing to say, "Well, that's not navigable water." Because if you looked at the regulations that determine whether water is navigable or not, by most standards it's completely navigable. However, one of the requirements is that you can navigate on that waterway from where you are to the ocean if you want to. And there are waters that are around the Great Lakes that the Corps of Engineers considers navigable that the Coast Guard does not consider navigable. In the case of Lake Winnipesaukee we examined all of the considerations, and the document that I got was prepared by the chief counsel.

One of the major considerations was the ability to get to another navigable waterway, which happened to be the Merrimack River. In order to get there, there had been consideration given and actual steps taken to make a canal with a lock from Lake

---

[*] "Live Free or Die" is the New Hampshire state motto.

Winnipesaukee into the Merrimack River. Having been approved as a project of I think two states at that time to get into the navigable Merrimack River, we said, "All right. It's navigable." The fact was that Lake Winnipesaukee is 100 feet higher than sea level, and so you could make as good a case where it's not navigable. Loeb did all he could to convince everyone in New Hampshire, "It's not navigable. The Coast Guard's just grabbing off more territory."

Loeb went to a Navy League meeting that I went to also in Boston, and during the afternoon, I guess I had lunch and then left and went out to inspect more Coast Guard units in Massachusetts. He was in the elevator with my wife. Didn't realize I think that everything that he was saying could be heard by my wife, and he felt that he was really putting the Coast Guard in its place. [Laughter] Anyway, we thought quite some time about taking steps to do the things that we would normally have done with navigable water, but about that time Brock Adams said, "Let's make everybody in New Hampshire happy and say it's not navigable." That was the end of that.

Paul Stillwell: So it just essentially remained status quo.

Admiral Siler: Yes, and I'm not sure what's being done today at all.

Paul Stillwell: Back in World War II, of course, the Coast Guard was absorbed into the Navy and was a fighting force. What can you say about the role of military preparedness and military equipment on board ships in the normal peacetime environments such as when you were Commandant?

Admiral Siler: Well, we had to do some military preparedness because we found out that the drug smugglers were doing things of a nature that we had to take that step. We didn't do anything that was overt, I believe, unless they did first. But I think it makes sense that an organization like the Coast Guard or the county police be prepared to take action if they have to.

Paul Stillwell: How much a factor was this in developing characteristics in aircraft and ships?

Admiral Siler: Well, our modern aircraft have no capability except very recently we have developed armed helicopters, and they've been effective in stopping some vessels that would not have stopped otherwise. But there's nothing of that nature built into the great majority of our aircraft.

Paul Stillwell: What about the ships?

Admiral Siler: They're slower reacting as far as having armament of a useful nature is concerned, so they have to have some capability built into them as they're developed. And so our vessels have some capability, and I think they should.

Paul Stillwell: How much contact did you have with the Navy during your tenure on the drug enforcement role?

Admiral Siler: Very little then.

Paul Stillwell: I gather that has grown since then.

Admiral Siler: Yes. We have Coast Guard teams on naval vessels. When we dispatch a team from a naval vessel they put up the Coast Guard ensign to identify themselves as a law enforcement vessel.

Paul Stillwell: This is because of the posse comitatus regulations?[*]

Admiral Siler: Yes.

---

[*] The Posse Comitatus Act of 1878 essentially bars the U.S. military from acting as a domestic police force.

Paul Stillwell: What can you say about the work of the NavGuard Board and the benefits that come from that?

Admiral Siler: I think they've improved a great deal over the last few years. We were just setting up the NavGuard Board when I was Commandant, and it wasn't very far along at all.

Paul Stillwell: What did you see as the function and role of that board?

Admiral Siler: It was primarily at that time keeping the Coast Guard informed as to how they could be of assistance. I doubt that there were times when the Navy felt that they could call on the Coast Guard for assistance. Yet probably the first year I was Commandant we had a military readiness exercise, and the Coast Guard rear admiral who was acting as the Commandant in that particular exercise said, "Why don't we do such and such?" boarding vessels or something of that nature.

And the Navy's reaction was, "Well, we couldn't do that. Posse Comitatus forbids any such action."

The response of the acting Coast Guard Commandant was, "Oh, but we can." [Laughter] So the Navy, I think, is more aware of what the Coast Guard brings to them because of those exercises, the joint exercises, and because of the NavGuard Board.

Paul Stillwell: So would you say the board was mostly an informational tool at that point?

Admiral Siler: At that point. I think now it's an operational type board.

Paul Stillwell: In the environmental protection program I read about such things as oil fingerprinting, pollution strike teams, construction regulations, and the creation of maritime safety offices. What can you say about that overall mission?

Admiral Siler: I think that the ability to fingerprint oil is a very worthwhile type of operation. We can get a sample of an oil spill at sea and identify it to a large degree as to where it came from. Then investigate what ships have been carrying that oil and very frequently fingerprint the oil that is in the ship and identify who pumped oil out there in the beautiful ocean.

Paul Stillwell: What sanctions do you have then after you find that out?

Admiral Siler: There are fines, penalties, listed in the regulations, and the EPA has established some of those regulations and some are the Coast Guard regulations.* For example, if oil is spilled accidentally and the owner of the ship reports it, he has to pay a penalty, but it's not a very large penalty. If he doesn't report it and it's discovered and identified completely, the penalty is doubled. So it makes it worthwhile for everyone to report it.

Paul Stillwell: What is the Coast Guard's role when there's a bigger spill than just something pumped overboard?

Admiral Siler: Well, if something is pumped overboard, the responsibility for the Coast Guard is pretty much the same as if they break the hull or something of that nature, so that in both cases the Coast Guard is very much involved in cleanup. If the owner of the vessel that spilled it admits to it, he's required to clean it up. If he doesn't admit it, then the Coast Guard goes ahead and cleans it up and tries at the same time to identify where it came from.

Paul Stillwell: And do you also try to recover the cost of the cleanup?

Admiral Siler: Absolutely, plus a penalty. [Laughter]

---

* EPA—Environmental Protection Agency.

Paul Stillwell: What can you say about the role of the Coast Guard Yard at Curtis Bay in supporting the overall fleet?

Admiral Siler: Well, it doesn't do much at all for West Coast ships, of course. We established a place in Seattle that most of the repair work is done for the icebreakers, because their homeport is Seattle, and they have most of the work done right in Seattle. But for East Coast ships and vessels that are moving around, the Coast Guard Yard is very helpful.

Paul Stillwell: And that's where the Eagle goes to get fixed.

Admiral Siler: That's right.

Paul Stillwell: Completely unrelated, I saw in your shadowbox the other day the Order of St. Olav that you got from the Norwegian government. What brought that about?

Admiral Siler: That was an effort just to recognize the Coast Guard. I didn't have anything to do with it. But there were a number of Norwegian ships that were in trouble, and the Coast Guard assisted them. One was a commercial vessel on the East Coast that just disappeared, and the Coast Guard searched for days and found traces of where the oil was and the vessel had gone down. There was also at least one ship that was in, I think, Alaskan waters and had trouble.

Then there was a vessel that was on the AMVER system, the merchant vessel reporting system, had been entirely until that voyage. They changed the master or something of that nature, and they didn't send position reports except the departure and the non-arrival. There were something like six people that were recovered after the ship sank, and they wanted to recognize the fact that AMVER was so helpful in at least letting the owners know that the ship had departed and did not arrive. They wanted to recognize the Coast Guard, and so I got the medal to commemorate that. Then it was suggested again by the embassy that if I found it practical that I call on the King of Norway when I next was over in Europe.* And so in the summer of '76 I believe it was, early summer, I stopped by and saw the King of Norway. He was an interesting person.

Paul Stillwell: What do you recall about him?

Admiral Siler: One very unusual thing that I was warned about was that he giggled frequently when he was talking. I had met him before at the dinner that was given, and I as the Commandant was invited to that dinner at the Blair House in Washington. Well, I went to the dinner at Blair House and met the King there, and the primary reason was simply that the Norwegians at that time were considering bidding on our next ships, which would have been the 270s. They did not bid on them, but there were apparently some shipbuilders that did consider it at least. And so knowing that he interspersed many of his conversations with this (sound of giggle) was a good thing, because my wife didn't know about it until it was pointed out that he did that. She said she would have been at least taken aback by that if she had not known about it ahead of time.

After I was given the medal at the Norwegian Embassy, I then asked the Department of State if I could wear it. And I didn't wear anything associated with it except the ribbon except when I was in full dress. And if I was in full dress I would wear the medal and usually let the Coast Guard people that were there know that this was given to the Coast Guard, not me personally.

Paul Stillwell: So it was a symbolic gesture?

Admiral Siler: Yes.

Paul Stillwell: One name we talked about the other day when the tape recorder wasn't running was Edith Head.† What role did she have with the Coast Guard?

---

* Olav V was King of Norway from 21 September 1957 until his death on 17 January 1991.
† Edith Head was a famous designer of costumes for movie actresses.

Admiral Siler: When Admiral Bender set up the new Coast Guard uniform, somehow we contacted Edith Head, and she designed the new Coast Guard women's uniform. It was interesting as far as skirt length was concerned, because at that time it was anywhere in here.

Paul Stillwell: Quite variable.

Admiral Siler: For non-uniform in particular. She rather smoothly suggested that the skirt should be at least to the middle of the kneecap, and that's where it was most of the time when I was Commandant. I remember some shorter ones, but [laughter] I tried not to notice them. [Laughter]

Paul Stillwell: And you can't always be successful in those things.

Admiral Siler: No.

Paul Stillwell: What do you remember about her personally?

Admiral Siler: Not very much.

Paul Stillwell: I saw some pictures of you in your file where you were being interviewed on board a cutter at Governors Island by Tom Brokaw.* What was the occasion for that? That was in early 1977.

Admiral Siler: Well, I think it was having to do with how successful were the fishery regulations out to 200 miles.

Paul Stillwell: Any other memorable cases of dealing with the news media?

---

* Brokaw is a long-time newsman with NBC television.

Admiral Siler: I was on the "Today Show" at least once when I was interviewed in Washington, and I went to I guess it was WRC there, and I was interviewed by someone other than Tom Brokaw. But I knew Tom Brokaw well enough that he greeted me, I remember, one time when both of us were attending a function at the Iranian Embassy in Washington. So our relationships were good with NBC at that time.

Paul Stillwell: Did you have much contact with the media on a regular basis?

Admiral Siler: No.

Paul Stillwell: What can you say about the role of public affairs and getting the word out about the Coast Guard?

Admiral Siler: Well, if it was something spectacular, they would accept it with no question. I think trying to keep the Coast Guard in the public eye was quite difficult. Had to have something like a 200-mile fishery law or something like that before we got their attention.

Paul Stillwell: Well, I think that was probably part of the thought behind the Coast Guard slash, wasn't it, to make the service more identifiable?

Admiral Siler: Oh, very definitely. Of course, that slash came about probably at least three years before I was Commandant. There was an interesting aspect of that that I was involved with, and that was one of suggestions with the slash was that we have signboards with the slash on them. The initial proposal was that the common name of the station be used rather than a formal name. For example the Coast Guard Air Station here in Savannah would be known as Savannah Air Station and not the Coast Guard Air Station. I objected strenuously to that and had some signs changed so that it would say "Coast Guard Air Station, Savannah, Georgia." I don't know that they all say that today.

Paul Stillwell: The chaplains that work with the Coast Guard are from the Navy. What sort of relationship, if any, did you have with Admiral O'Connor, who was the Chief of Chaplains?[*]

Admiral Siler: I had a very good relationship with him. He invited us to his quarters a few times, and he used to have some great poker games up in his quarters there in the Navy Yard. He was very helpful in establishing more and more Navy chaplains at Coast Guard units.

Paul Stillwell: What benefits did they bring?

Admiral Siler: Well, I think that it always helps to have someone that the enlisted personnel in particular feel comfortable talking to, and I'm sure that a good many enlisted personnel do not feel comfortable talking to senior officers who are not identified as a chaplain ahead of time. Now, and much of this has taken place after Chaplain O'Connor has left, but he probably started the wheels rolling on it, and we have Navy chaplains at many, many of the Coast Guard units. Here in Savannah we have a chaplain who is identified as a chaplain for the Coast Guard. Of course, we have two good-sized units here, the marine safety office and the air station. A chaplain is always present at a formal ceremony, a change of command or something of that nature.

Paul Stillwell: I was struck when it first hit me that Navy chaplains were serving with the Coast Guard. Everything about the uniform is Coast Guard except the cap device.

Admiral Siler: Yes, right.

Paul Stillwell: The medical services come from the Public Health Service. What can you say about how well that function is performed?

---

[*] Rear Admiral John J. O'Connor, CHC, USN, served as the Navy's Chief of Chaplains from July 1975 to June 1979.

Admiral Siler: Well, we don't have many doctors in locations where you might want to have a doctor, but the relationship has been improved in that we do have more doctors assigned to the Coast Guard than we did a few years ago. I guess we got to a very low point at one time. Dr. Harry Allen, who was the chief medical officer, reviewed the regulations in the Public Health Service and found that doctors with a certain amount of experience can be directly commissioned into the Public Health Service with a pretty good rank. In fact, the last one that I saw some headlines on was a captain who was at that point at Coast Guard headquarters, but he stayed in St. Petersburg and Clearwater for a good many years before he went to headquarters. And I don't think he ever served as a commander or a lieutenant commander. [Laughter] But he had served the requisite number of years as a doctor in the civilian world in St. Petersburg. He owned a yacht in St. Petersburg, and when he came to the Coast Guard he went to flight surgeon's school so that he was a flight surgeon in the Coast Guard. He was still with the Coast Guard when he was the last person who has served in World War II and was on active duty this year.

Paul Stillwell: Do you remember his name?

Admiral Siler: No, I'm afraid I don't.

Paul Stillwell: I once met a Navy doctor who had got a direct commission as a lieutenant. It was all brand new to him, and I said, "How do you even know whom to salute?"

He said, "Well, anybody with bars salutes me and anybody else I salute him." [Laughter]

What can you say about the work of the Navy League and your own particular relationships with it?

Admiral Siler: Well, we started the relationship with Navy League when Admiral Smith was Commandant, and we had had a Coast Guard League back in the '50s when Admiral Richmond was the Commandant, but it pretty much fell apart because there was so little interest in trying to establish a national Coast Guard League. They had one convention in Washington I remember when I was there, because I was Admiral Richmond's personal aide. But it pretty much fell apart, and Admiral Trimble, who was the Assistant Commandant, and Admiral Smith suggested that we make the relationship with the Navy League stronger and closer.

Over the years I think they have improved that situation so that part of the Sea Power magazine every August is of the Coast Guard. And there are a few items every time that have to do with the Coast Guard. They have done things to recognize units and the performance of the Coast Guard, and they've decorated and recognized the lifeboat training facility out at Cape Disappointment. The magazine has featured them several times. They always have big pictures of Coast Guard units in the August magazine. I think they try hard to get recognition there, and my wife and I have been recognized with the Distinguished Service Certificate from the Navy League.

Paul Stillwell: Speaking of another organization that I'm familiar with, the Naval Institute, what benefits does it provide for the Coast Guard?

Admiral Siler: Well, it usually makes the one issue each year on the Coast Guard and they will recognize the Coast Guard anytime that they have something to contribute.

Paul Stillwell: Well, I think also it serves as something of a professional forum to keep people up to date on what's happening and a way to express opinions.

Admiral Siler: Very definitely.

Paul Stillwell: How much did you keep flying as you became a more and more senior flag officer?

Admiral Siler: Not much. I received a letter from, interestingly, the chief of officer personnel when I was at the National War College that said as of the first of December of 1966 I was no longer required nor permitted to fly for proficiency. That was the standard letter; if you had more than a certain number of years and you were assigned a place where the only flying would be for proficiency it was not required any longer of you. I still got flight pay, and I got flight pay right up to the time when I was Commandant the first two years, I think. But I believe that I was the only Commandant who has ever gotten flight pay.

Paul Stillwell: How did you manage that?

Admiral Siler: Well, I still had that letter that said I was no longer required nor permitted to fly for proficiency, but I'd get flight pay. Now the system for flight pay is entirely different, so I stopped getting flight pay when that new arrangement took place. I flew as a pilot when I was a rear admiral out in St. Louis, but I flew Army airplanes because when I'd asked and my original idea was that they would make a training flight wherever I wanted to go and get transportation that way. But instead of setting it up the way I had envisioned it, they simply set up an airplane to go where I wanted to go, and I was the pilot. So I'd fly anyplace within the district, and most of the time I was the pilot. Now, I can recall one time when I was just a passenger, and they did exactly what I had in mind and that was a lieutenant colonel was taking an instrument check. He had to fly to the Army training base that's out in the middle of Missouri.

Paul Stillwell: Fort Leonard Wood?

Admiral Siler: Yes. And our Coast Guard people were taking small arms training, and I wanted to be there to see how they were being trained. I spent half a day with them, saw their efforts, and I don't think on that one I did have any firing of the pistols or the rifles, but I did that another time. That time I drove out, but most of the time I would be the pilot whenever we'd go someplace.

Paul Stillwell: Did you ever do recreational flying as a private pilot?

Owen W. Siler, Interview #5 (12/14/00) – Page 334

Admiral Siler: Once in Puerto Rico. The captain who was there had been in Coast Guard headquarters when I was there also, and he had bought a small plane in Puerto Rico where he was stationed, and I went to Puerto Rico just for a recreational trip. His wife and my wife went shopping someplace, and he and I went out to one of the lovely hotels in the vicinity to play golf. We flew out from the field that was at that time the Coast Guard Air Station, San Juan, out to where the hotel was, because it had a little field right next to the hotel. That's the only time I have ever seen a hole in one. He made a hole in one. All of us couldn't find the ball. It was in the hole. [Laughter]

Paul Stillwell: In October 1977 a task force was formed to prevent and prosecute vessel hijackings. What do you remember about that?

Admiral Siler: Not very much. Almost all of those were down in the Florida and Puerto Rico area. The Commandant didn't get involved with it.

Paul Stillwell: We've talked mostly about issues. What people stand out in your mind from serving with when you were Commandant? You've talked about the area commanders and Admiral Perry. What about other individuals?

Admiral Siler: Well, Admiral Benkert was really outstanding in the merchant marine safety area. I think Admiral Cueroni was a very helpful individual while I was Commandant. He was a speechwriter to begin with and then the administrative special assistant. We were trying to avoid "aide" in those days. I think the two or three people who were involved then with the Ancient Albatross were interesting to be aware of.[*] Admiral Chet Richmond was given all the trappings to become the Ancient Albatross very shortly after I became Commandant.[†]

Then Glenn Thompson, who got his wings the same day I did, became the next one, and he was the Ancient Albatross and I was not, simply because he was originally something like two numbers senior to me.[‡] [Laughter] Then the next Ancient Albatross

---
[*] "Ancient Albatross" is a title for the active duty Coast Guard aviator with the earliest date of designation.
[†] Rear Admiral Chester A. Richmond, USCG.
[‡] Rear Admiral Glenn O. Thompson, USCG.

was a man who was originally an AP, and I guess he was back again to chief aviation pilot at that time. He had great difficulty passing his flight physicals because he was getting so deaf from flying those noisy airplanes that he'd flown in his earlier years, and that was John Greathouse.* He was taking a physical one day when I was at Naval Air Station, Seattle, and he was trying to get through the ear test before he could finish his physical. Of course, I'd been flying the Martin 404 for five years so that was in effect a vacation from working on my ears. But he kept the title of Ancient Albatross until he retired, and he kept saying to me later that he would have retired earlier so that I could have been the Ancient Albatross, but he knew that Glenn Thompson was around, so he didn't do it.

Paul Stillwell: Wouldn't have helped you anyway.

Admiral Siler: No.

Paul Stillwell: One thing I've discovered in the last few days is that you're not a boastful person. Let me give you the opportunity. What would you like to brag about from your time as Commandant?

Admiral Siler: I don't know that there's an awful lot that I would boast about. I think my wife would boast about the fact that we sent women to sea. And I have to admit that I didn't do it without some pushing. The general counsel of the Department of Transportation was a woman, and she set up a meeting with the Secretary to discuss sending women to sea.† She said that she had gotten some letters, and she wasn't quite sure she could defend the Coast Guard if they ever did the ultimate they were threatening, which was sue the Coast Guard to send women to sea. So at that point we decided we'd send women to sea. [Laughter]

Paul Stillwell: You've made a gesture as if you were sort of dragged into it.

---

* ADCMAP John P. Greathouse, USCG.
† The general counsel was Linda H. Kamm.

Admiral Siler: Yes, indeed. The first thing we did was to decide how we would send them to sea on a trial basis initially. We ordered I think it was 12 enlisted women to sea, because by putting 12 women in one compartment on the big 327-foot cutters they could have a space to themselves. There were two women who were officers who were assigned to each ship. I'm quite certain that the one of the officers who was the first one to be ordered to the cutter on the East Coast later married the exec.

The women who were ordered to the ships on the Pacific Coast—I think I mentioned to you before one of those women became a very well qualified more senior officer. The funny thing about that was when they were ordered to the ship they were both ensigns, so they shared a stateroom. Then the one who'd been in the Coast Guard for some time made jaygee, and all the male jaygees had a room to themselves. She thought about it for a while, then went to the exec and said, "Shouldn't I have a room to myself?" Of course, this meant the other ensign was given a room by herself too. But that question didn't get into it. They just said, "Well, if you get a room to yourself, you'll have to share the head with a male officer." And she said, "I understand there's a lock on the door." [Laughter] So she got the room to herself.

Paul Stillwell: Do you recall which ship that was?

Admiral Siler: I can't remember now. It was based in Alameda at that time.

Paul Stillwell: It was a 327?

Admiral Siler: No, it was a 378. I don't remember which one it was.

Paul Stillwell: What else would you like to brag about?

Admiral Siler: Well, the fact that we set up the 200-mile fishing limit and had no problems, no real problems with that I think was something that the Coast Guard as whole should have been very proud of. We had one incident very shortly after we set that up when there was a huge Russian factory vessel that came inside the 200-mile limit.

That was not allowed either, because for them to do their operation they had to transfer fish from the catcher-type vessel to this big factory vessel. We apprehended the vessel and wanted to seize it and take it into port, and the penalty that was usually assigned for that was in theory we seized the vessel, and it became an American piece of property.

In actual practice, what we did was quickly get a judge to assess a penalty. They would pay the penalty, which was buying the vessel back. We had the vessel alongside of the Coast Guard ship and we were about to order it into Boston. Before we did that, we were told we should notify the White House. Well, quite a bit earlier we had had the situation where a Russian vessel and an American vessel were conferring and a Russian seaman named Simas Kudirka jumped over on the Coast Guard ship and didn't want to go back to the Russian vessel.*

So after that happened, we had a State Department person assigned to Coast Guard headquarters to always be available to channel information to the State Department when it seemed necessary. At the same time we had people assigned to the State Department, and one of the Coast Guard captains married the Assistant Secretary of State, Rozanne Ridgway. [Laughter] She's the only ambassador I've ever kissed. [Laughter] But I'd known her for some time because we'd worked so closely together, and this latter event occurred when she was appointed ambassador to East Germany.

But in these seizure cases we cleared them through the State Department, and apparently President Carter said, "Be sure you notify me before we do anything with a Russian vessel." So we went to the Secretary of State en route to the President, and the Secretary of State was Warren Christopher at the time, acting Secretary.† He was actually the Under Secretary of State.

He said, "Well, let's see what the President has to say about it." So we woke up Jimmy Carter and said, "The Coast Guard's about to seize this vessel."

He said, "Just give them a warning and let them go," each time, and it was about the third time, we actually got the authority to seize it and take it into Boston, and they

---

* Simas Kudirka was a radio operator on board the Soviet fishing trawler Sovietskaya Litva. On 23 November 1970 he leaped from his ship to the deck of the U.S. Coast Guard cutter Vigilant (WMEC-617), which was moored alongside in American waters, near Martha's Vineyard, Massachusetts. Ten hours later he was removed by force from the U.S. ship and returned to the Soviet vessel.
† Warren Christopher was Deputy Secretary of State from 26 February 26 to 20 January 1981.

were assessed a good-sized penalty.[*] Probably that captain never served as a captain again would be my guess. But anyway—

Paul Stillwell: Well, you said you thought they were testing the enforcement.

Admiral Siler: Oh, yes. The fact, that we had to go to the President, though, that's a perfect example of how Jimmy Carter liked to do things himself rather than delegating authority.

Paul Stillwell: You said earlier that you had the opportunity to serve beyond your four years as Commandant. Why did you choose not to?

Admiral Siler: Because I'd seen the feelings toward Admiral Richmond when he served eight years. I just said, "No, I will not take another appointment."

Paul Stillwell: Who made the offer?

Admiral Siler: Brock Adams.

Paul Stillwell: What sort of feeling was there toward Admiral Richmond?

Admiral Siler: Just a general resentment because the legislation was introduced at that time to limit captains' terms in office and admirals' terms. And other than Admiral Richmond, I don't think any admiral has served more than 35 years. It was 30 years for a captain. But Admiral Richmond was without doubt one of the most capable officers we had at that time.

---

[*] On 10 April 1977 a boarding party from the Coast Guard cutter Decisive (WMEC-629) seized the 275-foot Soviet trawler Taras Shevchenko 130 miles off Nantucket for violating the U.S. 200-mile fishing zone. This seizure, which was the first under the new law, resulted in the Soviet ship being taken to Boston. The captain of the Soviet ship was fined $10,000 and received a suspended nine-month jail sentence.

Paul Stillwell: Did you feel any emotional pangs taking off the uniform after all those years?

Admiral Siler: Not really. The last year gets a little bit tiresome.

Paul Stillwell: In what ways?

Admiral Siler: The hours that they call you and the fact that you feel you should be in New York or Miami or someplace. So you're in the airplane going to meetings when you really would prefer to be somewhere else.

Paul Stillwell: So you were psychologically ready to retire when you did.

Admiral Siler: Yes, I really was.

Paul Stillwell: Did you have anything else specific in mind at that point to go to?

Admiral Siler: No. I had been contacted by the Norwegian ambassador to see if I would be interested in a position on the board of directors of a Norwegian company, but I was still on active duty, and I wasn't about to go job hunting at that time. I know that a lot of people do, but that's not what the regulations say, and I took them to heart.

Paul Stillwell: What did you wind up doing after that?

Admiral Siler: Not much. [Laughter] After some time doing nothing, I took a position with ManTech International Corporation, and I feel certain in that case it was a manufactured job, but they felt that I could provide information about Coast Guard contracts that they might not have been considered for. There were some jobs of that nature, I'm sure. There were also some jobs that we did for the Navy that had a Coast Guard slant that should be considered.

For example, there was a proposal to use a tanker because of its greater stability and heavier weight, mount a frame on the deck of that and off-load ships at places—well, Saudi Arabia in particular—where the Saudis were very slow in building port facilities. It would have been practically impossible to do because it was in violation of all sorts of Coast Guard regulations. And I was able to point those out to the Navy when they were thinking about it. It would have been almost a necessity to make it a water tanker rather than an oil tanker. Whether they were willing to do that I'm not sure.

Paul Stillwell: When I came into your house I noticed the oil portrait that Albert Murray did of you.[*] Any recollections of working with him?

Admiral Siler: Yes, it was about as boresome as I can possibly think of. [Laughter] He had a studio, which was I think a rather good studio in that the light was exactly right, in New York. At the time that I was working on that portrait Jimmy Holloway gave him some photographs and said, "That's it." He would not pose. Bill Middendorf had a portrait made that I thought was very good, and he posed with a model of the Constitution there in the background.[†] And the painting of the model was just as good as Middendorf. So I thought that the example of what the portraits were like were interesting. He also had just recently gone to South Africa to paint a portrait of—would it have been DeBeers? I'm not sure.

Paul Stillwell: Could have been.

Admiral Siler: He was very short, and yet he's the ruler of a wonderful empire of diamonds. So in order to make that portrait work out Murray devised an arrangement to that this short man—and it may have been DeBeers, I'm not sure—was on a pedestal and was looking down at Murray when he painted because the looking down on the world because he was such a rich man made it an important part of the portrait.

---

[*] The oral history of Commander Albert K. Murray, USNR (Ret.), is in the Naval Institute collection.
[†] J. William Middendorf served as Secretary of the Navy from 20 June 1974 to 20 January 1977.

Paul Stillwell: My brief dealings with Murray I found he had a very lively personality.

Admiral Siler: I wish he'd had a lively personality while he was painting [laughter], because I almost went to sleep several times while I was sitting there. [Laughter]

Paul Stillwell: You had mentioned to me that you were on the Naval Aviation Museum board. What do you remember of that service?

Admiral Siler: Well, there were some very interesting people on that board. Of course, I started working with Admiral Mickey Weisner.* And very frequently the former Chief of Naval Operations would be there and give us some input, because he was very interested in developing the museum. Then it was downgraded a little as we made some real progress with the museum, and the museum I think is a fabulous place. The development of this museum over the years has been very interesting to see.

Paul Stillwell: Which CNO was it that was involved there?

Admiral Siler: Tom Moorer.† Tom, I think, had a lot to do with the establishment of the museum to begin with and worked with Weisner and a few others to get it started. And so he had a great personal interest in it.

Paul Stillwell: You were telling me but not yet on the record about a Coast Guard aviator that you pushed to get into the Hall of Fame.

Admiral Siler: Well, that was D. B. McDermott who had developed a lot of the techniques for open-sea landings in the PBM in particular in those days. He was practically given a Navy PBM-5A, the one with wheels on it. I don't know how much he flew it, but I don't think anyone else flew it, the one that was given to the Coast Guard.

---

* Admiral Maurice F. Weisner, USN (Ret.).
† Admiral Thomas H. Moorer, USN, a naval aviator, served as Chief of Naval Operations from 1 August 1967 to 1 July 1970. He was later Chairman of the Joint Chiefs of Staff from 3 July 1970 to 30 June 1974. His oral history is in the Naval Institute collection.

He had the facilities of Lindbergh Field in San Diego to operate from, and he would land on the land and then taxi over to the Coast Guard and they had a seaplane ramp there and he'd taxi down the seaplane ramp and take off from there. He eventually was training some rather junior birdman how to land in the open sea. They wrecked the airplane [Laughter] and it went down, so that was the end of the tests. It was not practical to have the PBM as a regular offshore landing plane, and so they went to the P5M rather than the PBM.

Paul Stillwell: And I think you told me you wanted to put him in ahead of Frank Erickson, because you thought Erickson would make it anyway.*

Admiral Siler: Yes. With helicopters being so much the thing today, I felt that open-sea landings which were determined to be impractical would not qualify if it were not done right then, so we made him the nominee at that time.

Paul Stillwell: What era was that when he was nominated?

Admiral Siler: I'm not sure of date offhand.

Paul Stillwell: Any other highlights from your retirement years that you want to mention? What different places have you lived since then?

Admiral Siler: Well, when I first retired we went to Mobile, Alabama, because I knew they had a big Coast Guard unit there, an air station. At the same time I didn't feel that I would be happy without employment of some kind, and I made several calls but didn't get much interest in employing me. So I went back to Washington, figuring that working in the beltway bandits would be a possibility.† Eventually I went to work for ManTech,

---

* In World War II Commander Frank A. Erickson, USCG, did pioneering work in the development of helicopters for Coast Guard missions. See Erickson's account, "The First Coast Guard Helicopters," U.S. Naval Institute Proceedings, July 1981, pages 62-66.
† "Beltway bandits" is a nickname for consultants that work for the Department of Defense. The name comes from their office locations near the Capital Beltway that surrounds Washington, D.C.

and I was in the division that was under the direct supervision of the president. Most of that division, though, was in Norfolk and dealing with the Navy and whatever they could develop with a contract.

The work that I did with the assistance of about two people in the Washington, D.C., area and then all of the staff that did the clerical work that was in the Washington area, too, had to do with the Navy R&D centered over in the Annapolis area.[*] We worked on some ideas to develop a standard hull that could be an auxiliary of any type for the Navy. I think it's feasible, but I'm not sure how practical it would be because of the expense of that kind of an operation. It was fun to work with, though.

Then I moved from there to their division, which was in Annapolis. It originally was a part of their computer aids design division, and then it broke off and became its own division and eventually a subsidiary company. I'm not sure whether it's still in Annapolis or whether it's even in business now, but it was dealing with legal aspects of analyses of accidents of any kind looking particularly at the engineering aspects of it for insurance companies and for attorneys. I worked with a couple of attorneys on cases that had to do with smaller boats, recreational-type boats, and then I guess for a while I was a vice president in their organization, and I was looking for engineering talent that could do these analyses too.

There were a tremendous number of people who were interested in that kind of thing. They had some very interesting cases of that type. There was one that had to do with the supertanker of a class that one of them went aground on the French coast and dumped a huge amount of oil there. This particular tanker got into trouble in the South Atlantic when it was headed, I think, to Durban, South Africa, to load oil there. So at the time it was pretty much empty except that it had partially ballasted one of its tanks but only partially ballasted it, and that tank was 300 feet long. It built up waves inside this tank so large that when the waves would hit a bulkhead, that bulkhead got knocked off its foundation. The steel was that thick.

Paul Stillwell: Two inches maybe.

---

[*] R&D—research and development.

Admiral Siler: I'm sure it was two inches at least.

Paul Stillwell: So a lot of free surface effect in that.

Admiral Siler: Tremendous amount of free surface, and it was so large that they knew they had to get that repaired before they could put any more oil in it.* So they stopped in Durban, South Africa, to inspect the tank and pumped it empty and then examined the tank. We used a person to look at the tank for this company, and I think it was Amoco but I'm not sure. The person we had was the professor of metallurgy at the Naval Academy, and it was summertime so he had enough free time. He went first to Durban, and then I don't remember whether he came back or not, but the ship went on to Singapore and could go into dry dock there and have that bulkhead welded into place again. That's when he cut out a sample of it, and you could see that the weld was just a little bit on this side, a little bit on that side, but not really welded.

Paul Stillwell: You mean the original weld?

Admiral Siler: Yes.

Paul Stillwell: As far as moves, then in 1987 you came to Savannah. What were the attractions here?

Admiral Siler: We had for some time decided that we had had enough of the Washington, D.C., area. We had lived in the Kensington area just outside the city limits up near the Mormon temple there. Each time that we would come down to visit our daughter, we would look for someplace south of Washington so there'd be less snow than I had shoveled in Washington a good many times. We started with Yorktown and Williamsburg and went to the Triangle area in North Carolina: Raleigh, Durham, and Chapel Hill.

---

* Free surface effect comes about when a ship's tank or other compartment is partially filled with liquid so that the liquid is free to move from side to side of the ship. Because the liquid goes to the low side of the compartment, a large amount of free surface can be dangerous to the ship's stability.

Then we looked in Columbia, South Carolina, because I had been on the Retired Officers Association board of directors, and one of the generals there said, "Well, you can't beat Columbia, South Carolina." But, of course, he'd been commanding officer of the training station there in Columbia, so he had a little advantage over me. We looked at Columbia, and I rather liked the development and the houses that we saw. We eventually put a down payment on a house but could get it back with interest if we backed out before they started construction. They changed the entire concept before they were ready to go ahead and build. So we backed out of that and started looking again and looked at Charleston and here and Ponte Vedra down in Florida. Both my wife and I liked this a great deal, so we decided that we'd make a try at this. It was not in the plans at all originally, except it was closer to our daughter.

Paul Stillwell: Well, please bring me up to date on Gregory and Marsha.

Admiral Siler: Well, Gregory went to the University of Connecticut. He did very well in school, and I'm not sure that the University of Connecticut was his choice for any particular reason. He was a very good swimmer, and he swam both on the freshman team and on the varsity team the next three years as their breaststroker. So he was doing quite well as a swimmer. He didn't do any swimming in high school, because we were in Alaska a good part of the time. The swimming pool that they had at that time was only active in the summertime, so he was never available for swimming during his high school years. He majored in accounting in college and got his degree in accounting. The only other subject that particularly appealed to him was microbiology, but the instructor was gay, so he didn't want to do anything there.

He had some interesting jobs in accounting, but at least one of the companies went bankrupt, and so his greatest task there was to declare bankruptcy properly. Now he's working as the chief financial officer for a building material or hardware firm, a mini-Home Depot, but nowhere near that big. Their only installation is just inside the district on the Maryland side, but he lives in Columbia. He's had two sons by two wives; now he's with his third wife, and they have no children.

Marsha thought she wanted to be a nurse when she went to college, and she decided very early that she wanted to go to the University of Florida. We sent her to the University of Florida, because at that time we claimed Florida as a residence. When she became a junior in the college, she said, "You promised me I could spend one year in Great Britain." She took all of her courses at the University of London, but she lived way out in the suburbs at Richmond College and had to take the subway all the time to get to the university. Richmond is out in the vicinity of Wimbledon. It's a college, I guess, of the University of London but she lived out there. She came back with the best figure she's ever had in her life. The food she could hardly stand [laughter], and particularly some of the food she developed an absolute detesting for it. But she did look good when she came home.

Then she went back to the University of Florida and decided that that was the man for her. When he graduated he was admitted to the bar in Florida and went to work in Tallahassee. So when Marsha graduated she wanted to go to Tallahassee. Before she went to Tallahassee she was offered a teaching job in the—I think it was Alachua County, I'm not sure—out in the suburbs, way out in the country. The kids were not very well behaved, to say the least.

She thought one day that she would maybe make some friends among the students, and so she made some cookies. They ended up having a cookie fight, throwing them across the room. When she came back from England, she had thought she would at that point major in English Literature and British History. Then she thought, "Now, how do I benefit from that?" Teaching was the only way that she could think of, so she majored in education the last year or so, but it was not in fact a year. And graduated with honors in those things. But after one semester of teaching, she said, "There must be something else."

So she went back to school and took counseling. She had a choice of three areas of concentration in counseling. One was mental counseling, and one was marriage counseling, and I guess the other was educational counseling. She had to take an internship one of those semesters, and she was assigned to the mental counseling, and she said that was shocking enough that she thought she would end up counseling herself. But when she graduated, she looked in Tallahassee then so that she could be where Jim was.

She took a job as director of counseling in a mental hospital. Then they gave her a promotion, and she was director of admissions as well as director of counseling and no raise in pay. So she stayed there for some time, and then she tried several other things, not in schools at all.

Now she is with Florida State University. Gets a salary high enough that it's too high to be in the faculty, so she's a special executive director at Florida State University. She has two children, a boy and a girl. The young man is now 20 years old, and I think last year he finally graduated from high school. Went to college over at St. Augustine and started dropping off courses as the semester went along, and I think he got credit for one course that he finished. Now he's taking another course at Tallahassee Community College, and at that rate he may finish college someday about the year of 2050. [Laughter] But he's making a little bit of money by delivering Chinese food to people, I think.

Paul Stillwell: Well, what about your granddaughter there, his sister?

Admiral Siler: His sister is doing beautifully. She has appeared in some musical performances. We went over to see her in "Carousel," and it was very well staged. She didn't have an outstanding part, but she was in it and very happy to be in it. And I think she's been in another one since then. But she does beautifully in everything she does.

Paul Stillwell: After all these questions is there something I should have asked but didn't? Is there something else you want to talk about?

Admiral Siler: Well, speaking of children and all, I mentioned my son had two boys. The older one had a daughter who lives with her mother in the Fairfax area, I'm not sure exactly where. But the grandson lives in Richmond, and the little girl now is 11 years old and again is a beautiful student. If she thins out a little bit, she'll be a very attractive girl.

Paul Stillwell: Anything on any other subject?

Admiral Siler: I don't think so.

Paul Stillwell: Well, I certainly appreciate your cooperation and friendliness and hospitality these last few days. It's been a real pleasure to get acquainted with you, and I very much appreciate this contribution to history.

Admiral Siler: Well, it's interesting that this becomes history, because I didn't ever think I was going to be history.

Paul Stillwell: Well, you're still making history.

Admiral Siler: I guess.

Paul Stillwell: Thank you very much.

Launched in 1969, the Naval Institute's oral history program is among the oldest in the country. Used in combination with documentary sources, oral histories offer a richer understanding of naval history. Often they contain candid recollections and explanations never entered into contemporaneous records. In addition, they can help depict the atmosphere of a particular event or era in a manner not available in official documents.

The Naval Institute gratefully accepts tax-deductible gifts to strengthen its oral history program. This support allows the Institute to preserve the hard-earned life lessons of today's service men and women so they may teach and inspire future generations.

For information about opportunities to underwrite Naval Institute oral history projects, please contact the Naval Institute Foundation at 291 Wood Road, Annapolis, Maryland 21402; by phone, (410) 295-1056; via e-mail, foundation@usni.org.

Index to the Oral History of
Admiral Owen W. Siler
U.S. Coast Guard (Retired)

Adams, Brock
From 1977 to 1979 served as Secretary of Transportation, 278, 309-311, 322, 338

Air Force, U.S.
A B-36 ran into trouble during a West Coast flight in the 1950s, so the crew bailed out, 120-121
Role in search and rescue operations around Alaska in the early 1960s, 191-192, 195
Transported Coast Guard Academy cadets to the West Coast for training in the late 1970s, 273
Air Force uniforms resemble those of the Coast Guard, 285-287

Alameda, California, Coast Guard Training Station
Siler served briefly in 1946 as a personnel officer while the service was demobilizing, 73-74, 77-78
In the late 1960s there were proposed changes to the status of the training station, 241-242

Alaska
Search and rescue incidents in the early 1960s, 191-193, 198-200
An earthquake hit the state in March 1964, 193-196
Difficult weather conditions for flying, 201-202
The Coast Guard was involved in fisheries enforcement off Alaska in the early 1960s, 202-203

Amphibious Warfare
In November 1943 the attack transport Hunter Liggett (APA-14) took part in the amphibious assault on Bougainville, 44-47, 60, 291
Amphibious warfare training by the Hunter Liggett in World War II, 49-50

AMVER
Automated system for tracking commercial ships, 154-155
In the mid-1970s Norway honored Siler for the work of the AMVER system, 326-327

Antisubmarine Warfare
Training in 1943 with Coast Guard 83-foot patrol boats, 39-40
During World War II a JRF Widgeon attacked a German submarine in the Gulf of Mexico, 84-85

Arctic
In 1967 the icebreaker Eastwind (WAGB-279) circumnavigated the North Pole, 293-294

Army, U.S.
Various elements stationed in the St. Louis area in the early 1970s, 259, 333

Atlantic
Schooner used for sail training at the Coast Guard Academy in the early 1940s, 21-22, 26, 272

B-17 Flying Fortress
The Coast Guard version, PB-1G, was used in the late 1940s-early 1950s, 103, 106-107, 124-125

B-36 Peacemaker
A B-36 ran into trouble during a West Coast flight in the 1950s, so the crew bailed out, 120-121

Barbers Point, Hawaii
Site of Coast Guard air operations in the early 1950s, 124-136
Living accommodations for service personnel and their families in the 1950s, 131
Navy and Coast Guard operations were both located at the air station in the early 1950s, 133

Barnum, John W.
   In the mid-1970s was Under Secretary of Transportation, 263-264, 268, 274

Bayfield, USS (APA-33)
   During and shortly after World War II was manned by a Coast Guard crew during various operations in the Pacific, 61-64, 67-72

Bear (WMEC-901)-Class Cutters
   Design of in the 1970s, 303-304

Beechcraft Baron
   Aircraft used by Siler to visit various elements of the Second Coast Guard District in the early 1970s, 259-260

Bender, Admiral Chester R., USCG (USCGA, 1936)
   In the late 1960s commanded the Coast Guard Western Area from San Francisco, 241
   Served as Coast Guard Commandant, 1970-74, 142, 244, 262-263, 265, 267-268, 284-286, 305, 313, 328
   In the early 1970s changed the Coast Guard uniform, 284-286

Benkert, Rear Admiral William M., USCG (USCGA, 1944)
   As a Coast Guard Academy cadet in the early 1940s, 293
   In the 1960s commanded the icebreaker Eastwind (WAGB-279) in arctic operations, 294-294
   Served in Coast Guard headquarters in the mid-1970s, 292-293, 297-301, 334

Bermuda
   Liberty stop during a Coast Guard Academy training cruise in the early 1940s, 24-26

Blanchard, Colonel Felix A., Jr., USA (USMA, 1947)
   In the mid-1960s was injured while on a National War College field trip to Guatemala, 217-218

Bougainville, Solomon Islands
   In November 1943 the attack transport Hunter Liggett (APA-14) took part in the amphibious assault on Bougainville, 44-47, 60, 291

Bowman, Commander Carl G., USCG (USCGA, 1929)
   Served as an aviator in World War II and as skipper of the cutter Taney (WPG-37) shortly after the war, 84-87, 91

Boxing
   At the Coast Guard Academy in the early 1940s, 28-30

Boyce, Lieutenant Commander George R., Jr., USCG (USCGA, 1936)
   In 1946 served as executive officer of the cutter Taney (WPG-37), 85-88

Brinegar, Claude S.
   From 1973 to 1975 served as Secretary of Transportation, 262-265, 268, 308-309

Budgetary Considerations
   Role of the programs division of Coast Guard headquarters in the late 1960s-early 1970s, 227, 236-238

Buoy Tending
   Managed by the Second Coast Guard District on inland waterways in the early 1970s, 246, 253-254

C-130 Hercules
    Aircraft that has had a long life in the Coast Guard, 146-147, 197-198, 203-204, 237, 307, 312

Canada
    In the early 1950s an Air Force B-36 crashed in western Canada, 120-121

Carter, President James E. Jr.
    His administration in the late 1970s took a less military approach to the Coast Guard than did the previous Ford Administration, 309-311
    Requirement for personal permission for seizure of Soviet fishing vessels, 311, 337-338

Christopher, Warren
    Was Deputy Secretary of State during a fisheries enforcement case in the 1970s, 337

Coast Guard, U.S.
    Coast Guard Academy in the early 1940s, 11-39
    Sail training in the early 1940s 21-24
    Manned Navy attack transports in World War II, 41-68
    Ocean station patrols during various periods, 81-95, 153, 281-282
    Air station operations in the 1950s and 1960s, 102-136, 165-167, 175-187, 205-215, 226
    Commandant's office in the late 1950s, 137-174
    Headquarters in Washington in the 1950s, 144-145
    Proposals to provide quarters for the Commandant, 170-171
    Role of the 17th District in Alaska in the early 1960s, 191-204
    Fisheries enforcement, 202-203, 311-312, 336-338
    No black Coast Guard Academy cadets before the 1960s, 17-18
    In the 1960s Coast Guard headquarters moved to the Department of Transportation building in Washington, 229
    Management division of Coast Guard headquarters, 1967-71, 227-244
    Role of the Second District in St. Louis in the early 1970s, 245-262
    Ship replacement actions initiated in the mid-1970s, 270, 303-304, 308-309
    Aircraft replacement actions initiated in the mid-1970s, 305-307
    Law enforcement operations against drug smuggling in the mid-1970s, 316-318, 322-323
    Increasing use of the Coast Guard slash in the 1970s as a service identifier, 274-275, 329
    In 1977 women began serving on board Coast Guard ships, 277-280, 335-336

Coast Guard Academy, U.S.
    Swab summer of 1940, 11-16
    Hazing, 16
    Response to perceived cheating in class, 16-17
    Academics, 16-20, 34-35
    Athletics in the early 1940s, 14, 26-31
    Training cruises in the early 1940s, 21-26
    Social life for cadets in the early 1940s, 31
    News of the 1941 Japanese attack on Pearl Harbor, 32-33
    During World War II served as the site for Officer Candidate School, 33-34
    Shortened courses during World War II, 34-35
    Leave periods for cadets in the early 1940s, 35-37
    The class of 1944 graduated in 1943, 38-39
    No black cadets before the 1960s, 17-18
    The bark Eagle (WIX-327) made a training cruise to the West Coast in 1978, 272-273
    Women were admitted for the first time in 1976, 277-278, 313
    Operation of in the mid-1970s, 312-313

Coast Guard Auxiliary
    Role over the years in augmenting the active service, 151, 193, 314-315

Coast Guard Districts
    Role of the 11th District at Long Beach in 1947, 95-97
    Role of the 17th Coast Guard District in Alaska, 1962-64, 191-204
    Role of the Second Coast Guard District in St. Louis, 1971-74, 245-262

Coast Guard Reserve, U.S.
    Provided a great deal of manpower in World War II, 68
    Gained extra pilots from other services in the 1950s, 115-117
    Over the years its existence has been threatened, 149, 257-258
    Reservists were recalled to active duty to deal with flooding in the Midwest in 1973, 255-257
    Transformation of its role in the 1970s, 313-314

Coleman, William T., Jr.
    Served as Secretary of Transportation, 1975-77, 301, 309, 311

Commercial Ships
    AMVER is an automated system for tracking commercial ships, 154-155
    In December 1976 the tanker Argo Merchant ran aground on Nantucket Shoals, 299-301
    Operations by Soviet fishing vessels in the mid-1970s, 311, 336-338
    Coast Guard law enforcement operations against drug smuggling in the mid-1970s, 316-318, 322-323

Communications
    Radio capability of the cutter Taney (WPG-37) in 1946, 92
    By the 11th Coast Guard District in 1947, 95-97
    By the Coast Guard air station at Port Angeles, Washington, in the late 1940s, 111
    In the wake of the Alaska earthquake of March 1964, 195

Computers
    Introduction in Coast Guard headquarters in the late 1960s, 228-230, 236
    Used in the COMDAC for the Coast Guard's Bear (WMEC-901)-class cutters, designed in the 1970s, 304

Congress
    Testimony by various Coast Guard Commandants, 141-142, 164, 175, 300-302
    Proposed a nuclear-powered Coast Guard icebreaker in the 1950s, 156
    The Coast Guard took congressmen on various trips in the 1950s, 168-170
    Confirmation of Siler as Commandant in 1974, 267-268

Corpus Christi, Texas, Coast Guard Air Station
    Site of Coast Guard air operations in the late 1950s-early 1960s, 165-167, 175-187, 226
    Relationship with district headquarters in New Orleans, 186-187

Corpus Christi, Texas, Naval Air Station
    Site of flight training in the late 1940s, 98
    Site of instrument training in 1952, 123-125
    Relationship with the Coast Guard in the late 1950s-early 1960s, 165-166, 184-185

Crea, Rear Admiral Vivien S., USCG
    Aviator who served in the White House in the 1980s and subsequently made flag rank, 279

Cuba
    In the mid-1960s was patrolled by Coast Guard aircraft from Florida, 206-209
    In late 1965 refugees left Cuba for the United States, 207-208, 211-212

Cuban Missile Crisis
  During the crisis in October 1962 the Coast Guard patrolled the North Pacific to track Soviet ships, 203-204

Cueroni, Rear Admiral Richard P., USCG (USCGA, 1953)
  Served in the mid-1970s as the Commandant's speechwriter, 271, 277, 334
  From 1986 to 1989 was superintendent of the Coast Guard Academy, 313

Danmark
  Danish square-rigger used for sail training at the Coast Guard Academy in the early 1940s, 23, 26, 272

Disciplinary Matters
  Court-martial for a crew member of the attack transport Hunter Liggett (APA-14) during World War II, 56

Disney, Walt
  In the mid-1950s hosted a visit in California by Coast Guard leaders, 137-138

Drugs
  Coast Guard law enforcement operations against drug smuggling in the mid-1970s, 316-318

Eagle, USCGC WIX-327)
  Square rigger that was present during the Commandant change of command in Washington, D.C., in May 1974, 271-272
  In the mid-1970s received the Coast Guard slash on her hull, 274-275
  In July 1976 participated in a bicentennial sailing review in New York City, 275-276
  In 1978 made a training cruise to the West Coast, 272-273

Eastwind, USCGC (WAGB-279)
  Operations in the Arctic in 1967, 293-294

Egan, William
  Served as governor of Alaska in the early 1960s, 190, 195, 197

Eleventh Coast Guard District, Long Beach
  Operation of the district office at Long Beach in 1947, 95-97

Elizabeth City, North Carolina, Coast Guard Air Station
  In the 1950s served as a supply and training base, 117-118

Emigh, Lieutenant (junior grade) Ward, USCG (USCGA, 1944)
  Served in the San Francisco area shortly after World War II, 79, 81

Enlisted Personnel
  In the crew of the attack transport Hunter Liggett (APA-14) during World War II, 54-58
  Communication with in the mid-1970s, 318-320

Evans, Captain Stephen H., USCG (USCGA, 1927)
  In 1945 was stationed in the assignment section at Alameda, California, 61-62

Federal Aviation Administration
  Had a large role when the Transportation Department was formed in 1967, 232
  Certification of new aircraft in the mid-1970s, 306-307

Fire
    The passenger ship Yarmouth Castle burned during a Caribbean cruise in 1965, 213-215

Fishing
    The Coast Guard was involved in fisheries enforcement off Alaska in the early 1960s, 202-203
    In the mid-1970s U.S. fisheries enforcement was moved out to 200 miles from the coasts, 237, 311-312, 336-338

Flight Training
    At Corpus Christi, Texas, in the late 1940s, 98-100
    At Pensacola, Florida, in the late 1940s, 100-101

Floyd Bennett Field, Brooklyn, New York
    In the 1950s was used by both Navy and Coast Guard aircraft, 160-162

Flues, Abram Gilmore
    Served 1957 to 1961 as Assistant Secretary of the Treasury, 145-146, 160, 163

Football
    Siler's experiences as a player in junior college, late 1930s, 8-9
    At the Coast Guard Academy, early 1940s, 14, 26-27

Ford, President Gerald R.
    Sworn in as President in August 1974, 285, 289-290
    Interactions with Admiral and Mrs. Siler in the mid-1970s, 288-290

France
    Role in the manufacture of the Coast Guard's HU-25 aircraft in the 1970s, 307

Gambling
    Poker games on board the cutter Taney (WPG-37) in 1946, 88

German Navy
    During World War II a JRF Widgeon attacked a German submarine in the Gulf of Mexico, 84-85

Glomar Explorer
    Coast Guard inspection of the ship that attempted to recover a Soviet submarine in the 1970s, 268-269

Goehring, Rear Admiral Robert W., USCG (USCGA, 1939)
    In 1970 headed a flag selection board, 242

Goldman, Cadet Ernest H., USCG (USCGA, 1944)
    Graduated from the Coast Guard Academy in the early 1940s, 17

Greathouse, ADCMAP John P., USCG
    Served 1977-79 as the Coast Guard's Ancient Albatross, 334-335

Grumman Aircraft Company
    Around 1960 supplied the Coast Guard with the upgraded UF-2 Albatross, 175-177

Guam, Marianas Islands
    Siler spent two weeks on the island during the summer of 1945, 62-63

Guatemala
   Visited by Coast Guard Commandant Alfred Richmond in the 1950s, 169
   In the mid-1960s students from the U.S. National War College had a terrifying bus ride while on a field trip to this nation, 217-218

Gunnery–Naval
   By the attack transport Hunter Liggett (APA-14) during the invasion of Bougainville in 1943, 45

HH-52 Seaguard
   Helicopter used in the mid-1960s by Coast Guard Air Station Miami, 210, 212-214

HNS
   Helicopter from the icebreaker Northwind (WAGB-282) was dropped off in the late 1940s at Port Angeles, Washington, 102, 118

HO3S
   Helicopter flown from Port Angeles, Washington, in the late 1940s-early 1950s, 104-105, 118

HU-16 Albatross
   Flying boat used by the Coast Guard in the mid-1960s, 205-206, 210, 305
   See also: UF-1/UF-2 Albatross

HU-25 Guardian
   Chosen in the mid-1970s as a patrol aircraft for the Coast Guard, 305-307

Hahn, Commander Edward E., Jr., USCG
   During World War II commanded the attack transport Hunter Liggett (APA-14), 53-54, 61

Haley, JOC Alex, USCG (Ret.)
   Black enlisted man who wrote the bestselling book Roots, 18, 295-296
   The cutter Alex Haley (WMEC-39) is named in his honor, 296

Hansen, Knud L.
   During World War II served as master of the Danmark, an interned Danish square-rigger used by the Coast Guard Academy as a training ship, 23

Hayes, Admiral John B., USCG (USCGA, 1947)
   In the mid-1970s served as Commander 17th District in Alaska, 193, 312
   Served 1978-82 as Commandant of the Coast Guard, 319

Hayward, Admiral Thomas B., USN (USNA, 1948)
   Future Chief of Naval Operations attended the National War College as a captain in the mid-1960s, 215-217

Healy, Captain Michael A., USRCS
   Officer who operated in Alaskan waters for many years in the 19th century, 295

Helicopters
   An HNS from the icebreaker Northwind (WAGB-282) was dropped off in the late 1940s at Port Angeles, Washington, 102, 118
   The HO3S was flown from Port Angeles, Washington, in the late 1940s-early 1950s, 104-105
   The HH-52 was used in the mid-1960s by Coast Guard Air Station Miami, 210, 212-214

Hirshfield, Rear Admiral James A., USCG (USCGA, 1925)
   In the 1950s served as chief of personnel for the Coast Guard, 142-143

Holloway, Admiral James L. III, USN (USNA, 1943)
    In August 1974 attended the swearing-in of new President Gerald Ford, 285-286
    Relationship with Siler, 290-292

Honduras
    Visited in the 1950s by Coast Guard Commandant Alfred Richmond, 152

Honolulu, Hawaii
    Facilities for Coast Guard personnel in the area in the early 1950s, 132
    Tourist attractions, 132-133

Howarth, Commander George E., USCG (USCGA, 1938)
    In the early 1950s commanded the Coast Guard aviation detachment at Barbers Point, Hawaii, though he had cataract problems, 134-135

Hunter Liggett, USS (APA-14)
    Characteristics of this converted merchant ship, 41-42, 52, 57
    During World War II was manned by a Coast Guard crew during operations in the Pacific, 41-61
    In November 1943 took part in the amphibious assault on Bougainville, 44-47, 60, 291
    Enlisted crew members, 54-58
    Did Magic Carpet runs after World War II ended, 57

Imlay, Captain Miles H., USCG (USCGA, 1926)
    Taught seamanship at the Coast Guard Academy in the early 1940s, 20

Inchon, Korea
    The attack transport Bayfield (APA-33) visited shortly after World War II, 71-72

Ing, Commander Edwin B., USCG (USCGA, 1938)
    In the early 1950s commanded the Coast Guard aviation detachment at Barbers Point, Hawaii, 134

Instrument Flight
    Training at Corpus Christi, Texas, in 1952, 123-125

JRF Widgeon
    During World War II a JRF attacked a German submarine in the Gulf of Mexico, 84-85
    Flew in the late 1940s from Port Angeles, Washington, 103-107, 119-121

James, General Daniel, Jr., USAF
    In the mid-1970s attended a reception given by President and Mrs. Gerald Ford, 288-289

Japan
    Visited by the attack transport Bayfield (APA-33) shortly after World War II, 64, 67-68, 72
    American visitors to Japan were well received in the 1950s, 130-131

Jenkins, Lieutenant Commander William A., USCG (USCGA, 1942)
    In the early 1950s served as pilot for the Coast Guard Commandant, 137

Johnson, President Lyndon B.
    Was in office when the Transportation Department was established in 1967, 233

Johnson, Commander Roger R., USCG
    In the late 1940s commanded the Coast Guard air station at Port Angeles, Washington, 112

Juneau, Alaska
    Local activities in the early 1960s, 189-195

Kamm, Linda H.
    In the 1970s was general counsel of the Department of Transportation, 335

Kelly, Lieutenant (junior grade) Beverly, USCG
    In 1979 became the first woman to command a Coast Guard cutter, 278-279

Kennedy, President John F.
    Observed at his 1961 inauguration that the Coast Guard Academy had no black cadets, 17-18

Kinnard, Brigadier General Leo D., USA (USMA, 1944)
    Attended the Coast Guard Academy in the early 1940s before transferring to West Point and graduating, 14-15

Korea
    The attack transport Bayfield (APA-33) visited Inchon shortly after World War II, 71-72

Korean War
    Coast Guard planes patrolled the Pacific from Port Angeles, Washington, 103, 105-106
    Resulted in a buildup of Coast Guard air stations, 112-113

Lake Winnipesaukee, New Hampshire
    Controversy in the 1970s over whether it should be considered navigable from a legal standpoint, 320-322

Leave and Liberty
    For Coast Guard Academy cadets in the early 1940s, 23-25, 35-37

Loran
    Use of in the mid-1940s for navigation, 50, 73
    On board the cutter Taney (WPG-37) in 1946, 82
    Various stations in the Pacific operated in the 1950s, 127-128
    Installation of loran stations early in the Vietnam War, 234-235, 315
    Upgrades in the 1970s, 315

Louisville, Kentucky
    In 1972 the Coast Guard had to aid a barge of hazardous materials that was hung up on McAlpine Dam, 247-249

Magnuson, Warren
    Service in the U.S. Senate in the mid-1970s, 300-301

Marine Corps, U.S.
    Amphibious warfare training by the attack transport Hunter Liggett (APA-14) in World War II, 49-50

Martin 404 Skyliner
    Aircraft used in the mid-1950s for transporting Commandant Alfred Richmond, 129, 139-140, 152-153, 158, 169

McClelland, Vice Admiral Joseph J., USCG (USCGA, 1940)
    Candidate for Commandant in 1974, 264-267, 297
    In 1974 became Commander Pacific Area, 298-299

McClernon, Lieutenant Commander Harry K., USCG
During World War II coached at the Coast Guard Academy and then had sea duty, 28

McDermott, D. B.
Coast Guard aviator who developed techniques for open-sea landings in a PBM flying boat, 341-342

McGovern, Lieutenant Commander Gerald E., USCG
In the early 1950s flew as part of the Coast Guard air detachment at Barbers Point, Hawaii, 134-135

Medical Problems
Right after World War II Siler had considerable problems getting a satisfactory chest X-ray, 73-74
In the early 1950s Commander George Howarth commanded a Coast Guard air detachment in Hawaii even though he had cataracts, 134-135
In the early 1960s boards were held in Texas to decide cases of individuals with mental difficulties, 185-186

Miami, Florida, Coast Guard Air Station
Operations in the mid-1960s included patrols of Cuba and the rescue of passengers from the burning passenger ship Yarmouth Castle, 205-215

Middendorf, J. William
Mid-1970s Secretary of the Navy whose portrait was painted by Albert Murray, 340

Midway Atoll
Flight operations were plagued by gooney birds in the 1950s, 114

Military Academy, U.S., West Point, New York
During World War II Leo Kinnard dropped out of the Coast Guard Academy and then graduated with honors from West Point, 14-15

Mississippi River
Role of the Coast Guard on the river and its tributaries in the early 1970s, 245-253

Moorer, Admiral Thomas H., USN (Ret.) (USNA, 1933)
Spoke at a graduation ceremony for the Coast Guard Academy, 38
Role on behalf of the Naval Aviation Museum, 341

Movies
In the mid-1950s the Disney studio made a movie, Men Against the Arctic, about icebreaker operations, 138

Murray, Commander Albert K., USNR (Ret.)
In the 1970s painted Siler's portrait, 340-341

N2S Kaydet
Used for primary flight training at Corpus Christi in the late 1940s, 99-100

National Transportation Safety Board
The Coast Guard got a seat on the board following the 1965 fire on board the passenger ship Yarmouth Castle, 214-215

National War College, Washington, D.C.
In the mid-1960s students had a curriculum and papers at the school and made field trips, 215-225
The student body included future leaders of their services, 215-216, 219-221

Naval Aviation Museum, Pensacola, Florida
  Role in honoring the achievements of naval aviators, 341-342

NavGuard Board
  Established in the 1970s to deal with issues of interest to the Navy and Coast Guard, 324

Navigation
  Use of radar for navigation by the attack transport Hunter Liggett (APA-14) during World War II, 50
  Use of loran during various periods, 50, 73, 82, 127-128, 234-235, 315
  On board the cutter Taney (WPG-37) in 1946, 82-83

Navy League of the United States
  Provides benefits to the Coast Guard, 331-332

New York City
  On 4 July 1976 hosted a sailing ship review in New York Harbor, 275-276

New Zealand
  The attack transport Hunter Liggett (APA-14) visited Wellington during World War II, 42-44, 51

News Media
  In 1977 the media covered the advent of Coast Guard women serving in ships, 278
  Interviewed Siler during his time as Commandant in the mid-1970s, 328-329

Nicaragua
  Visited in the 1950s by Coast Guard Commandant Alfred Richmond, 152

Nixon, President Richard M.
  Met people in a receiving line early in his presidency, circa 1970, 287-288

Northwind, USCGC (WAGB-282)
  An HNS helicopter from this icebreaker was dropped off in the late 1940s at Port Angeles, Washington, 102, 118

Norway
  In the mid-1970s honored Siler for the work of the AMVER system, 326-327

Nuclear Power
  Proposal in the 1950s for a nuclear-powered Coast Guard icebreaker, 156

O'Connor, Rear Admiral John J., CHC, USN
  Served 1975-79 as the Navy's Chief of Chaplains, 330

Ohio River
  Role of the Coast Guard on the river in the early 1970s, 248-250

Oil Pollution
  The Coast Guard role in the mid-1970s in dealing with oil spills, 284, 324-325
  In December 1976 the tanker Argo Merchant ran aground on Nantucket Shoals, 299-301

Olav V
  King of Norway, was visited by Siler in the mid-1970s, 326-327

Olsen, Rear Admiral Carl B., USCG (USCGA, 1928)
  In the 1950s was selected for flag rank the same week he was dropped from aviation, 144
  Commanded the Eighth Coast Guard District in New Orleans around 1960, 186

P5M Marlin
    Characteristics of the plane, 109

PB-1G
    Coast Guard version of the B-17 was used in the late 1940s-early 1950s, 103, 106-107, 124-125

PBM Mariner
    Used during flight training at Corpus Christi, Texas, in the late 1940s, 101-102
    Characteristics of the plane, 108-109
    Operated from Port Angeles, Washington, in the early 1950s, 121
    Capability for open-sea landings, 341-342

PBY Catalina
    Used during flight training at Pensacola, Florida, in the late 1940s, 100-101

PB4Y/P4Y Liberator
    Aircraft used by the Coast Guard in the late 1940s-early 1950s, 113, 125-127

Panama
    In the mid-1960s was visited by students from the National War College, 219-220, 223-224

Pan American Airways
    Dinner Key, Florida, was one of the bases for flying boat operations, 205
    During the 1950s used Wake Island as a way station in the Pacific, 129-130

Patch, Captain Roderick S., USCG (USCGA, 1915)
    During World War II commanded the attack transport Hunter Liggett (APA-14), 52-54

Pay and Allowances
    Siler continued to receive flight pay up through the early part of his tenure as Commandant in the 1970s, 332-333

Pensacola, Florida, Naval Air Station
    Site of operational flight training in the late 1940s, 100-101

Perry, Vice Admiral Ellis L., USCG (USCGA, 1942)
    In the early 1970s served as the Coast Guard's chief of personnel, 242
    Candidate for Commandant in 1974, 264-265
    Service in the mid-1970s as Assistant Commandant of the Coast Guard, 266, 270, 274, 298

Pfeiffer, Lieutenant Commander Arthur, USCG (USCGA, 1938)
    In 1946 served as chief engineer of the cutter Taney (WPG-37), 88-89, 91

Polar Sea, USCGC (WAGB-11)
    Icebreaker commissioned in 1976 with Mrs. Siler as sponsor, 308

Polar Star, USCGC (WAGB-10)
    Icebreaker commissioned in 1976 with Mrs. Claude Brinegar as sponsor, 308
    Ran aground during early trials in Puget Sound, 308-309

Pollution
    The Coast Guard role in the mid-1970s in dealing with oil spills, 284, 324-325
    In December 1976 the tanker Argo Merchant ran aground on Nantucket Shoals, 299-301

Port Angeles, Washington, Coast Guard Air Station
    Various aircraft at the station in the late 1940s-early 1950s, 102-108, 118-119
    Base for patrol flights in the Pacific during the Korean War, 103, 105-106
    Search and rescue and medevac flights, 103-108, 112-113, 119-121
    Command arrangement in the late 1940s-early 1950s, 111-112

Promotion of Coast Guard Officers
    In the 1950s officers had to take promotion exams, 142-143
    In the 1960s selection boards did not always go according to expectations, 297

Propulsion Plants
    Steam turbine plant in the cutter Taney (WPG-37) in 1946, 91-92
    In the mid-1970s Admiral Hyman Rickover asked Siler about gas turbines in 378-foot Coast Guard cutters, 156-157
    Considerations that went into equipping the Bear (WMEC-901)-class cutters with diesels, 303-304

Public Health Service, U.S.
    Role in providing medical services for the Coast Guard, 330-331

Public Relations
    Siler had a number of speaking engagements as Commandant in the mid-1970s, 271, 277
    Increasing use of the Coast Guard slash in the 1970s as a service identifier, 274-275, 329

R5D Skymaster
    Used in the late 1950s to transport Coast Guard Commandant Alfred Richmond to various places, 159-160, 168-169

Racial Issues
    No black Coast Guard Academy cadets before the 1960s, 17-18
    Operation of the equal rights division of Coast Guard headquarters in the late 1960s, 230-231
    Coast Guard minority recruiting efforts in the 1970s, 295

Radar
    Use of by the attack transport Hunter Liggett (APA-14) during World War II, 50-51

Radio
    Communications capability of the cutter Taney (WPG-37) in 1946, 92, 95

Rea, Vice Admiral William F. III, USCG (USCGA, 1942)
    In the late 1960s was selected for flag rank sooner than expected, 297
    In the mid-1970s served as Commander Atlantic Area, 298-299

Recruiting
    The Midwest has long been a fertile recruiting ground for the Coast Guard, 282-283
    Coast Guard minority recruiting efforts in the 1970s, 295

Richards, Captain Walter R., USCG (USCGA, 1925)
    Commanded the attack transport Bayfield (APA-33) in 1945, 69

Richmond, Vice Admiral Alfred C., USCG
    Personal characteristics, 137, 140-142, 148, 158-159, 244
    In the early 1950s served as Assistant Commandant of the Coast Guard, 136-137
    Trips in the 1950s during his time as Commandant, 92, 137-141, 152-153, 159-164, 168-170, 173-174
    Duties as Commandant, 142-164, 168-175, 331-332, 338
    Sons of, 148

Richmond, Rear Admiral Chester A., USCG (USCGA, 1941)
  In the 1970s was the Coast Guard's Ancient Albatross, 334

Rickover, Admiral Hyman G., USN (Ret.) (USNA, 1922)
  Contact with Siler about Coast Guard cutters in the mid-1970s, 156-157

Riedel, Captain William R., USCG (USCGA, 1939)
  Served as assistant chief of staff of the Coast Guard until his 1969 retirement, 230, 235-236

Roland, Admiral Edwin J., USCG (USCGA, 1929)
  Service in Coast Guard headquarters in the 1950s, 143
  Congressional testimony as Commandant in 1962-66, 142

SNJ Texan
  Used for primary flight training at Corpus Christi in the late 1940s, 99

Sailing
  Coast Guard Academy sail training in the early 1940s, 21-26, 272
  In the early 1960s Siler built a sailboat from plans in a magazine, 179-181
  Coast Guard Academy sail training in the 1970s, 272-273
  On 4 July 1976 the United States hosted a sailing ship review in New York Harbor, 275-276

St. Louis, Missouri
  Floods in the vicinity in the spring of 1973, 254-257
  Relationship between the city and the Coast Guard in the early 1970s, 260-261

Salvage
  Rescue of a barge of hazardous material hung up on a dam at Louisville in 1972, 248-250

San Francisco, California
  Events in the city around the time World War II ended in August 1945, 64-67
  In 1946 the cutter Taney (WPG-37) entered the port at high speed during a shipping strike, 91-92

Sargent, Rear Admiral Thomas R. III, USCG (USCGA, 1938)
  During the Vietnam War traveled to the Pacific to see about loran stations, 234-235
  In the late 1960s-early 1970s served as Coast Guard chief of staff, 230, 234-235, 242

Scheiderer, Rear Admiral Edward D., USCG (USCGA, 1943)
  In the late 1960s headed the programs analysis division of Coast Guard headquarters, 227, 236
  In the 1970s served as Coast Guard chief of staff but declined a job as district commander, 236

Search and Rescue
  Flights from Port Angeles, Washington, in the late 1940s-early 1950s, 103-108, 119-120
  Various incidents in Alaska in the early 1960s, 191-193, 198-200
  In waters near Cuba in the mid-1960s, 207-209
  Rescues from the burning passenger ship Yarmouth Castle in November 1965, 213-215

Seattle, Washington
  Site of a world's fair in 1962, 187-189

Second Coast Guard District, St. Louis, Missouri
  Role in the early 1970s in working with river traffic in the Midwest, 245-253
  Rescue of a barge of hazardous material hung up on a dam at Louisville in 1972, 248-250
  Dealt with flooding in the Midwest in the spring of 1973, 254-257
  The Midwest has long been a fertile recruiting ground for the Coast Guard, 282-283

Seventeenth Coast Guard District, Juneau, Alaska
    Search and rescue incidents in Alaska in the early 1960s, 191-193, 198-200
    Role in helping provide relief after an earthquake hit Alaska in March 1964, 193-196
    Operation of the district headquarters in the early 1960s, 197-198
    During the Cuban Missile Crisis in October 1962 patrolled to track Soviet ships, 203-204

Shields, Rear Admiral William D., USCG (USCGA, 1931)
    In the early 1960s commanded the 17th Coast Guard District in Alaska, 197

Siler, Admiral Owen W., USCG (Ret.)
    Parents of, 1-3, 5-6, 8, 10, 180, 280
    Siblings of, 1-4, 10, 35-36, 76, 180-181
    Wife Betty, 32, 38-39, 65-66, 71, 79-80, 85, 122-123, 131, 133, 136-137, 141, 187-190, 194-195, 197, 203, 242-245, 262, 264, 266, 308, 322, 327, 335, 345
    Children of, 78, 80, 85, 131, 165, 179, 199-200, 244-245, 262, 344-347
    Grandchildren, 345, 347
    Father-in-law Clarence Walford, 121-122
    Youth in California in the 1920s and 1930s, 2-10
    Attended Santa Maria (California) Junior College, 1938-40, 6-8
    As a cadet at the Coast Guard Academy, 1940-43, 11-39
    Served 1943-45 in the attack transport Hunter Liggett (APA-14), 41-61
    Served 1945-46 in the attack transport Bayfield (APA-33), 61-73, 76
    Served briefly in 1946 as a personnel officer in Alameda, California, 73-74, 77-79
    In 1946 was navigator of the cutter Taney (WPG-37), 79-95
    Shore duty in 1947 at the 11th Coast Guard District, Long Beach, 95-97
    Took flight training at Corpus Christi and Pensacola in 1947-48, 98-102
    Duty in 1948-52 at Port Angeles, Washington, 102-123
    Instrument training at Corpus Christi in 1952, 123-125
    Duty in 1952-54 at Coast Guard Air Detachment, Barbers Point, Hawaii, 124-136
    Served 1954-59 as aide and pilot for the Commandant, Admiral Alfred Richmond, 92, 128-129, 137-165, 168-174
    From 1959 to 1962 commanded Coast Guard Air Station Corpus Christi, 165-167, 175-187, 226
    Served 1962-64 in the 17th Coast Guard District office in Alaska, 191-204
    In 1964-66 was executive officer and then commanding officer of Coast Guard Air Station Miami, 205-215
    In 1966-67 was a student at the National War College in Washington, 215-225
    From 1967 to 1971 was in the management division of Coast Guard headquarters, 226-244, 287-288
    In 1971 was selected for rear admiral, 242-243
    From 1971 to 1974 commanded Second Coast Guard District in St. Louis, 245-262
    Commandant selection process in 1974, 262-269
    Served as Commandant of the Coast Guard, 1974-78, 142, 216, 269-339
    Post-Coast Guard activities, 339-348

Smith, Admiral Willard J., USCG (USCGA, 1933)
    Service as Coast Guard Commandant in the late 1960s, 142, 227-228, 234, 265, 267, 331-332

Snyder, Commander William H., USCG (USCGA, 1932)
    In the late 1940s commanded the Coast Guard air station at Port Angeles, Washington, 111-112

Sonar
    Antisubmarine exercises in 1943 with Coast Guard 83-foot patrol boats, 39-40

Sorensen, Commander Ellen M., USCG (Ret.)
    Long-time friend of Siler's who asked about his selection for flag rank in 1971, 242-243

Soviet Union
    In 1967 refused permission for the icebreaker Eastwind (WAGB-279) to go north of some Russian islands, 293-294
    Operations by Soviet fishing vessels in the mid-1970s, 311, 336-338

Sperry Corporation
    In the 1970s was involved in the design of COMDAC for the Coast Guard's Bear (WMEC-901)-class cutters, 304

State Department
    In the 1970s maintained a person at Coast Guard headquarters to provide a channel of information, 337

Steele, Rear Admiral Joseph R., USCG (USCGA, 1944)
    Graduated number two in his class at the Coast Guard Academy, 20
    Selected for flag rank in 1971, 243-244

Stephens, Captain Irvin J., USCG (USCGA, 1932)
    In the 1950s served as assistant to the Commandant, Admiral Alfred Richmond, 169-170, 173

Synon, Rear Admiral George D., USCG (USCGA, 1932)
    In the early 1960s commanded the 17th Coast Guard District in Alaska, 197-199

Taney, USCGC (WPG-37)
    In 1946 served on ocean station patrol in the Pacific, 81-85, 87, 90-93
    Shortly after World War II conducted a sort of boot camp on board, 86-87
    Off-duty entertainment for the crew, 87-88
    In 1946 was converted from her wartime role back to a Coast Guard cutter, 88-90
    Weather station patrol in the 1970s, 90, 281
    Steam turbine propulsion plant, 91-92
    Ship's store, 93-94
    Gunnery, 94-95
    After retirement from active service became a museum in Baltimore, 81

Thayer, Rear Admiral Louis M., USCG (USCGA, 1933)
    Investigated the fire on board the passenger ship Yarmouth Castle in 1965, 214

Thompson, Rear Admiral Glenn O., USCG
    In the 1970s was the Coast Guard's Ancient Albatross, 334-335

Tinian, Marianas Islands
    Hit by a typhoon shortly after the end of World War II, 70-71

Training
    Cruises by Coast Guard Academy cadets in the early 1940s, 21-26
    Antisubmarine exercises in 1943 with Coast Guard 83-foot patrol boats, 39-40
    Amphibious warfare training by the attack transport Hunter Liggett (APA-14) in World War II, 49-50
    Shortly after World War II the cutter Taney (WPG-37) conducted a sort of boot camp on board, 86-87
    Flight training at Corpus Christi, Texas, and Pensacola, Florida, in the late 1940s, 98-101

Transportation Department
    In 1967 the department was formed and included the Coast Guard, which moved from Treasury, 229-233
    Claude S. Brinegar as Secretary from 1973 to 1975, 262-265, 268, 308-309
    William T. Coleman as Secretary from 1975 to 1977, 301, 309, 311
    Brock Adams as Secretary from 1977 to 1979, 278, 309-311, 322, 338

Treasury Department
Relationship with the Coast Guard in the late 1950s, 145-146, 154-155, 171-172

Trimble, Commander Paul E., USCG (USCGA, 1936)
Service in the late 1950s in Coast Guard headquarters, 178
In the late 1960s was Assistant Commandant of the Coast Guard, 332

Tugboats
Operation of towboats on U.S. rivers in the early 1970s, 245-253

UF-1/UF-2 Albatross
Coast Guard flying boat that went into service in the early 1950s and had a long service life, 114-116, 166-167, 175-177, 182-185, 191, 204
After 1962 was designated HU-16, 205, 278, 309-311, 322, 338

Uniforms–Coast Guard
During World War II some enlisted Coastguardsmen still wore surfman uniforms, 57-58
Change in the style of blue uniforms in the early 1970s, 284-285
In the 1970s Edith Head designed uniforms for Coast Guard women, 328

Unimak, USCGC (WHEC-379)
In 1977 was recommissioned briefly to aid in fisheries enforcement, 237, 302-303

Venzke, Captain Norman C., USCG (USCGA, 1950)
In the mid-1970s was the first commanding officer of the icebreaker Polar Star (WAGB-10), 308-309

Vessel Traffic Systems
Installation of in various locations in the 1970s, 255, 315-316

Vietnam War
Early in the war the Coast Guard stepped up loran coverage in the Pacific, 234-235, 315
Use of Coast Guard patrol boats off the Vietnam coast, 237-238

Volpe, John A.
Served 1969-73 as Secretary of Transportation, 287-288

Waesche, Rear Admiral Russell R., Jr., USCG (USCGA, 1936)
Service in the late 1950s in Coast Guard headquarters, 178, 244
Ended his active service in the 1970s as Commander Second Coast Guard District, 244

Wake Island
In the 1950s still had remnants from World War II, 128-129
Was used in the 1950s as a way station by the Coast Guard and Pan American Airways, 129-130, 136

Walsh, Captain Quentin R., USCG (USCGA, 1933)
As an instructor at the Coast Guard Academy in World War II, 31-32
Duty as an aide in the Treasury Department in the 1950s, 145, 171-172

Warner, John
In 1976 headed the national bicentennial celebration, 275

Waters, Captain John M., Jr., USCG (USCGA, 1943)
Was a Coast Guard Academy cadet in the early 1940s, later wrote books, 26-27

Weather
    A typhoon hit Tinian in the Marianas shortly after the end of World War II, 70-71
    At various periods the cutter Taney (WPG-37) provided weather reports while on ocean station patrol, 81-82, 281
    Prevailing winds at the Coast Guard air station in Port Angeles, Washington, 110
    Difficult weather conditions for flying in Alaska in the early 1960s, 201-202

Weisner, Admiral Maurice F., USN (Ret.) (USNA, 1941)
    Role on behalf of the Naval Aviation Museum, 341

Wellington, New Zealand
    The attack transport Hunter Liggett (APA-14) visited during World War II, 42-44, 51

Whalen, Vice Admiral Mark A., USCG (USCGA, 1937)
    In the late 1960s served as chief of staff of the Coast Guard, 227, 230, 234
    In the early 1970s was Commander Pacific Area, 299

White, Commander Justus P., USCG (USCGA, 1935)
    In 1945 was executive officer of the attack transport Bayfield (APA-33), 69

Wilson, General Louis H., Jr., USMC
    Served in World War II and later was Commandant of the Marine Corps in the 1970s, 291

Women in the Coast Guard
    During World War II women received officer candidate training at the Coast Guard Academy, 33-34
    In the 1970s Edith Head designed uniforms for Coast Guard women, 328
    Vivien Crea was a pioneer naval aviator in the 1970s, 294
    In 1976 women were first admitted to the Coast Guard Academy, 277-279
    In 1977 women began serving on board Coast Guard ships, 277-280, 335-336

Yarmouth Castle
    Passenger ship that burned during a Caribbean cruise in 1965, 213-215

www.ingramcontent.com/pod-product-compliance
Lightning Source LLC
Chambersburg PA
CBHW080620170426
43209CB00007B/1475